HABITAT Jaguars live in North, Central, and South America. Their habitats are swamplands, rainforests, dry grasslands, scrub, and deserts.

Atlantic Ocean

Pacific Ocean

Pacific Ocean

Indian Ocean

BODY COVERING Most jaguars have brownish-yellow fur with dark rosettes, or spots, that look like paws.

SELF-PROTECTION Jaguars are one of only four wild cats that roar. A jaguar roars to scare other animals away from its territory.

TEETH The strong jaws and sharp teeth of a jaguar allows it to bite into prey.

New York City Edition
Science

Jaguar

Harcourt
SCHOOL PUBLISHERS

Visit the Learning Site!
www.harcourtschool.com

Jaguar

Consulting Authors

Michael J. Bell
Associate Professor of Early Childhood Education
College of Education
West Chester University of Pennsylvania

Michael A. DiSpezio
Curriculum Architect
JASON Academy
Cape Cod, Massachusetts

Marjorie Frank
Former Adjunct, Science Education
Hunter College
New York, New York

Gerald H. Krockover
Professor of Earth and Atmospheric Science Education
Purdue University
West Lafayette, Indiana

Joyce C. McLeod
Adjunct Professor
Rollins College
Winter Park, Florida

Barbara ten Brink
Science Specialist
Austin Independent School District
Austin, Texas

Carol J. Valenta
Senior Vice President
St. Louis Science Center
St. Louis, Missouri

Barry A. Van Deman
President and CEO
Museum of Life and Science
Durham, North Carolina

Dear Students,

What's special about this Science textbook? It has been specially printed just for students in New York City. Inside you will put your hands on exciting Science Investigations and your minds on engaging science content! You will find special features like Science Spin from Weekly Reader and lots of links to online exploration.

Using this special book will help ensure that you are meeting the Major Understandings in the New York State Science Core Curriculum and the New York City Scope and Sequence. This is because the book includes only the content that matches with the Science Scope and Sequence for New York City. This will help you and your classmates focus on those science topics the New York City Department of Education requires.

We hope that you have a successful and exciting year in SCIENCE!

Sincerely,
Harcourt School Publishers

CONTENTS

UNIT 3 Food and Nutrition

How does nutrition and exercise affect our health?

UNIT 4 Exploring Ecosystems
How are plants and animals in an ecosystem connected?

The Nature of Science

Getting Ready for Science

○○○ Experimental Aircraft Association Fly-In

TO: kurt@hspscience.com

FROM: rhonda@hspscience.com

RE: weather planes

Dear Kurt,

Have you ever wondered where the warnings about dangerous weather patterns begin? I went to the air show here in Oshkosh, Wisconsin, and found out that the National Weather Service provides this information. How do they get it? A lot of radar is used, of course. But, I also saw a Strike Commander 500S at the air show. This is one of the airplanes used to track potential snowstorms. Other aircraft are used to fly into the eye of a hurricane! I never realized that the National Weather Service used aircraft so much to gather information. As a future pilot, I thought you'd want to know!

Your big sister,

Rhonda

TO: bill@hspscience.com

FROM: diana@hspscience.com

RE: rocket center

Dear Bill,

I know the biggest thing we have in common is our dream of becoming astronauts some day! The U.S. Space and Rocket Center is right down the road from our new home in Huntsville, Alabama. My parents took me there over the weekend. The Shuttle Park has many of the rockets used to go into space. Seeing them up-close makes me want to be an astronaut more than ever. I hope you can visit soon, so we can take you there.

Your former classmate,

Diana

Experiment!

Modern Rocket Stages

Scientists study the universe from Earth and from space. Studying the universe from space requires rockets that can send heavy payloads deep into space. What rocket design will carry heavy payloads the farthest? For example, is one large rocket more powerful than several smaller rockets? Plan and conduct an experiment to find out.

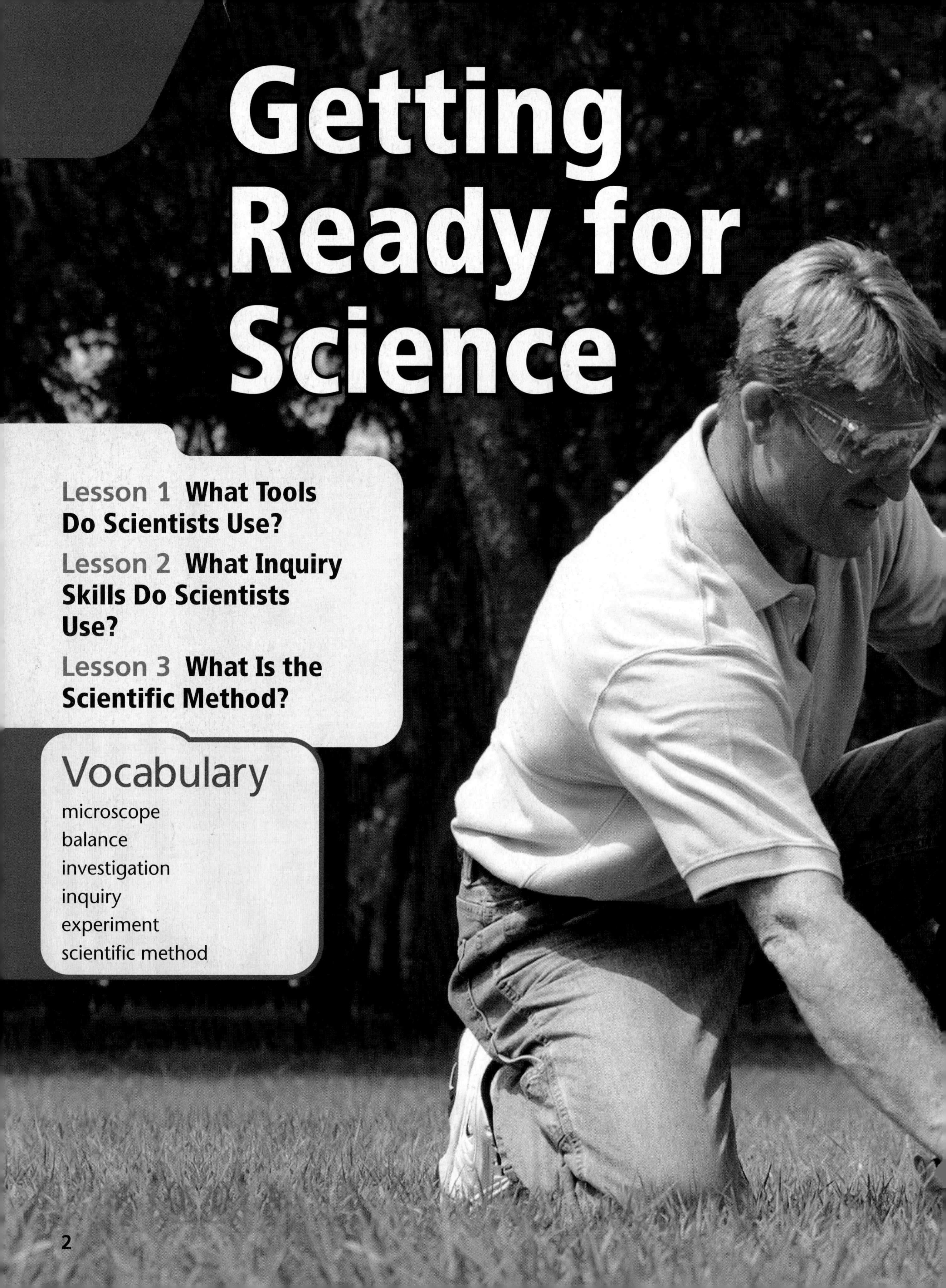

Getting Ready for Science

Lesson 1 **What Tools Do Scientists Use?**

Lesson 2 **What Inquiry Skills Do Scientists Use?**

Lesson 3 **What Is the Scientific Method?**

Vocabulary

microscope
balance
investigation
inquiry
experiment
scientific method

What do YOU wonder?

This rocket won't travel into space, but it works in the same way as the rockets that carried people to the moon. How do rocket scientists try out their designs? What variables can they test to make a rocket fly farther and faster?

3

What Tools Do Scientists Use?

That's a BIG Kite! One of the largest kites ever flown is the Megabite. It is 64 m (210 ft) long (including tails) and 22 m (72 ft) wide. That's only about 6 m (20 ft) shorter than a 747 jet airliner! Kite fliers around the world are always trying to set new records. How high can a kite go? How big or small can a kite be? Setting a record depends on accurate measurements. In the Investigate, you'll practice several different ways of measuring objects.

Measuring Up!

Materials
- balloon
- ruler
- tape measure
- hand lens
- string
- spring scale

Procedure

1. Observe the empty balloon with the hand lens. Copy the chart, and record your observations.

2. Measure the length and circumference of the balloon. Record your measurements.

3. Use the spring scale to measure the weight of the balloon. Record its weight.

4. Now blow up the balloon.

5. Match a length of string to the length of the balloon. Measure that string length with the ruler or tape measure. Record the length.

6. Measure the circumference of the balloon as in Step 5. Record your measurement.

7. Measure the weight of the balloon with the spring scale. Record your measurement.

Draw Conclusions

1. How did the measurements change when you blew up the balloon? Why?

2. Do you think that your measurement of the length of the empty balloon or the blown-up balloon was more accurate? Why?

3. **Inquiry Skill** Work with another group to identify variables in your measurements. What variables caused different groups to get different measurements?

Step 2

	Balloon	Balloon with Air
Hand lens		
Length		
Circumference		
Weight		

Investigate Further

How can you find the volume of a blown-up balloon? Plan and conduct a simple investigation to find out.

Reading in Science

VOCABULARY
microscope p. 8
balance p. 11

SCIENCE CONCEPTS
▶ how tools are used to make better observations
▶ why a balance and a scale measure different things

READING FOCUS SKILL

MAIN IDEA AND DETAILS Look for details about how and when each tool is used.

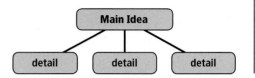

Using Science Inquiry Tools

People in many jobs must use tools. Cooks use pots and pans. Mechanics use screwdrivers and wrenches. Scientists use tools to measure and observe objects in nature.

Inquiry tools include a dropper to move liquids, as well as forceps to pick up solids. A hand lens and a magnifying box help you see details. You can measure temperature with a thermometer, length with a ruler or tape measure, and volume with a measuring cup. A spring scale measures weight.

 MAIN IDEA AND DETAILS What are four tools you can use to measure objects?

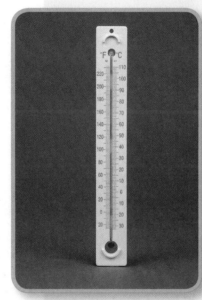

◀ A thermometer measures the temperature of liquids and the air. It measures in degrees Celsius (°C).

A tape measure helps you measure the length of curved or irregular surfaces. ▶

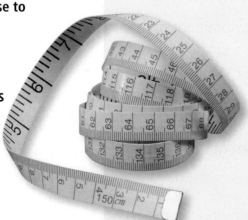

▲ Use a dropper to move small amounts of liquid or to measure volume by counting drops.

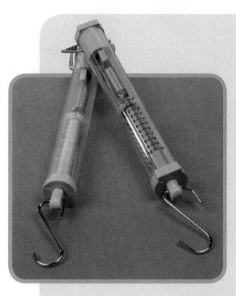

◀ A spring scale measures forces, such as weight or friction. It measures in units called newtons (N).

▲ A ruler measures the length and width of objects in centimeters (cm) and millimeters (mm).

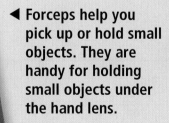

▲ You can place an insect, pebble, or other small object in the magnifying box. Looking through the lid helps you see the object clearly.

▲ A measuring cup is used to measure the volume of liquids. It measures in liters (L) and milliliters (mL).

◀ Forceps help you pick up or hold small objects. They are handy for holding small objects under the hand lens.

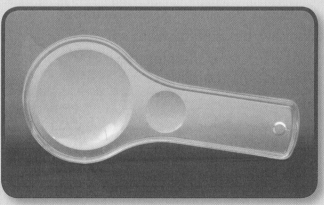

▲ A hand lens makes objects look larger and helps you see more detail.

Microscopes

Without a telescope, you can't identify what look like tiny objects in the sky. In the same way, you can't see tiny parts of an insect, colored particles in a rock, or cells in a leaf without a microscope. A **microscope** is a tool that makes small objects appear larger. It lets you see details you couldn't see with your eyes alone.

People have known for a long time that curved glass can *magnify,* or make things look larger. An early Roman scholar read books through a glass ball filled with water. People started making eyeglasses a thousand years ago. They called the curved glass a *lens* because it looked like a lentil—a bean!

An early scientist named Anton van Leeuwenhoek (LAY•vuhn•hook) used a lens to see creatures in a drop of pond water. He called them animalcules.

In the late 1500s, a Dutch eyeglass maker put a lens in each end of a hollow tube. Changing the length of the tube made tiny objects look three to nine times their actual size. This was probably the first "modern" microscope.

In the 1600s, Robert Hooke used a microscope to study thin slices of cork. To describe the tiny, boxlike structures he saw, he used the word *cell,* the name now used for the smallest unit of living things.

Today, microscopes can magnify objects thousands of times. So a tiny "animalcule" might look as large as a whale!

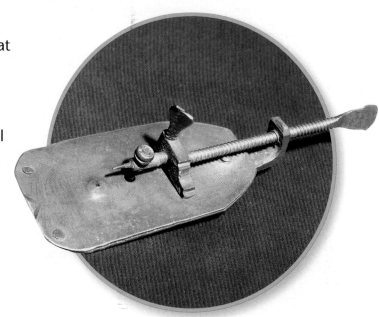

▲ Van Leeuwenhoek was the first person to see microscopic organisms. He placed tiny samples on the tip of a needle and looked at them through a single lens.

Using a simple microscope, you can make things look up to 400 times their actual size! ▼

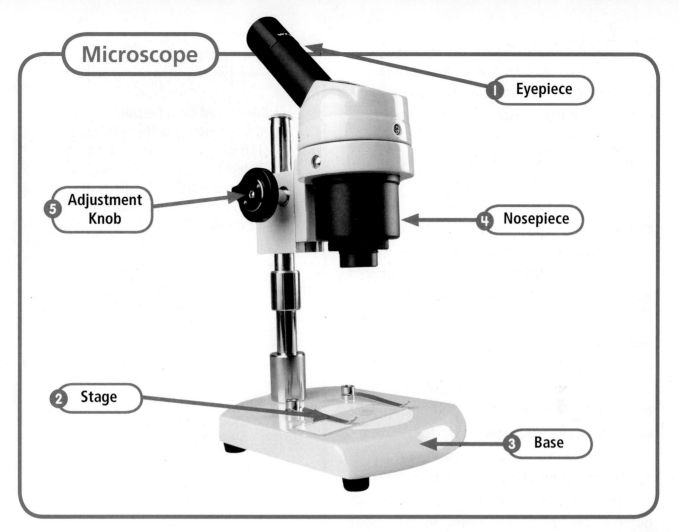

Microscope

1. Eyepiece
5. Adjustment Knob
4. Nosepiece
2. Stage
3. Base

Most classroom microscopes have several main parts:

1. The eyepiece contains one lens and is mounted at the end of a tube.

2. The stage holds the slide or object you are looking at.

3. The base supports the microscope. It usually holds a lamp or mirror that shines light through the object.

4. A nosepiece holds one or more lenses that can magnify an object up to 400 times.

5. Adjustment knobs help you focus the lenses.

Focus Skill **MAIN IDEA AND DETAILS** What are the main parts of a microscope?

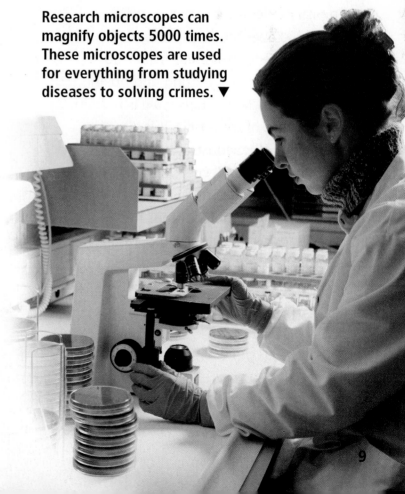

Research microscopes can magnify objects 5000 times. These microscopes are used for everything from studying diseases to solving crimes. ▼

Measuring Temperature

"Boy, it's hot today! It feels much hotter than yesterday." Without a thermometer, temperature isn't much more than how a person feels.

In 1592, an Italian scientist named Galileo found that a change in temperature made water rise and fall in a sealed tube. This device, a simple thermometer, helped Galileo study nature in a more precise way.

In the early 1700s, a German scientist named Fahrenheit sealed mercury in a thin glass tube. As it got warmer, the liquid metal took up more space. The mercury rose in the tube. As it cooled, the mercury took up less space. So the level of liquid in the tube fell. But how was this thermometer to be marked? What units were to be used?

Fahrenheit put the tube into freezing water and into boiling water and marked the mercury levels. Then he divided the difference between the levels into 180 equal units—called degrees.

In 1742, a Swedish scientist named Celsius made a thermometer with 100 degrees between the freezing and boiling points of water. The Celsius scale is used in most countries of the world. It is also the scale used by all scientists.

Thermometers can't measure extreme temperatures. For example, many metals get to several thousand degrees before they melt. Scientists have other temperature-sensing tools to measure very hot and very cold objects.

 MAIN IDEA AND DETAILS How does a thermometer work?

Temperature Scales

Measured on a Celsius thermometer, water boils at 100 degrees and freezes at 0 degrees. On a Fahrenheit thermometer, water boils at 212 degrees and freezes at 32 degrees.

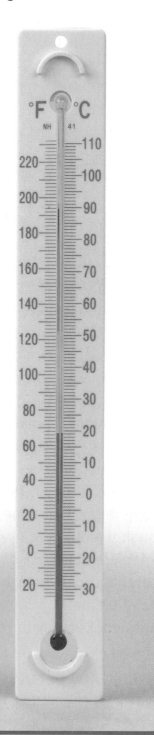

Balance or Spring Scale?

Suppose you're a merchant in Alaska in the early 1900s. A man wants food in exchange for some gold he got from the bottom of a river. But how much is the gold worth?

To find out, you use a tool that looks like a small seesaw. You place the gold at one end of a beam. Then you add objects of known mass at the other end until the beam is level. The objects balance! A **balance** is a tool that measures the amount of matter in an object—the object's *mass*.

The balance in your classroom measures mass by balancing an unknown object with one or more objects of known mass. Mass is measured in grams (g) or kilograms (kg).

When you want to measure an object's weight, you use a spring scale. You hang an object from a hook on the scale and let gravity pull it down. Gravity is a force that pulls on all objects on or near Earth. Weight is a measure of the force of gravity's pull. The unit for this measurement is the newton (N).

People often confuse mass and weight. But think what happens to the mass of an astronaut as he or she goes from Earth to the International Space Station. Nothing! The astronaut's mass stays the same, even though his or her weight goes down. The pull of gravity from Earth is countered by the space station's great speed in orbit.

 MAIN IDEA AND DETAILS What does a balance measure? What does a spring scale measure?

▲ Find an object's mass, or amount of matter, by first placing the object on one pan. Then add a known mass to the other pan until the pointer stays in the middle.

▲ When you hang an object on the hook of the spring scale, you measure the force of gravity pulling on the object. This is the object's weight.

Insta-Lab

Do They Balance?

Place a blown-up balloon on one pan of a balance and an empty balloon on the other pan. Do they have the same mass? Why or why not?

Safety in the Lab

Working in the lab is fun. But you need to be careful to stay safe. Here are some general rules to follow:

- Study all the steps of an investigation so you know what to expect. If you have any questions, ask your teacher.
- Be sure you watch for safety icons and obey all caution statements.

Scientists in the lab wear safety goggles to protect their eyes. Smart students do the same thing! When you work with chemicals or water, a lab apron protects your clothes.

Be careful with sharp objects!

- Scissors, forceps, and even a sharp pencil should be handled with care.
- If you break something made of glass, tell your teacher.
- If you cut yourself, tell your teacher right away.

Be careful with electricity!

- Be especially careful with electrical appliances.
- Keep cords out of the way.
- Never pull a plug out of an outlet by the cord.
- Dry your hands before unplugging a cord.
- If you have long hair, pull it back out of the way. Roll or push up long sleeves to keep them away from your work.
- Never eat or drink anything during a science activity.
- Don't use lab equipment to drink from.
- Never work in the lab by yourself.
- Wash your hands with soap and water after cleaning up your work area.

 MAIN IDEA AND DETAILS What are four ways to keep safe in the lab?

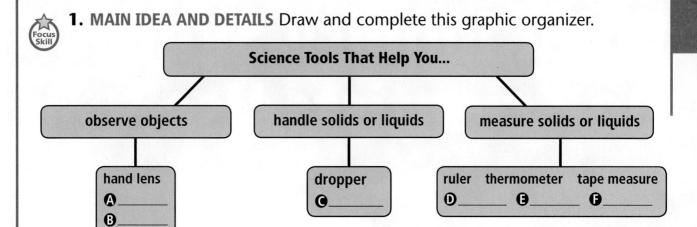

1. MAIN IDEA AND DETAILS Draw and complete this graphic organizer.

Science Tools That Help You...

observe objects	handle solids or liquids	measure solids or liquids

hand lens
Ⓐ_____
Ⓑ_____

dropper
Ⓒ_____

ruler   thermometer   tape measure
Ⓓ_____ Ⓔ_____ Ⓕ_____

2. SUMMARIZE Write two sentences that tell the most important information in this lesson.

3. DRAW CONCLUSIONS Why are different tools used to measure mass and weight?

4. VOCABULARY Write one sentence describing each vocabulary term.

Test Prep

5. Critical Thinking You are doing an investigation and accidentally spill water on the floor. How could this be a safety problem?

6. Why is using a thermometer or measuring cup more scientific than estimating temperature or volume?

   A. It is easier.

   B. It is more accurate.

   C. It looks more scientific.

   D. It uses up more class time.

Links

Writing

Narrative Writing

Use reference materials to learn about the life of Anton van Leeuwenhoek. Write a **story** that includes what he is famous for and what kinds of things he observed using his microscope.

Math

Choose Measuring Devices

A bottle is half full of water. Describe three things you could measure about the water, and name the tools to use for the measurements.

Health

Measuring for Health

Which science tools are also used by doctors, nurses, lab workers in hospitals, or others involved in health care? Describe how they are used.

For more links and activities, go to **www.hspscience.com**

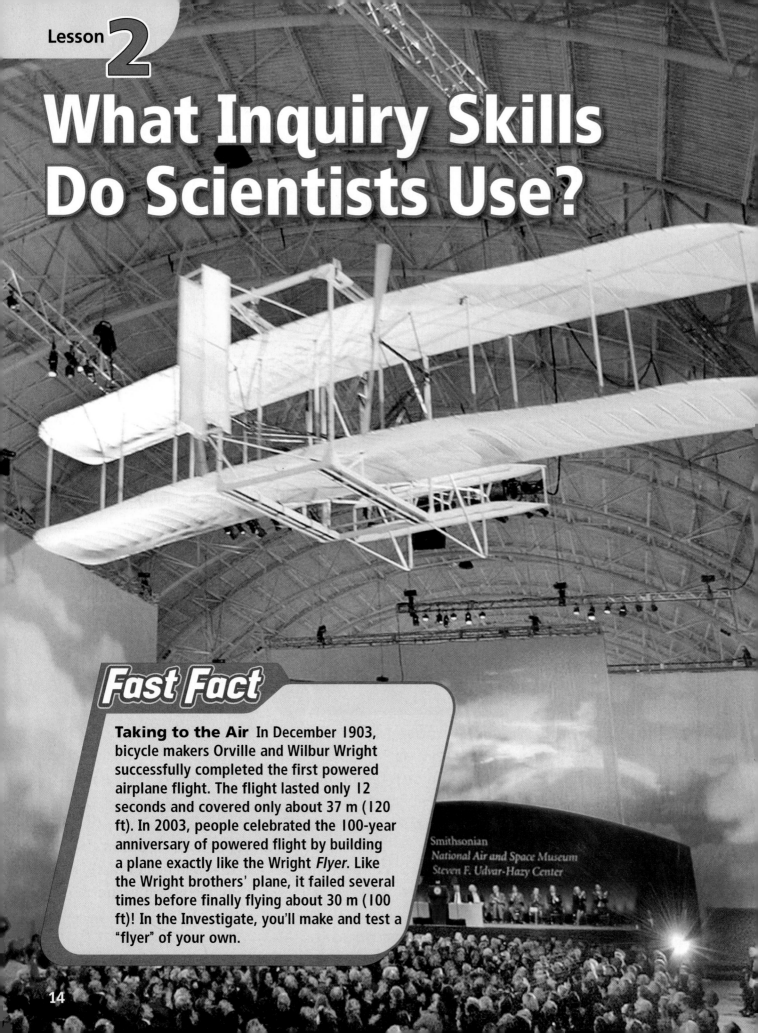

What Inquiry Skills Do Scientists Use?

Fast Fact

Taking to the Air In December 1903, bicycle makers Orville and Wilbur Wright successfully completed the first powered airplane flight. The flight lasted only 12 seconds and covered only about 37 m (120 ft). In 2003, people celebrated the 100-year anniversary of powered flight by building a plane exactly like the Wright *Flyer*. Like the Wright brothers' plane, it failed several times before finally flying about 30 m (100 ft)! In the Investigate, you'll make and test a "flyer" of your own.

Smithsonian
National Air and Space Museum
Steven F. Udvar-Hazy Center

Design an Airplane

Materials
- thick paper
- tape
- stopwatch
- tape measure

Procedure

1. Design a paper airplane. Then fold a sheet of thick paper to make the plane.

2. Measure a distance of 10 m in an open area. Mark one end of the distance as a starting line, and place a stick or stone every half meter from the starting line.

3. Test-fly your plane. Have a partner start the stopwatch as you're releasing the plane and stop it when the plane lands. Record the flight time in a table like the one shown.

4. Measure the distance the plane flew. Record the distance in the table.

5. Repeat Steps 3 and 4 for a second and a third trial.

6. Make a second airplane, with wings half as wide as your first plane.

7. Test-fly your second plane three times. Record all your measurements in the table.

Step 1

Data Table		Airplane 1	Airplane 2
Trial			
1	time		
	distance		
2	time		
	distance		
3	time		
	distance		

Draw Conclusions

1. How did changing the width of the wings affect the way your plane flew?

2. **Inquiry Skill** Why did some students' planes fly farther or longer than those of others? Write a hypothesis to explain your thinking.

Investigate Further

On one of your planes, add a paper-clip weight. Then fly the plane. What happens to the distance and time it flies? Infer the weight's effect on the plane.

Reading in Science

VOCABULARY
investigation p 16
inquiry p 16
experiment p 19

SCIENCE CONCEPTS
▶ how inquiry skills help you gather information
▶ how an investigation differs from an experiment

READING FOCUS SKILL

MAIN IDEA AND DETAILS Look for information on when to use different inquiry skills.

```
        Main Idea
       /    |    \
  detail  detail  detail
```

What Is Inquiry?

Suppose you wanted to learn about the way parachutes work. How would you begin? You might read a book about parachutes. Or you might investigate the subject on your own. An **investigation** is a procedure that is carried out to gather data about an object or event. An investigation can be as simple as measuring an object or observing a response to a stimulus. In this lesson, you investigated the way in which wing size affected flight.

So how can you begin your investigation about parachutes? Scientists usually begin an investigation by asking questions. Then they use inquiry skills to answer their questions. **Inquiry** is an organized way to gather information and answer questions. What questions do you have about parachutes?

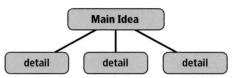

Inquiry Skills

Observe—Use your senses to gather information about objects and events.

Measure—Compare the length, mass, volume, or some other property of an object to a standard unit, such as a meter, gram, or liter.

Gather, Record, and Display Data—Gather data by making observations and measurements. Record your observations and measurements in an organized way. Display your data so that others can understand and interpret it.

Use Numbers—Collect, display, and interpret data as numbers.

How does a parachute enable a person to jump from an airplane without getting hurt? ▶

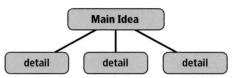

How can you get answers to your questions? First, you might observe how parachutes are made. Look for diagrams in books or on the Internet. Go to a local airport, and ask to see some parachutes. Then gather, record, and display the data you collected. Measure and use numbers to express the data if possible.

You might wonder how a round parachute compares to a parachute like the one pictured on the previous page. What do they have in common? How are they different? What other shapes can a parachute have?

Once you compare different shapes, you can classify them. Some parachutes are used for doing tricks. Others are used to gently land heavy objects, such as space capsules. Some help sky divers land on a small target.

Now you've gathered a lot of data. The next step is to interpret the data. For example, how does the size or shape of the parachute relate to its use? Is there any pattern in the data? What shape of parachute appears easiest to control?

Data and observations can be used in many ways. It all depends on what questions you want to answer. You can use the data and logical reasoning to draw conclusions about things you haven't directly observed. For example, you might notice that narrow parachutes are used for tricks. From that, you can infer that this shape is easier to control. Or you might predict which parachute might win a sky-diving contest.

 MAIN IDEA AND DETAILS What are inquiry skills used for?

Inquiry Skills

Compare—Identify ways in which things or events are alike or different.

Classify—Group or organize objects or events into categories based on specific characteristics.

Interpret Data—Use data to look for patterns, to predict what will happen, or to suggest an answer to a question.

Infer—Use logical reasoning to come to a conclusion based on data and observations.

Predict—Use observations and data to form an idea of what will happen under certain conditions.

How does the size or shape of a parachute affect the way it works? ▶

Using Inquiry Skills

Suppose you were in a contest to find a way to drop a raw egg from a balcony without breaking the egg. What kind of parachute would you use?

First, you might plan and conduct a simple investigation. You might make parachutes of different shapes and sizes. You could tie weights on them, drop them, and see how they behave. How long do they stay in the air? How gently do they land? You could make observations and take measurements.

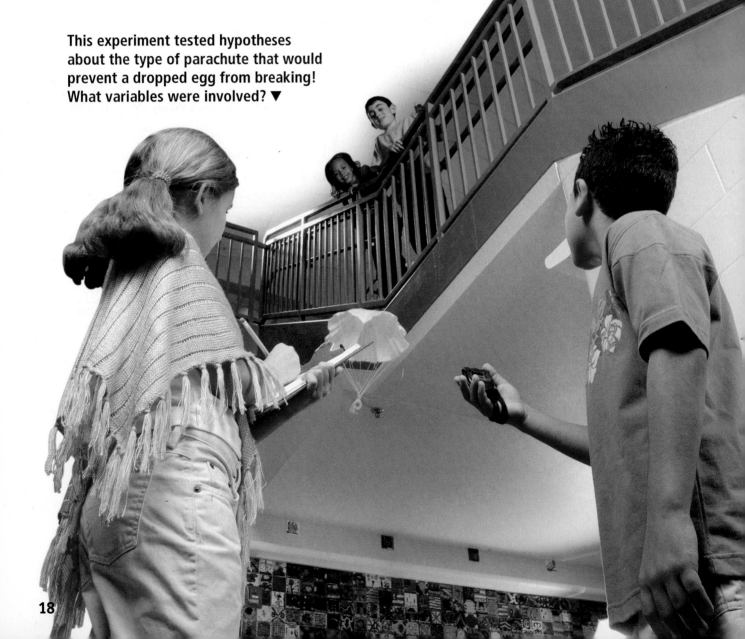

This experiment tested hypotheses about the type of parachute that would prevent a dropped egg from breaking! What variables were involved? ▼

Control Variables—Identify and control the factors that can affect the outcome of an experiment.

Draw Conclusions—Use data and experimental results to decide if your hypothesis is supported.

Communicate—Share results and information visually, orally, or electronically.

With that information, you could hypothesize. What design has the best chance to protect the egg? You may think that a large, round parachute is the best design. You could experiment to test your hypothesis. An **experiment** is a procedure you carry out under controlled conditions to test a hypothesis.

An experiment has more steps than a simple investigation. You have to decide what you will test. Then you have to be sure you control variables.

What are variables, and how can they be controlled? A variable is a factor, such as size, that can have more than one condition, such as large and small. You wouldn't test both the size and shape of parachutes at the same time. Why not? You wouldn't know whether the size or the shape caused the results. Suppose you compared a small, square parachute and a large, round one. How would you know if the size or the shape made a difference?

To test your hypothesis that large, round parachutes are best, you could first test round parachutes of different sizes. Everything except parachute size would be the same. You'd use the same egg size for each drop. You'd drop the eggs from the same height. And you'd drop each one several times to check the results. Then you'd do the whole thing again, using parachutes with different shapes instead of sizes! As before, you'd control all other variables.

During the experiment, you'd be careful to write down exactly what you did and how you did it. You'd record all observations and measurements.

The final step in an experiment is to draw conclusions. Did your experiment support your hypothesis? Was a large, round parachute the best way to protect the egg? What did the experiment show?

Finally, you'd write up your experiment to communicate your results to others. You might include tables for your data or draw diagrams of your parachute design.

 MAIN IDEA AND DETAILS Why do you have to control variables in an experiment?

Insta-Lab

What Causes Lift?

Cut a strip of newspaper or notebook paper about 2–3 cm wide and 10 cm long. Hold the end of the strip in your hand, and blow gently over the top of it. What happens? How might the result relate to airplane wings?

Models, Time, and Space

Have you ever watched a leaf fall from a tree? You might think of a falling leaf as a model for a parachute. It could give you ideas for a parachute design. Or you might make a model and test it before making an actual parachute. That can be very practical. Companies that build rockets, for example, save a lot of time and money by making and testing models before building the real things.

How will your parachute interact with what is attached to it? Thinking about time and space relationships is an important inquiry skill. For example, how do you make sure the parachute in a model rocket pops out at the right time? There's a lot to think about! Inquiry skills are ways to make sure your thinking and tests really work.

 MAIN IDEA AND DETAILS How do models help an investigation?

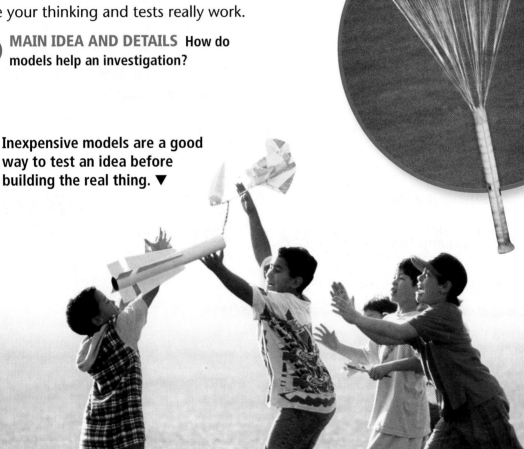

Inexpensive models are a good way to test an idea before building the real thing. ▼

1. MAIN IDEA AND DETAILS Draw and complete this graphic organizer.

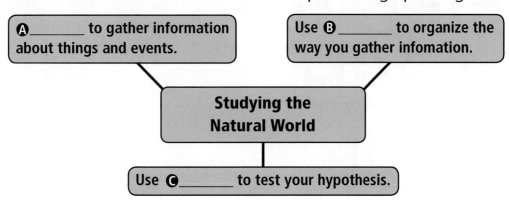

A_____ to gather information about things and events.

Use **B**_____ to organize the way you gather infomation.

Studying the Natural World

Use **C**_____ to test your hypothesis.

2. SUMMARIZE Use your completed graphic organizer to write a lesson summary.

3. DRAW CONCLUSIONS If you wanted to learn more about birds, would you be more likely just to make observations first or to experiment first?

4. VOCABULARY Use the vocabulary terms in a paragraph describing how scientists study the natural world.

Test Prep

5. Critical Thinking Alberto shines red light on one group of plants and blue light on another. He measures the height of the plants each day. What hypothesis is he testing?

6. A factor that can affect the outcome of an experiment is called a
- **A.** hypothesis.
- **C.** variable.
- **B.** prediction.
- **D.** model.

Links

Writing

Narrative Writing
What inquiry skills do you use in everyday life? Write a screenplay about a day in your life. **Describe** how you use inquiry skills.

Math

Displaying Data
Make three different charts, tables, or graphs that show how many of your classmates were born in each month of the year.

Social Studies

Making Inferences
Use reference materials to find out how archaeologists make inferences. What information do they use to infer what life was like hundreds of years ago?

For more links and activities, go to www.hspscience.com

What Is the Scientific Method?

Fast Fact

Reaching for the Stars In October 2004, *SpaceShipOne* traveled nearly 112 km (70 mi) above the surface of Earth. The ship reached a speed of Mach 3—three times the speed of sound. However, *SpaceShipOne* wasn't built or launched by a government or a major aerospace company. It was the first successful launch of a private spaceship! In the Investigate, you too will build your own rocket.

Build a Rocket!

Materials
- string, 5 m
- goggles
- drinking straw
- 2 chairs
- balloon
- tape
- timer/stopwatch
- tape measure

Procedure

1. **CAUTION: Wear safety goggles.** Thread one end of the string through the straw.

2. Place the chairs about 4 m apart, and tie one end of the string to each chair.

3. Blow up the balloon, and pinch it closed.

4. Have a partner tape the balloon to the straw, with the balloon's opening near one chair.

5. Release the balloon. Use the stopwatch to time how long the balloon keeps going.

6. Measure and record the distance the balloon traveled. Also record its travel time.

7. Repeat Steps 3–6 with more air in the balloon. Then repeat Steps 3–6 with less air in the balloon than on the first trial.

Draw Conclusions

1. Why did the balloon move when you released it?

2. How did the amount of air in the balloon affect the travel time and distance?

3. **Inquiry Skill** Would changing the shape of the balloon affect the distance it travels? Predict what would happen if you used a large, round balloon and a long, skinny balloon with the same amount of air.

Step 2

Step 4

Investigate Further

Plan an investigation to find out how the angle of the string affects the travel time and distance. How do you think the results will change when the angle is varied?

VOCABULARY
scientific method p. 24

SCIENCE CONCEPTS
- ▶ what steps are in the scientific method
- ▶ how scientists use the scientific method

READING FOCUS SKILL

MAIN IDEA AND DETAILS Look for information on the steps of the scientific method.

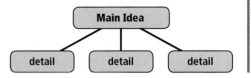

The Scientific Method

In the Investigate, you predicted what would happen if you changed the shape of the balloon. How can you tell if your prediction is right? You could just play around with some balloons and see what happens. But a true experiment involves a series of steps that scientists use. The steps are called the **scientific method**.

Scientists use the scientific method to plan and carry out experiments. Some of the steps are the same as inquiry skills. And some inquiry skills are used in planning experiments.

There are five steps in the scientific method:

1. Observe, and ask questions.
2. Form a hypothesis.
3. Plan an experiment.
4. Conduct an experiment.
5. Draw conclusions, and communicate the results.

① Observe, and Ask Questions

- Use your senses to make observations.
- Record *one* question that you would like to answer.
- Write down what you already know about the topic of your question.
- Do research to find more information on your topic.

② Form a Hypothesis

- Write a possible answer to your question. A possible answer to a question is a *hypothesis*. A hypothesis must be a statement that can be tested.
- Write your hypothesis in a complete sentence.

Suppose you follow the steps of the scientific method. You form a hypothesis, and your experiment supports it. But when you tell other people your results, they don't believe you!

This is when the scientific method works especially well. You recorded your procedures. You have all your observations and data. All that another person has to do is repeat exactly what you did. That's one way scientists can check each other's experiments. If another person doesn't get the same results, you can try to figure out why. You can ask, "Did I do something differently? Were there variables I didn't control?"

Scientists can use the scientific method to repeat the experiments of other scientists. This helps them make sure that their conclusions are correct.

 MAIN IDEA AND DETAILS What are the steps of the scientific method?

③ Plan an Experiment

- Decide how to conduct a fair test of your hypothesis by controlling variables. Variables are factors that can affect the outcome of the experiment.
- Write down the procedure you will follow to do your test.
- List the equipment you will need.
- Decide how you will gather and record data.

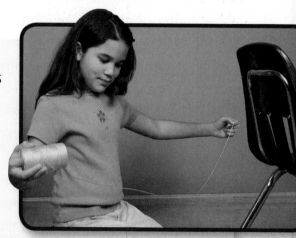

④ Conduct an Experiment

- Follow the procedure you wrote down.
- Observe and measure carefully.
- Record everything that happens, including what you observe and what you measure.
- Organize your data so it is easy to understand and interpret.

⑤ Draw Conclusions/ Communicate Results

- Make charts, tables, or graphs to display your data.
- Analyze your observations and the data you collected.
- Write a conclusion. Describe the evidence you used to determine whether the experiment supported your hypothesis.
- Decide whether your hypothesis was supported or not.

25

Before and After

People don't always start with the scientific method. Suppose you have questions about something scientists have already studied. All you need to do is read about it. But when studying the natural world, you often find new problems that puzzle you. You think, "I wonder what would happen if. . . " That's when inquiry skills, investigations, and experiments come in handy.

What happens after you've done an experiment? Even if an experiment supports your hypothesis, you might have other questions—about the same topic—that can be tested. And if your hypothesis wasn't supported, you might want to form another hypothesis and test that.

Scientists never run out of questions. The natural world is filled with things that make people wonder. By asking questions and using the scientific method, scientists have learned a lot. They've learned how to send people to the moon. They've learned to cure many diseases. But there are still many things to be learned. Who knows? Maybe you're the one to make the next big discovery!

 MAIN IDEA AND DETAILS What do scientists do when experiments show their hypotheses to be incorrect?

▲ Computers can be used to research a problem, display data, and share the results of experiments with scientists all over the world.

Tables and charts make it easy for other people to understand and interpret your data. ▼

Insta-Lab

Make a Helicopter

Cut a piece of paper 3 cm wide and 13 cm long. Draw lines on the paper like those on the diagram above. Cut along all the solid lines. Fold one flap forward and one flap to the back. Fold the base up to add weight at the bottom. Drop your helicopter, and watch it fly. How does adding a paper clip to the bottom change the way the helicopter flies?

1. MAIN IDEA AND DETAILS Draw and complete this graphic organizer.

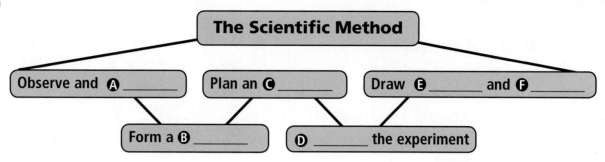

The Scientific Method

Observe and **A** _____

Plan an **C** _____

Draw **E** _____ and **F** _____

Form a **B** _____

D _____ the experiment

2. SUMMARIZE Use your graphic organizer to write a paragraph telling the steps of the scientific method.

3. DRAW CONCLUSIONS During which step of the scientific method would you identify variables and figure out how to control them?

4. VOCABULARY For each letter in *scientific method,* write a science-related word starting with the same letter. Skip repetitions of a letter.

Test Prep

5. Critical Thinking Karla heard that for making ice cubes, hot water is better than cold water because it freezes faster. How could she test that idea as a hypothesis?

6. What does an experiment test?

  A. a fact   **C.** a theory

  B. a hypothesis   **D.** a variable

Links

Writing

Expository Writing
Write a letter to a friend, **explaining** how he or she could use the scientific method to test a balloon rocket.

Math

Display Data
Make a table to display how long the balloon rockets flew in the Investigate. Then make a graph of the results.

Social Studies

Scientific Method
Use reference materials to compare how the Greeks studied science and what Francesco Redi added to their method. Write a story about what he showed.

For more links and activities, go to **www.hspscience.com**

Review and Test Preparation

Vocabulary Review

Use the terms below to complete the sentences. The page numbers tell you where to look in the chapter if you need help.

microscope p. 8 **inquiry** p. 16
balance p. 11 **experiment** p. 19
investigate p. 16 **scientific method** p. 24

1. An organized way to gather information is called _____.

2. A tool used to measure the mass of an object is a _____.

3. To test a hypothesis, you plan and conduct a(n) _____.

4. A tool that makes objects appear larger is a _____.

5. A series of steps used by scientists to study the physical world is the _____.

6. When you gather information about an object or event, you _____.

Check Understanding

Write the letter of the best choice.

7. Which tool is used to measure volume in the metric system?
   A. balance **C.** spring scale
   B. measuring cup **D.** thermometer

8. **MAIN IDEA AND DETAILS** Which of the following steps to solve a problem is done first?
   F. test a hypothesis
   G. interpret data
   H. form a hypothesis
   J. observe, and ask questions

9. Which inquiry skill can be used to save time and money before doing an experiment?
   A. form a hypothesis
   B. make and use models
   C. classify objects
   D. draw conclusions

The diagram shows four tools. Use the diagram to answer questions 10 and 11.

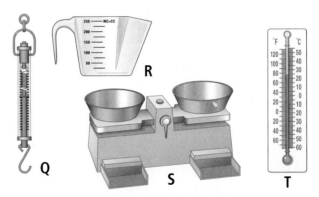

10. Which tool is used to measure the weight of an object?
    F. Tool Q **H.** Tool S
    G. Tool R **J.** Tool T

11. Which tool measures in grams?
    A. Tool Q **C.** Tool S
    B. Tool R **D.** Tool T

12. MAIN IDEA AND DETAILS Comparing, measuring, and predicting are examples of what process?

    F. communicating **H.** inquiry

    G. hypothesizing   **J.** investigating

13. When conducting an experiment, which is the best way to record data?

    A. Make a bar graph while taking the measurements.

    B. Write everything down after you are finished.

    C. Make a table to record your data as you collect it.

    D. Write things down on a sheet of paper and organize it later.

14. Juan is making and flying airplanes with different shaped wings. What is he doing?

    F. experimenting **H.** investigating

    G. hypothesizing   **J.** communicating

15. Why do scientists do each part of their investigation several times?

    A. to be sure their data is accurate

    B. to make their experiment look more impressive

    C. to use up all of their materials

    D. because it's fun

16. If you wanted to see more detail on the surface of a rock, what tool would you use?

    F. dropper   **H.** microscope

    G. forceps   **J.** thermometer

Inquiry Skills

17. Andrea is testing balloon rockets by using balloons with different amounts of air. **Identify three variables** Andrea will need to control.

18. Which boat would you **predict** will finish second in the race?

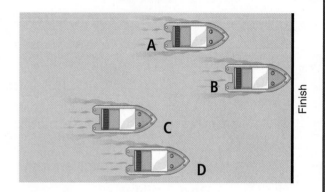

Critical Thinking

19. Why are safety goggles important when students are doing an investigation with scissors or glass?

20. The diagram shows an experiment. Different amounts of water were placed in 4 beakers. The beakers were heated at the same rate. The data shows how long it took each beaker to boil.

2.0 min   4.0 min   6.0 min   7.9 min

Part A What conclusion is supported by the experiment? Explain.

Part B What variables were controlled in the experiment?

EARTH SCIENCE

Earth Science

Chapter 1	**The Rock Cycle**	
Chapter 2	**Changes to Earth's Surface**	

Lava Beds National Monument

TO: emily@hspscience.com

FROM: toby@hspscience.com

RE: mighty volcanoes

Dear Emily,

I'm having a great time on my scout trip to the Lava Beds National Monument in Tulelake, California. Yesterday we went into some really cool caves. Mushpot Cave was my favorite. A park ranger taught us many interesting things about the caves. We learned that the caves were formed by volcanoes and are lava tubes. Lava once flowed through the lava tubes during volcanic eruptions. We also learned that the monument lies on the Medicine Lake Volcano.

See you in school this fall!

Toby

TO: colton@hspscience.com

FROM: cody@hspscience.com

RE: great caverns

Colton,

Can you imagine a house seven stories tall? Earth's processes made the Meramec Caverns in Stanton, Missouri, just that large. You see the 400-million year history of a changing Earth inside the caverns. You can also walk miles of passages. You'll see fossils, stalactites, and limestone formations in these really great caverns. The inside of the caverns is so large, it has a full restaurant and a grand ballroom.

What an amazing place!

Your best bud,

Cody

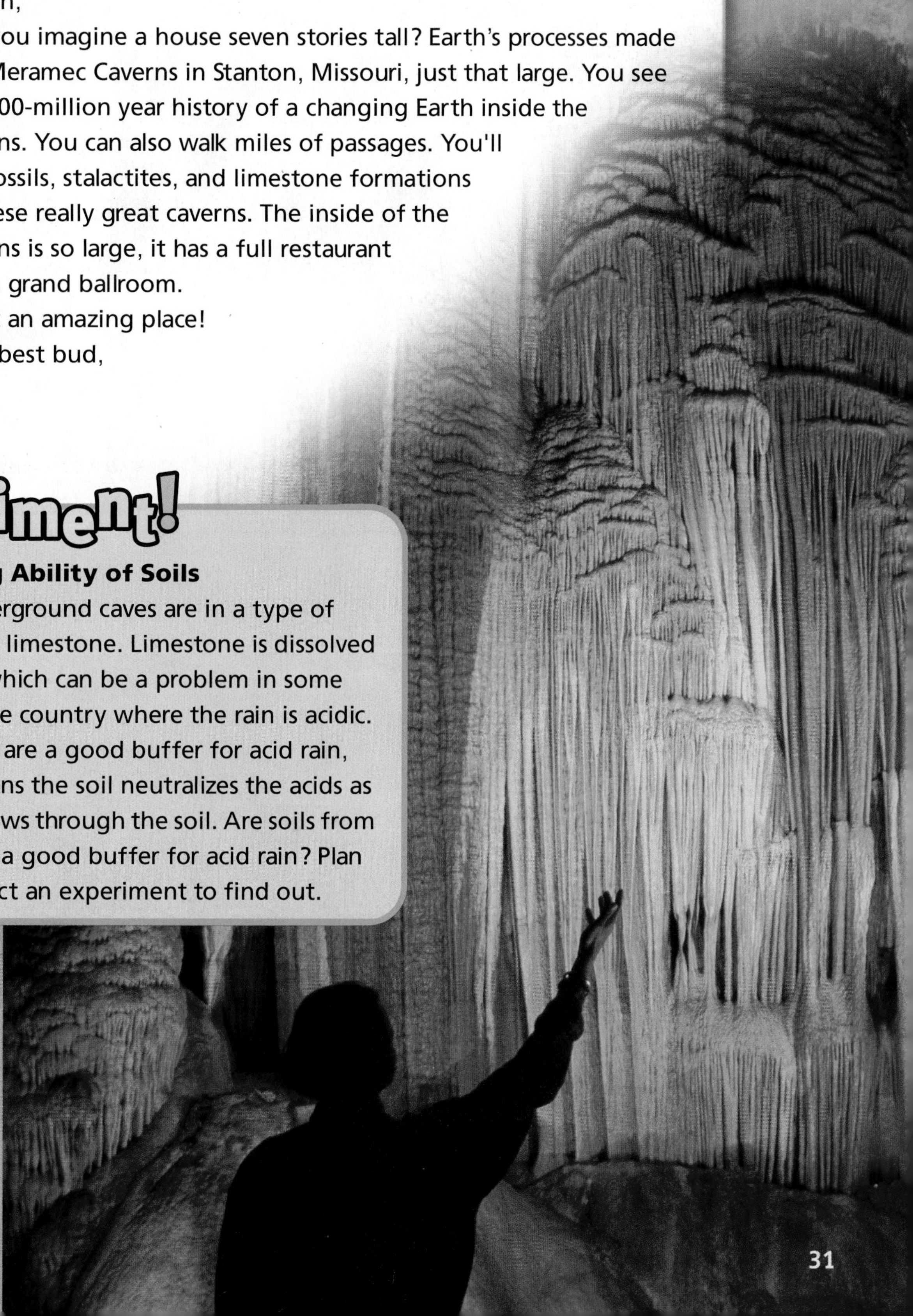

Experiment!

Buffering Ability of Soils

Most underground caves are in a type of rock called limestone. Limestone is dissolved by acids, which can be a problem in some parts of the country where the rain is acidic. Some soils are a good buffer for acid rain, which means the soil neutralizes the acids as the rain flows through the soil. Are soils from your town a good buffer for acid rain? Plan and conduct an experiment to find out.

Chapter 1

The Rock Cycle

Lesson 1 **What Are Minerals?**

Lesson 2 **How Do Rocks Form?**

Lesson 3 **How Are Rocks Changed?**

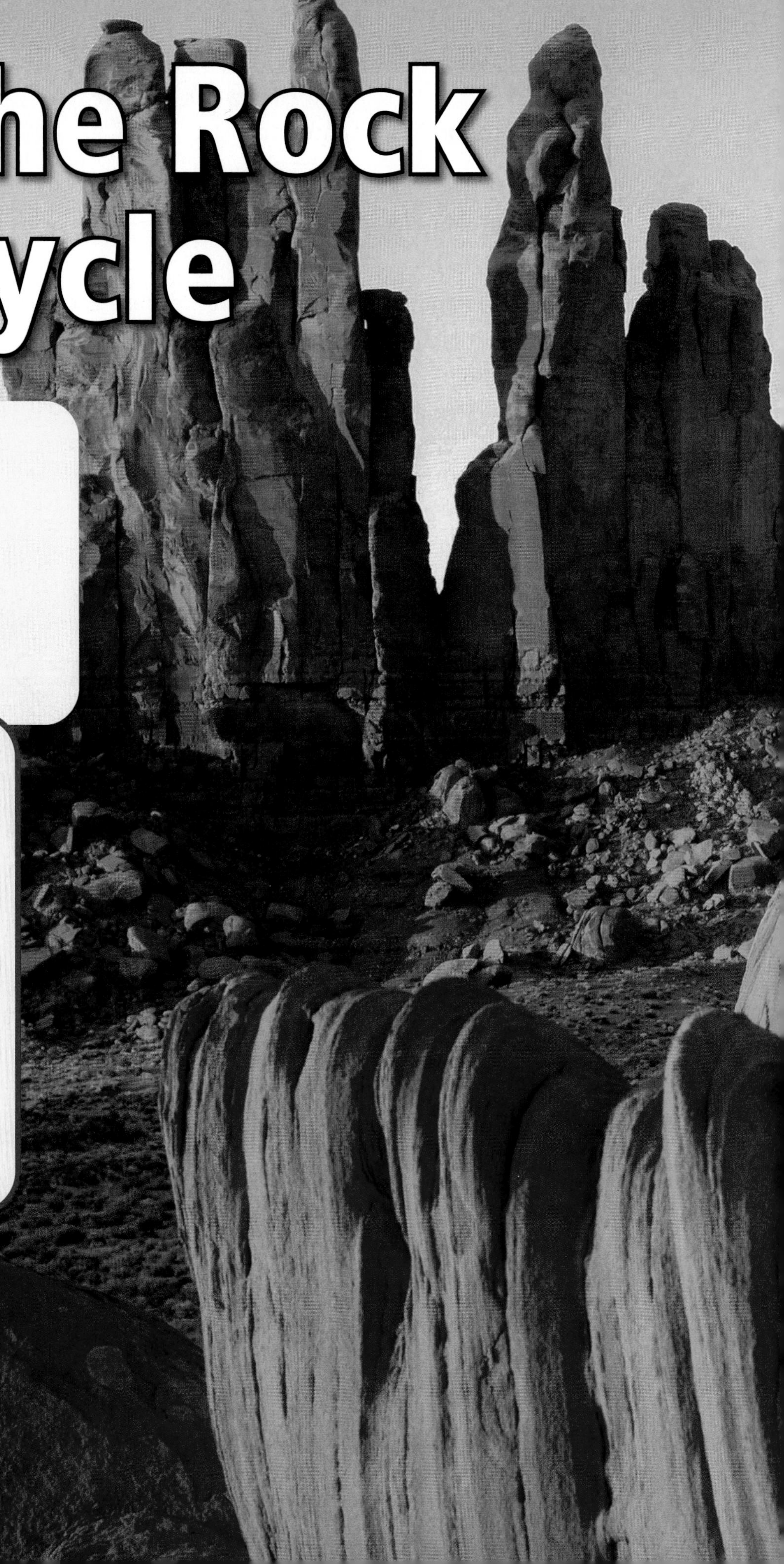

Vocabulary

mineral
streak
luster
hardness
rock
igneous rock
deposition
sedimentary rock
metamorphic rock
weathering
erosion
rock cycle

What do YOU wonder?

Joshua Tree National Park, in California, has rocks shaped like arches, soccer balls, and even skulls! What do you think could cause rocks to look like those in this photo?

What Are Minerals?

Fast Fact

Giant Gems! The Crown Jewels of Great Britain are set with thousands of diamonds, rubies, and sapphires. One diamond weighed 621.2 g (21.9 oz) before it was cut! A diamond is the hardest mineral known. That's one property that makes it a valuable gem. What property might make tanzanite, shown here, valuable? You'll learn about other mineral properties in the Investigate.

Mineral Properties

Materials
- 6 labeled mineral samples
- hand lens
- streak plate
- pre-1983 penny
- steel nail

Procedure

1. Copy the table.

2. Use the hand lens to observe each mineral's color. Record your observations in the table.

3. With each mineral, draw a line across the streak plate. What color is each mineral's streak? Record your observations.

4. CAUTION: **Use caution with the nail. It's sharp.** Test the hardness of each mineral. Try to scratch each mineral with your fingernail, the penny, and the steel nail. Then try to scratch each mineral with each of the other minerals. Record your observations in the table.

5. Classify the minerals by using the properties you tested: color, streak, and hardness. For each mineral, make a label that lists all three properties.

Draw Conclusions

1. How are the mineral samples different from one another?

2. **Inquiry Skill** Scientists classify objects to make them easier to study. How do you think scientists classify minerals?

Step 3

Mineral Sample	Color of the Mineral Sample	Color of the Mineral's Streak	Things That Scratch the Mineral
A			
B			
C			
D			
E			
F			

Investigate Further

Obtain five additional mineral samples. Classify each sample according to its color, streak, hardness, and one new property.

Reading in Science

VOCABULARY
mineral p. 36
streak p. 37
luster p. 37
hardness p. 38

SCIENCE CONCEPTS
▶ what minerals are
▶ how to identify minerals

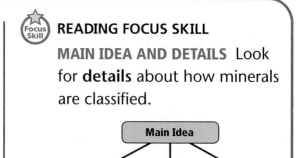

READING FOCUS SKILL

MAIN IDEA AND DETAILS Look for **details** about how minerals are classified.

Some Mineral Properties

You probably have heard the word *mineral* before. Foods that are healthful for you are full of vitamins and minerals. Bottled mineral water is often sold at the grocery store. Beautiful minerals such as diamonds and rubies are used in jewelry. But what exactly is a mineral? A **mineral** is a naturally occurring, nonliving solid that has a specific chemical makeup and a *crystalline*, or repeating, structure.

You may already be familiar with several kinds of minerals. Quartz, diamond, and salt are all minerals. So are the ores of metals such as copper, silver, and iron. There are hundreds of different minerals. So how do scientists identify all these minerals? Scientists use *mineral properties*, or characteristics, to identify and classify the more than 2000 different minerals that have been found on Earth.

One property of minerals that's easy to see is color. Minerals come in a rainbow of colors.

Mineral Color

Some minerals, such as quartz, are found in a variety of colors.

Rose quartz

Clear quartz

Amethyst quartz

Smoky quartz

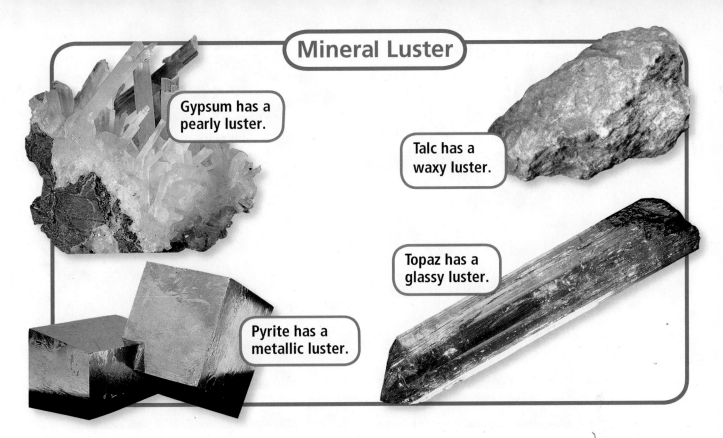

Gypsum has a pearly luster.

Talc has a waxy luster.

Topaz has a glassy luster.

Pyrite has a metallic luster.

But color alone cannot be used to identify a mineral. For example, some minerals, such as quartz, are found in many different colors. Scientists need to use additional properties when classifying most minerals.

Another mineral property is streak. **Streak** is the color of the powder left behind when you rub a mineral against a rough white tile, or a streak plate. Many minerals make a streak that is the same color as the mineral. However, some minerals do not. For instance, hematite is silver, black, or dark brown. But its streak is red-brown. Streak is a better property for mineral identification than color, because—unlike color—streak does not vary. All colors of quartz make the same streak.

The way a mineral's surface reflects light is a property called **luster**. Many minerals have a metallic luster. Think of how light reflects off metals such as gold, silver, and copper. Pyrite, or fool's gold, has a metallic luster. Other minerals have a nonmetallic luster. The luster of a nonmetallic mineral can be described as dull, glassy, pearly, waxy, and so on. For examples of different lusters, look at the minerals pictured above.

 MAIN IDEA AND DETAILS What are three visible properties of minerals?

Mineral Streak

The colors of these two pieces of hematite are different, but their streak is the same.

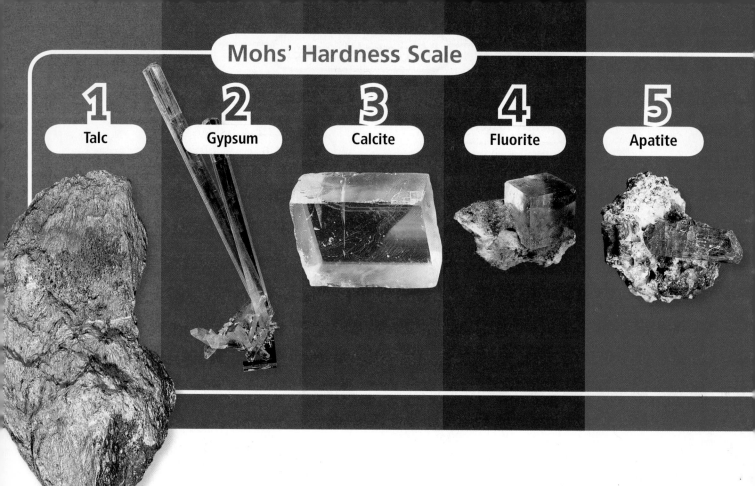

Mohs' Hardness Scale

1 Talc

2 Gypsum

3 Calcite

4 Fluorite

5 Apatite

Insta-Lab

Pass the Salt, Please!

Most minerals are crystalline in structure. Examine some grains of table salt with a hand lens. Note whether individual grains look like tiny crystals. Describe their shape.

Mineral Hardness

Most people would agree that objects such as rocks, nails, and glass are hard. An important property of minerals is hardness. **Hardness** is a mineral's ability to resist being scratched. Some minerals are so hard that they can't be scratched by anything. Others scratch easily. A German scientist, Friedrich Mohs (MOHZ), found that minerals can be classified by how hard they are to scratch. He came up with a scale that ranks minerals from 1 to 10 according to their hardness.

The scale is called the *Mohs' hardness scale.* On this scale, the softest mineral—talc—is classified as a 1. Diamond, the hardest mineral, is classified as a 10. Any mineral higher on the scale can scratch any mineral lower on the scale.

| **6** | **7** | **8** | **9** | **10** |
| Orthoclase | Quartz | Topaz | Corundum | Diamond |

The Mohs' scale is easy to use. If you have several minerals for which you know the hardness, you can use them to determine the hardness of an unknown mineral. You can also use common materials to test a mineral's hardness. For example, your fingernail has a hardness of about 2.5. That means your fingernail should be able to scratch any mineral that has a hardness of 1 or 2. A copper penny has a hardness of 3. (Be sure the penny was made before 1983. Pennies made after that are mostly zinc.) Steel nails have a hardness of about 5.5, and ordinary glass has a hardness of about 6.

 MAIN IDEA AND DETAILS How can you determine the hardness of a mineral?

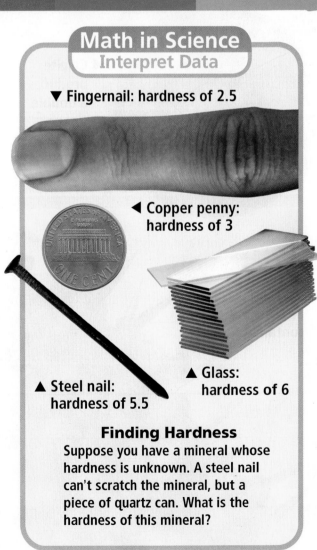

Math in Science
Interpret Data

▼ **Fingernail: hardness of 2.5**

◄ **Copper penny: hardness of 3**

▲ **Steel nail: hardness of 5.5**

▲ **Glass: hardness of 6**

Finding Hardness
Suppose you have a mineral whose hardness is unknown. A steel nail can't scratch the mineral, but a piece of quartz can. What is the hardness of this mineral?

Unique Properties of Minerals

You have unique characteristics that make you different from everyone else. Some minerals have unique properties that make them different, too. For example, the crystal structure of calcite (KAL•syt) refracts, or bends, light a certain way. If you place a picture behind a piece of calcite, you will see a double image of the picture.

The mineral magnetite (MAG•nuh•tyt) is magnetic. Magnetite is also called lodestone, after the word *lode*, which means "way." Lodestone can be used in a compass to help you find your way.

Some kinds of minerals glow under ultraviolet, or "black" light. Just as quartz can be found in many different colors, certain minerals glow in different colors. For example, corundum can glow red, yellow, green, or blue.

A few minerals—such as quartz—develop an electric potential when pressure is applied to them. This will also happen to quartz when the temperature changes. Because of this property, quartz is often used in computers, cell phones, radios, televisions, and watches.

Focus Skill **MAIN IDEA AND DETAILS** What are four special properties of minerals?

◄ Calcite produces a double image.

◄ Fluorite glows, or fluoresces, under certain kinds of light.

Magnetite attracts materials containing iron. ▶

Focus Skill

1. MAIN IDEA AND DETAILS Draw and complete the graphic organizer.

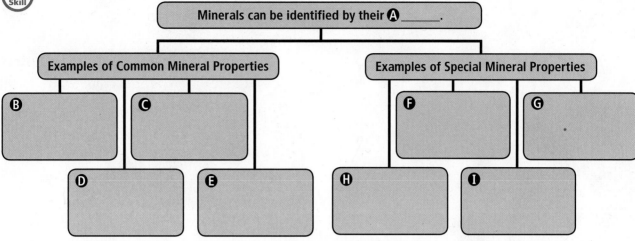

Minerals can be identified by their **A** _____.

Examples of Common Mineral Properties

B

C

D

E

Examples of Special Mineral Properties

F

G

H

I

2. SUMMARIZE Use the graphic organizer to write a lesson summary.

3. DRAW CONCLUSIONS Suppose you have two mineral samples with the same hardness. What other mineral properties could you use to decide whether the two samples are the same mineral?

4. VOCABULARY Choose a mineral, and write a short paragraph describing its streak, luster, and hardness.

Test Prep

5. Critical Thinking What characteristic of a mineral does the term *luster* describe?

6. Which of the following mineral properties can be expressed by a number?

A. color **C.** luster

B. hardness **D.** streak

Links

Writing

Expository Writing
Write two paragraphs **comparing and contrasting** different ways minerals can be classified.

Math

Use Measuring Devices
Collect several mineral samples that are about the same size. Use a balance to find the mass of each sample. Explain why minerals that are the same size may have very different masses.

Social Studies

Mineral Collage
Cut out pictures of minerals from old magazines. You may find minerals shown in many things, such as buildings, jewelry, and coins. Use the mineral pictures to make a mineral collage.

 For more links and activities, go to **www.hspscience.com**

How Do Rocks Form?

Fast Fact

The Sands of Time This rock formation in Arizona is part of the famous Vermillion Cliffs. It is a 200-million-year-old sand dune that has turned to rock! In the Investigate, you'll identify some other kinds of rock.

Identifying Rocks

Materials
- hand lens
- 5 labeled rock samples
- safety goggles
- dropper
- vinegar
- paper plate

Procedure

1. Copy the table. In the column labeled *Picture*, make a drawing of each rock.

2. Use the hand lens to observe each rock. In the table, record each rock's color.

3. Look at the grains that make up each rock. Notice their sizes. Are their edges rounded or sharp? How do the grains fit together? Under *Texture* in the table, record your observations.

4. CAUTION: **Put on the safety goggles.** Vinegar makes bubbles form on rocks that contain calcite. Put the rocks on the paper plate. Use the dropper to slowly drop some vinegar onto each rock. Observe the results, and record your findings.

5. Classify the rocks into two groups so that the rocks in each group have similar properties.

Rock Sample	Color	Texture	Picture	Bubbles When Vinegar Added
1				
2				
3				
4				
5				

Step 4

Draw Conclusions

1. What properties did you use to classify the rocks?

2. **Inquiry Skill** Scientists classify objects to make them easier to study. One way scientists classify rocks is by how they form. Choose one of the rocks, and describe how it might have formed.

Investigate Further

Hypothesize **about the best property to use to identify rocks.** Plan and conduct an investigation **to test your hypothesis.**

Reading in Science

VOCABULARY
rock p. 44
igneous rock p. 44
deposition p. 46
sedimentary rock p. 46
metamorphic rock p. 48

SCIENCE CONCEPTS
▶ how rocks form
▶ how people use rocks

 READING FOCUS SKILL

CAUSE AND EFFECT Look for what **causes** rocks to form.

| cause | → | effect |

Igneous Rocks

What are mountains, valleys, hills, beaches, and the ocean floor made of? Rocks! Rocks are found almost everywhere on Earth. You've probably seen many different kinds of rocks. But all rocks have one thing in common— minerals. A **rock** is a natural solid made of one or more minerals. In fact, you might think of most rocks as mineral mixtures.

Rocks are classified into one of three groups depending on how they form. Rock that forms when melted rock cools and hardens is called **igneous rock** (IG•nee•uhs). Igneous rocks can form underground, or they can form on Earth's surface.

Igneous rocks that form underground cool much more slowly than those that form on the surface. Below ground, the surrounding rocks hold in the heat. On the surface, melted rock cools quickly.

This igneous rock, called *rhyolite,* forms above ground. It contains the same minerals as granite, but the mineral crystals are smaller.

This igneous rock, called *granite*, forms below ground. It has large mineral crystals.

When melted rock cools slowly, mineral crystals have time to grow. Because of this, igneous rocks that form underground have large crystals.

When melted rock cools quickly, it hardens before any mineral crystals can grow large. As a result, igneous rocks that form above ground have small or no crystals.

The size of mineral crystals is not the only difference among igneous rocks. Different igneous rocks contain different amounts or different kinds of minerals. That's because not all melted rock beneath Earth's surface is the same.

For example, igneous rocks that form from melted rock containing a lot of silica will also have a lot of silica. One way it shows up in the rocks is as the mineral quartz. Igneous rocks that form from melted rock with little silica will have other kinds of minerals and will be different rocks.

 CAUSE AND EFFECT What causes igneous rocks to form?

Igneous Rocks

▲ *Basalt* (buh•SAWLT) is the most common type of igneous rock. It forms above ground. It has small mineral crystals.

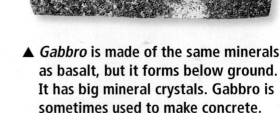

▲ *Gabbro* is made of the same minerals as basalt, but it forms below ground. It has big mineral crystals. Gabbro is sometimes used to make concrete.

▲ *Pumice* (PUHM•is) has a lot of air spaces and is very light. Some people use pumice stones to smooth their skin.

▲ *Obsidian* is also called volcanic glass. Surgeons once used blades made of obsidian because it breaks into sharp pieces.

Sedimentary Rocks

Picture a rock at the top of a hill. Every spring, rain falls on the rock, dissolving some of its minerals. In summer, the heat of the sun causes the rock to crack, and small pieces flake off. Fall arrives, and windblown dust slowly scratches the rock's surface. In winter, water seeps into cracks in the rock and freezes. The ice expands, breaking off more pieces of the rock. This rock is slowly being worn away.

What happens to all the little pieces of rock, called *sediment,* that have worn away? Sediment is carried off by water and wind. It is often set down, or *deposited,* in another place. This process in which sediment settles out of water or is dropped by the wind is called **deposition** (dep•uh•ZISH•uhn).

Over time, sediment piles up, one layer on top of another, pressing together tightly. Some minerals dissolved in water come out of solution, forming a kind of cement. This makes the sediment stick together. Cemented sediment forms a type of rock called **sedimentary rock** (sed•uh•MEN•tuh•ree).

Sedimentary rocks form from any rock that is worn down. Sediment of any size can be found in sedimentary rocks. Some sedimentary rocks have big pieces of sediment in them. Others contain grains of sand, or even smaller pieces. Some

Sedimentary Rocks

▲ A conglomerate (kuhn•GLAHM•er•it) rock is a sedimentary rock that is formed from sand, rounded pebbles, and larger pieces of rock.

▲ Shale is a sedimentary rock made up of tiny, dust-size pieces of sediment.

▲ Sandstone is a sedimentary rock made up of sediment pieces the size of sand grains.

▲ Limestone is a sedimentary rock that is usually formed in oceans from seashells, which are largely made of the mineral calcite. There is often more calcite between shells, cementing them together.

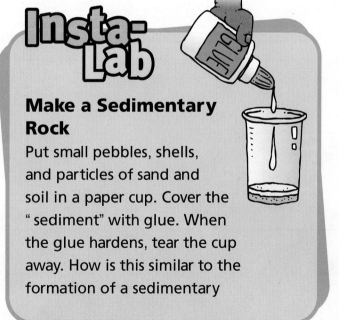

◀ As water moves through Florida Caverns, it dissolves minerals from the rocks. As this mineral-rich water drips, some of it forms icicle-like *stalactites* (stuh•LAK•tytz). Drops pile up on the floor and harden to form *stalagmites* (stuh•LAG•mytz).

sedimentary rocks have the remains of living things, such as shells, within the sediment. Other sedimentary rocks form when mineral-rich water evaporates. Try placing a pan of salt water in a warm area. When the water dries up, you will have salt. When this happens in nature, the mineral formed is called *halite*. Large deposits of halite are rock salt, a sedimentary rock.

After a sedimentary rock forms, it might be worn away. Sediment from the rock may be deposited in a different location or in a different way, forming a completely different sedimentary rock. This is one way that rocks are constantly changing. In the next section and in Lesson 3, you'll learn about other ways that rocks change.

 CAUSE AND EFFECT How do sedimentary rocks form?

Insta-Lab

Make a Sedimentary Rock

Put small pebbles, shells, and particles of sand and soil in a paper cup. Cover the "sediment" with glue. When the glue hardens, tear the cup away. How is this similar to the formation of a sedimentary

Metamorphic Rocks

Have you ever seen a caterpillar change into a butterfly? This process is called *metamorphosis* (met•uh•MAWR•fuh•sis), from the Greek words *meta*, meaning "change," and *morphosis,* meaning "form." Rocks, too, can change form under certain conditions. When rock is changed by heat and pressure, the new rock is called **metamorphic rock**. Metamorphic rocks can form from any other rock—including igneous rocks, sedimentary rocks, and other metamorphic rocks.

Where is there enough pressure and heat to change rocks? Metamorphic rocks are found in every mountain range on Earth. Picture the processes working there. Suppose you have a ball of clay. You place a book on top of the clay, and then another and another book. Soon you have a dozen books piled on top of the clay. What happens to the clay? As you can imagine, it becomes flat and very, very thin!

Now suppose the ball of clay is a rock somewhere in northern New Mexico. Instead of a pile of books on top of it, there is a huge mountain with a mass of millions and millions of kilograms. The weight of the mountain squashes the rock. The rock also gets very hot, because as pressure increases, temperature rises. All this heat and pressure changes the old rock into a new rock—a metamorphic rock.

Metamorphic rocks form in other places, too. Imagine an ocean floor where layers of sediment are constantly being piled on top

These layers of metamorphic rock, called Vishnu Schist, were formed in the Grand Canyon when sandstone was changed by pressure and heat. ▼

Metamorphic Rocks

▲ Schist (SHIST) may form from sandstone. As mountains build up, they put a huge amount of pressure on sedimentary rocks.

▲ Gneiss (NYS) can form when granite, an igneous rock, is subjected to a lot of pressure.

▲ Slate is formed from a small-grained sedimentary rock such as shale.

▲ Quartzite is formed from sandstone that is made almost entirely of the mineral quartz.

Marble forms from calcite-rich limestone, so it is often white. Small amounts of other minerals give marble its colors. ▶

of one another. Stuck together by minerals that act as cement, sedimentary rocks form. In time, these rocks may be pushed under other rocks, causing them to change into metamorphic rocks.

Metamorphic rocks also form near some volcanoes. Volcanoes are places where melted rock rises above Earth's surface.

The melted rock is extremely hot—not hot enough to melt nearby rocks, but hot enough to change them into metamorphic rocks. Even igneous rocks can become metamorphic rocks.

 CAUSE AND EFFECT What causes metamorphic rocks to form?

How Rocks Are Used

Rocks have always been an important natural resource for people. Thousands of years ago, people used rocks called *flint* to make hand tools. Even today, rocks are used to make tools of many kinds—from sandpaper to surgical instruments.

People also use rocks such as sandstone, granite, limestone, and marble to build buildings and monuments. The Capitol building of the United States contains both sandstone and marble. The Great Pyramid of Giza in Egypt was made out of sandstone covered with limestone. In fact, everywhere in the world, you'll find important buildings and monuments made of rocks. Rocks are also used to make cement, glass, gravel, and other building materials.

Remember that rocks are made of minerals. Many minerals and the metals they contain are used in products such as cell phones, cars, and computers.

Rocks and minerals are natural resources, and so they must be conserved. People can conserve them by recycling metal products, such as cans, and by reusing rock from buildings. Recycling and reusing also protect the environment by reducing the need to dig into Earth for more resources.

CAUSE AND EFFECT How does the durability of rocks affect the way people use them?

Many things are made from granite, an igneous rock, including buildings, monuments, and kitchen countertops. ▼

▲ **This garden wall is made of limestone, a sedimentary rock. Pieces of the wall may have been used in an earlier wall or building.**

The Taj Mahal in India, like many grand buildings and monuments, is made of marble, a metamorphic rock. ▶

1. CAUSE AND EFFECT Draw and complete the graphic organizer.

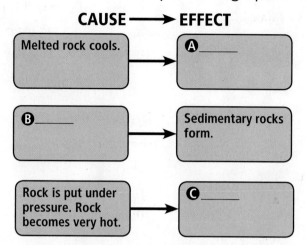

CAUSE ⟶ EFFECT

Melted rock cools. → **Ⓐ**_____

Ⓑ_____ → Sedimentary rocks form.

Rock is put under pressure. Rock becomes very hot. → **Ⓒ**_____

2. SUMMARIZE Write a summary of this lesson by using the lesson vocabulary in a paragraph.

3. DRAW CONCLUSIONS You find an igneous rock with large crystals in it. Where was the rock formed? Explain your answer.

4. VOCABULARY Write three sentences that describe the three main types of rock. Give an example of each type.

Test Prep

5. Critical Thinking How can different kinds of igneous rocks be classified?

6. What kind of rock is gneiss?
- **A.** igneous
- **B.** marble
- **C.** metamorphic
- **D.** sedimentary

Links

Writing

Narrative Writing
Write a poem using as many adjectives as you can to **describe** how rocks form and change.

Math

Use Mental Math
If it takes 150 years for a mountain to grow 2.5 cm, how many years will go by before the mountain is 10 cm taller?

Art

Stone Sculptures
Over the centuries, sculptors have made many beautiful works of art from rock. Choose a sculpture. Make a fact sheet listing who made the sculpture and when, where, and why.

 For more links and activities, go to **www.hspscience.com**

How Are Rocks Changed?

Fast Fact

A Window on the World North Window in Arches National Park, Utah, is a natural bridge—a hole worn through a rock. The hole was carved by water. In the Investigate, you'll see what it takes to change rocks!

Molding Rocks

Materials
- small objects—gravel, sand, pieces of paper, several fake gems
- 3 pieces of modeling clay, each a different color
- 2 aluminum pie pans
- water

Procedure

1 Suppose the small objects are minerals. Press two different kinds of "minerals" into each piece of clay. Now you have three different "igneous rocks."

2 What happens when wind and water wear down rocks? To model this process, break one of the rocks into pieces and drop the "sediment" into a pie pan filled with water.

3 On top of the sediment pile, drop pieces of the second rock. Then drop pieces of the third rock. Press the layers together using the bottom of the empty pie pan. Now what kind of rock do you have?

4 Squeeze and mold the new rock between your hands to warm it up. What is making the rock change? Which kind of rock is it now?

Draw Conclusions

1. How did the igneous rocks change in this activity?

2. **Inquiry Skill** Scientists often use models to help them understand processes that occur in nature. What process did you model in Step 4 of this activity?

Step 1

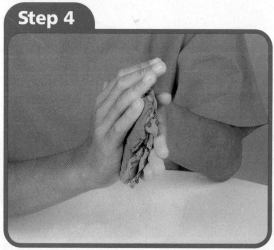

Step 4

Investigate Further

Can any type of rock change into any other type? Make a model to explore this question.

Reading in Science

VOCABULARY
weathering p. 54
erosion p. 55
rock cycle p. 56

SCIENCE CONCEPTS
▶ how rocks change over time
▶ how rocks move through the rock cycle

 READING FOCUS SKILL

SEQUENCE Look for **sequences** in which rocks change.

Processes That Change Rocks

After a volcano erupts, molten rock hardens into igneous rock. But this isn't the end of the story for the newly formed rock. As you learned in Lesson 2, rocks are constantly being formed and worn away.

Igneous rocks, like all rock on Earth's surface, are exposed to wind, water, ice, sunlight, and more. All of these factors break down rocks into sediment. The process of wearing away rocks by natural processes is called **weathering**.

All rocks on Earth's surface are weathered. But not all rocks weather at the same rate. In Lesson 1, you discovered that minerals have different degrees of hardness. Some minerals, such as corundum and diamond, can't be easily scratched because they're hard. Others, such as talc, can be easily scratched because they're soft. Rocks that contain mostly hard minerals weather much more slowly than rocks that contain mostly soft minerals. So granite, which contains feldspar and quartz, weathers more slowly than limestone, which contains mostly calcite.

Weathering is only the beginning of a process that changes rocks on Earth's

After rock has been weathered, what remains may look unusual.

As soon as igneous rock cools, it begins to weather.

54

◀ The Colorado River erodes sediment from one area and moves it downstream. Some of the sediment is deposited at the river's mouth, forming a delta.

surface. The wind and water that weather rocks are part of another process. Wind and water move sediment from one place to another. The process of wearing away and removing sediment by wind, water, or ice is called **erosion**.

After erosion, sediment can be deposited, pressed together, and cemented, forming sedimentary rock. As more layers of sediment are deposited, processes that cement the sediment speed up.

Processes using pressure and heat, which form metamorphic rock, can take place where mountain ranges have formed. Rock layers in mountain ranges are often folded, broken, and upturned, showing that the rocks have been through many changes.

 SEQUENCE What happens to sediment after weathering?

The rock layers exposed by this road cut were bent and folded as this mountain formed.

The Rock Cycle

Weathering, erosion, deposition, heat, and pressure can all change rocks. Together, these processes make up the rock cycle. The **rock cycle** is the continuous process in which one type of rock changes into another type. Study the Science Up Close feature to see how the rock cycle works.

 SEQUENCE What sequence of events would have to take place to change a metamorphic rock into an igneous rock?

Squashing Stones

Use your metamorphic " rock" from the Investigate. Fold it in half and then in half again. Squeeze it tightly between your hands. Then cut through it with a plastic knife. How is this " rock" like the rock layers found in mountains?

The Rock Cycle

Just as you recycle aluminum cans and waste paper, Earth recycles rocks through the rock cycle.

Igneous Rock

Granite, an igneous rock, can be changed into sandstone, a sedimentary rock, through weathering and erosion. Heat and pressure can change granite into a metamorphic rock. With enough heat, granite can melt and harden into a new igneous rock.

Sedimentary Rock

Heat and pressure can change sandstone, a sedimentary rock, into gneiss, a metamorphic rock. If sandstone is melted, it hardens into an igneous rock when it cools. If sandstone is weathered and eroded, it can form a new sedimentary rock.

Metamorphic Rock

Gneiss (NYS), a metamorphic rock, can be weathered, eroded, deposited, and cemented into a sedimentary rock. If a metamorphic rock is melted and then hardens again, it will become an igneous rock. With heat and pressure, a metamorphic rock can become a new metamorphic rock.

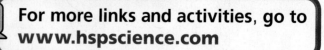

For more links and activities, go to
www.hspscience.com

Soil Formation

The next time you're outside, take a close look at the soil under your feet. Soils around the world are very different from one another. They have many different colors and textures.

Some soils are good for farming. They contain the right amounts of both large and small particles. But some soils contain too much sand, which makes them dry out quickly. Other soils contain too much clay, which keeps them too wet. No matter how different soils are, though, they have one thing in common: they all come from weathered rock.

Soil can form from weathered rock right under it, or it can form from eroded sediment carried from far away. Because soils are made from rocks, they contain minerals. The kinds of minerals found in any soil depend on the kind of rock from which the soil formed. Certain minerals are needed for plant growth.

Most soil is made up of more than weathered rock. Rich farming soil also contains small pieces of decayed plant and animal matter, called *humus* (HYOO•muhs). Humus provides additional nutrients that plants need to grow. If these nutrients are missing, fertilizers must be added to the soil to meet the plants' needs.

Focus Skill **SEQUENCE** What must happen first for soil to form?

Soil often forms layers, with the smallest particles and the most humus in the top layer, or topsoil. Layers below the topsoil have larger and larger pieces of weathered rock.▶

◀**Plowing gets soil ready for planting by breaking up hard clumps and mixing the layers.**

1. SEQUENCE Draw and complete the graphic organizer.

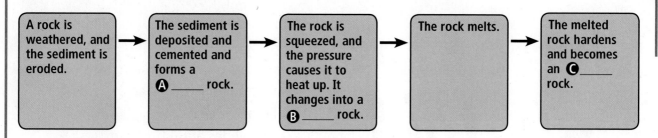

A rock is weathered, and the sediment is eroded. → The sediment is deposited and cemented and forms a **A** _____ rock. → The rock is squeezed, and the pressure causes it to heat up. It changes into a **B** _____ rock. → The rock melts. → The melted rock hardens and becomes an **C** _____ rock.

2. SUMMARIZE Draw a diagram that summarizes this lesson.

3. DRAW CONCLUSIONS How might a sedimentary rock change into another sedimentary rock?

4. VOCABULARY Write two or three sentences using terms from this lesson to explain how soil formation could be considered part of the rock cycle.

Test Prep

5. Critical Thinking What determines how quickly a rock is weathered?

6. Which of the following processes can change a metamorphic rock into a sedimentary rock?

   A. adding pressure

   B. increasing temperature

   C. melting

   D. weathering

Writing

Expository Writing

Write a newspaper article **describing** the erosion of a local valley or river bank.

Math

Subtract Fractions

If $\frac{1}{4}$ of a granite rock is quartz, $\frac{5}{8}$ of the rock is feldspar, and the rest is mica, what fraction of the rock is mica?

Social Studies

Time Line

Research a famous landform. How old is it? How fast is it eroding? Make a time line showing the landform's changes.

 For more links and activities, go to www.hspscience.com

King of the Mountain

When Jerod Minich prepares to climb a mountain or scale a rock cliff, he makes sure he has all the right equipment. That equipment includes ropes, hammers, and his high-tech artificial legs and feet.

Minich is an experienced climber who had both his legs amputated below the knees when he was a child. He suffered from a disease called *diabetes,* and doctors had to cut off his legs to save his life.

In the past few years, Minich, of East Stroudsburg, Pennsylvania, has climbed some of the most dangerous and unforgiving rocks in the United States. He has scaled Devils Tower in Wyoming and, most recently, a 70-foot wall of rock called "the Column" in Minnesota.

Not Stopping

New technology has helped Minich do the sport he loves so much. Minich can hike with the help of new superstrong and lightweight carbon-fiber feet.

The feet are attached to artificial legs that are specially designed to reduce the pressure Minich feels when climbing up a rock face.

Minich isn't the only athlete who relies on high-tech artificial legs to climb mountains. In Nepal, a country in Asia, doctors fit climber Nawang Sherpa with an artificial leg after he was injured in a motorcycle accident.

Nawang received his first artificial leg in 2001. After getting used to that for a year, Nawang later received an artificial climbing leg. Nawang's climbing leg is lighter than his regular leg, which allows him to climb farther and more comfortably.

Nawang brought two of these legs with him when he attempted to climb Mount Everest, Earth's tallest mountain. Nawang changed the leg when he lost weight during the climb, which is normal. The foot that was attached to the leg was designed so that it would allow Nawang to get traction on the rough terrain of Everest.

Using the high-tech leg worked so well that Nawang became the first amputee to climb Mount Everest.

Think About It

1. What do you think engineers had to keep in mind when designing an artificial climbing foot?
2. What is the toughest challenge you have ever had to overcome?

 Find out more! Log on to
www.hspscience.com

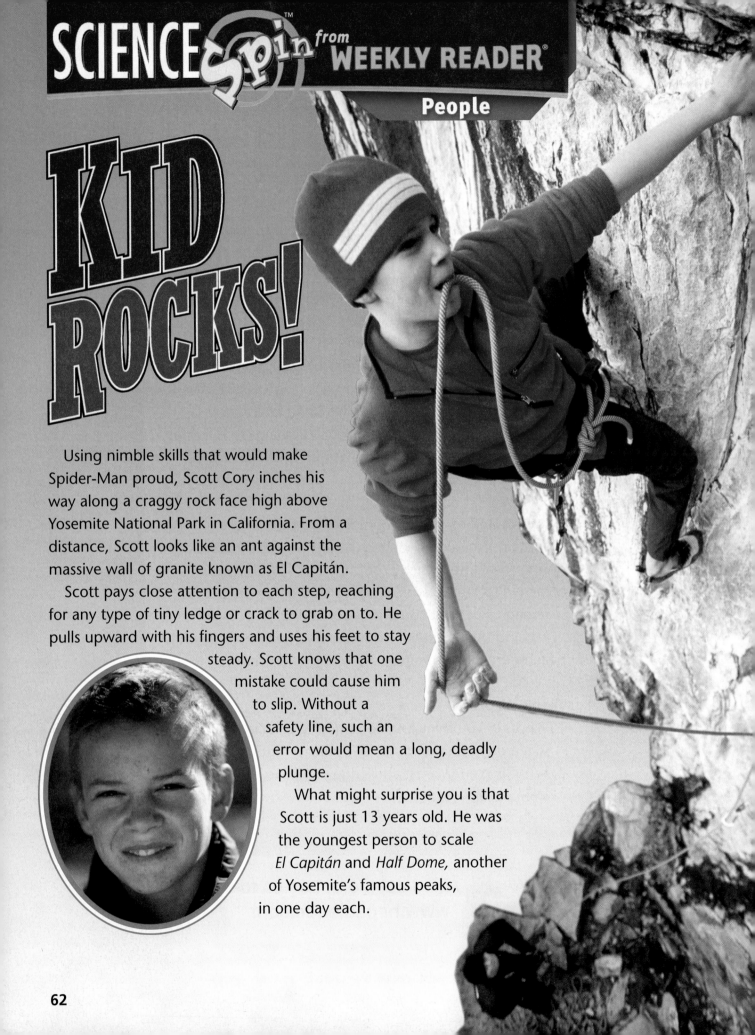

KID ROCKS!

Using nimble skills that would make Spider-Man proud, Scott Cory inches his way along a craggy rock face high above Yosemite National Park in California. From a distance, Scott looks like an ant against the massive wall of granite known as El Capitán.

Scott pays close attention to each step, reaching for any type of tiny ledge or crack to grab on to. He pulls upward with his fingers and uses his feet to stay steady. Scott knows that one mistake could cause him to slip. Without a safety line, such an error would mean a long, deadly plunge.

What might surprise you is that Scott is just 13 years old. He was the youngest person to scale *El Capitán* and *Half Dome,* another of Yosemite's famous peaks, in one day each.

Materials
- 3 soil samples
- 3 sheets of white paper
- hand lens
- toothpicks

Quick and Easy Project

Observing Soil

Procedure
1. Obtain soil samples from three different places.
2. Pour each sample onto a separate sheet of paper.
3. Examine each sample with the hand lens. Record your observations.
4. Use the toothpicks to separate the grains in each sample into piles of soil particles, rock, and plant matter.
5. Classify each sample by its contents.

Draw Conclusions
Compare and contrast the three soils. What do the contents of soil tell you about its formation? Which of the three soil samples would be best to grow plants in? Explain your answer.

Design Your Own Investigation

Weathering Rocks

Decide how you can test which agent of weathering erodes rocks the fastest. For example, you may decide to place some rocks in water, freeze them, and then thaw them out again. You might place other rocks in a container and shake it. Collect small rocks to use for your experiment. Remember that different rocks weather at different rates, so be careful to collect rocks of the same type. Record your observations. You may want to present your findings to the class.

Review and Test Preparation

Vocabulary Review

Use the terms below to complete the sentences. The page numbers tell you where to look in the chapter if you need help.

mineral p. 36   metamorphic
streak p. 37   rock p. 48
luster p. 37   weathering p. 54
igneous rock p. 44   erosion p. 55
deposition p. 46   rock cycle p. 56
sedimentary
    rock p. 46

1. The way a mineral reflects light is its _____.

2. Rocks are broken down into sediment during _____.

3. Rock changed by heat and pressure is known as _____.

4. Rocks continually change into other types of rocks in the _____.

5. Pieces of sediment settle out of water or wind during _____.

6. You can rub a mineral against a white tile to see its _____.

7. A naturally occurring solid with a crystalline structure is a _____.

8. Pieces of sediment that have been pressed and cemented together form _____.

9. Melted rock cools to form _____.

10. Wind and water carry sediment from one place to another during _____.

Check Understanding

Write the letter of the best choice.

11. What property describes a mineral's ability to resist being scratched?
    A. erodibility   **C.** luster
    B. hardness   **D.** streak

12. Which of the following is a good definition of the word *rock*?
    F. A rock is any nonliving solid found in nature.
    G. A rock is anything found in the ground.
    H. A rock is a hard object.
    J. A rock is a mineral mixture.

13. You find an igneous rock with no visible mineral crystals. Where did this rock most likely form?
    A. deep underground
    B. in a cave
    C. on Earth's surface
    D. under a mountain

14. MAIN IDEA AND DETAILS Look at the picture below. What kind of rock is this an example of?

    F. basalt rock
    G. igneous rock
    H. metamorphic rock
    J. sedimentary rock

15. CAUSE AND EFFECT Which of the following lead to weathering?
    A. high temperatures
    B. mineral type and color
    C. pressure and light
    D. wind and rain

16. Which of the following are the main ingredients of soil?
    F. humus and weathered rock
    G. minerals and water
    H. sedimentary and igneous rocks
    J. soft minerals and cement

Inquiry Skills

17. Explain some ways in which minerals are **classified**.

18. What changes might you **observe** in a rock as it is weathered?

Critical Thinking

19. Monica found a clear mineral crystal. She wanted to identify its hardness. She tried to scratch it with her fingernail, a penny, and a steel nail. But none of these worked. Then she tried topaz, which did leave a scratch. The mineral was able to scratch glass. What mineral could Monica have found? Explain your answer.

20. Examine the pictures of the two rock samples.
Part A How did Rock A form? Where did Rock A form? Explain your answer.
Part B How did Rock B form? Could Rock B have formed from Rock A? Explain your answer.

ROCK A   **ROCK B**

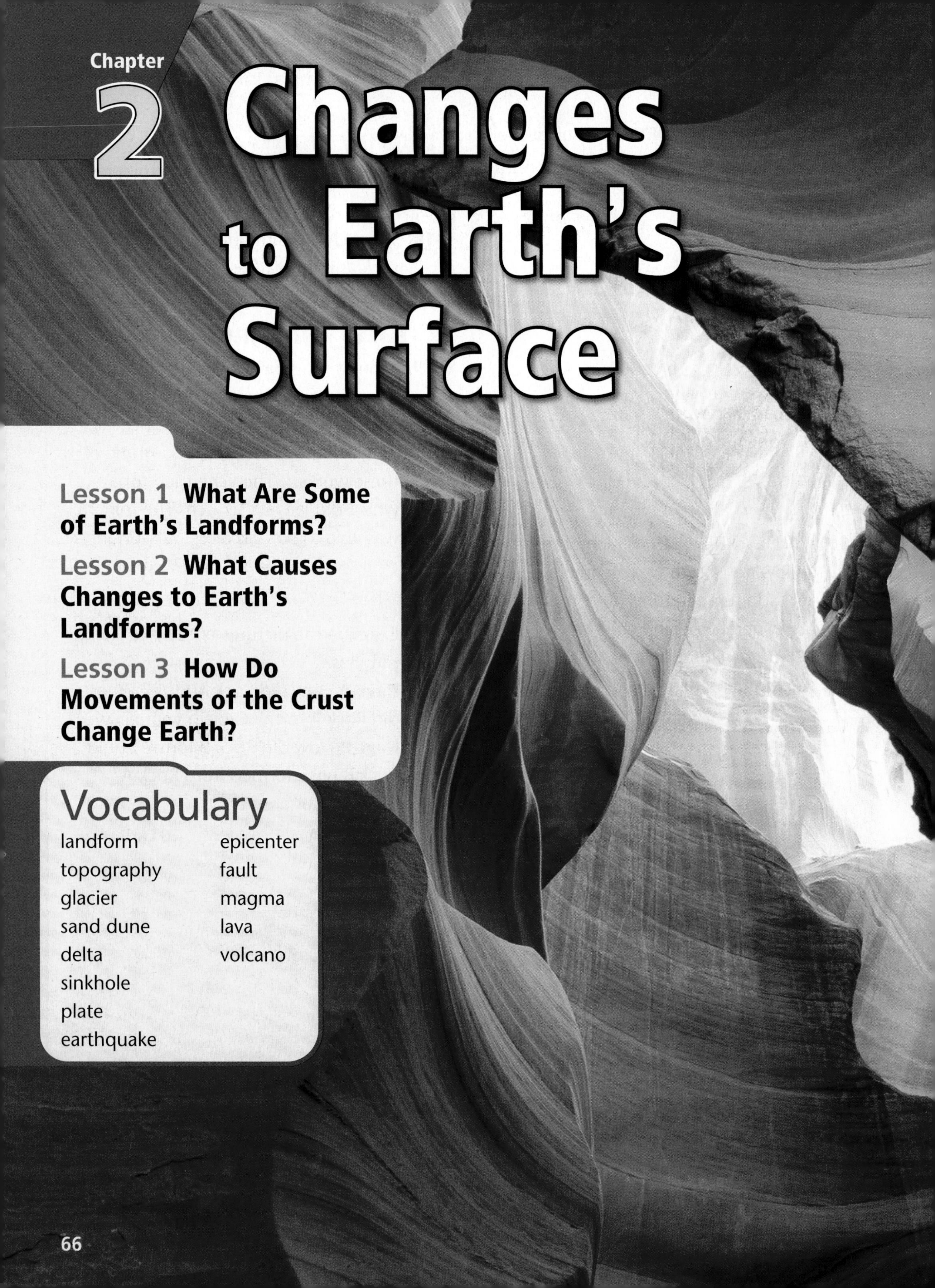

Chapter 2

Changes to Earth's Surface

Lesson 1 **What Are Some of Earth's Landforms?**

Lesson 2 **What Causes Changes to Earth's Landforms?**

Lesson 3 **How Do Movements of the Crust Change Earth?**

Vocabulary

landform
topography
glacier
sand dune
delta
sinkhole
plate
earthquake
epicenter
fault
magma
lava
volcano

In 1931, a young Navajo girl was exploring the countryside near her home in Arizona. She noticed a small slit in the ground. That small slit led to a canyon 40 m (130 ft) deep and more than 5 km (3 mi) long! Today, the canyon is called Antelope Canyon. What do you think could have made this landform?

What Are Some of Earth's Landforms?

Fast Fact

Mitten of Rock The landform shown here is called Right Mitten. Its unusual shape made it a popular location for car commercials. Vehicles were flown in by helicopter and placed on the top. How did Right Mitten form? Earth's surface seems to stay the same, but wind and water change landforms into interesting shapes. You can model some of these changes in the Investigate.

Modeling Earth's Landforms

Materials ● clay ● plastic tray ● forceps ● cup

Procedure

① With a partner, form the clay into pea-size balls. Use the balls to model a landform, such as a mountain or a plain, in the tray.

② One partner should close his or her eyes. Then the other partner should change the landform by removing one clay ball with the forceps and putting the ball into the cup.

③ After the ball is removed, the partner whose eyes were closed should observe the landform carefully. Can that person see any change? Switch roles and repeat Step 2.

④ Take turns removing clay balls and observing until one of you can describe a change in the landform.

⑤ Count the clay balls in the cup. If each ball represents a change that takes place in 1000 years, how long did it take before a change was observed?

Step 1

Step 3

Draw Conclusions

1. Why might changes in hills and mountains be seen sooner than changes in plains?

2. **Inquiry Skill** Scientists often use models to help them understand natural processes. Why might a model be useful for understanding how landforms change?

Investigate Further

Build a model of a landform. Then show how the landform may look in 10,000 years.

Reading in Science

VOCABULARY
landform p. 70
topography p. 70
glacier p. 72
sand dune p. 73

SCIENCE CONCEPTS
▶ what landforms are
▶ what makes each landform different from others

READING FOCUS SKILL

MAIN IDEA AND DETAILS Look for examples and details for each type of landform.

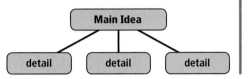

Mountains, Hills, and Plains

What is the land around your town like? Is it wide and flat? Does it have rolling hills or steep mountains? Land has many different shapes. A natural land shape or feature is called a **landform**. When you describe the landforms around your town, you're describing the area's topography. **Topography** is all the kinds of landforms in a certain area.

The jagged peaks of the Rocky Mountains are many thousands of feet higher than the surrounding land. ▼

Look at the pictures below. How would you describe the topography of the two areas? Both areas have mountains. A *mountain* is a landform that is much higher than the surrounding land. Often, mountains occur in groups called ranges. Mountain ranges can be very different from each other. The Rocky Mountains, for example, form tall, jagged peaks that rise thousands of feet above the surrounding land. The Appalachian Mountains are lower and more rounded. They are still thousands of feet high, but much lower than the Rocky Mountains.

The Appalachians are mountains, too, but their peaks are lower and more rounded than the peaks of the Rockies. ▼

▲ The Great Plains covers much of the middle of the United States. Because plains are flat, they are often good farming areas.

So, although these two areas have similar landforms—mountains—their topographies are very different.

The topography of volcanic areas differs in another way. Volcanoes usually occur as individual mountains, not in ranges. They may have steep sides or rounded slopes.

Hills are landforms that are like mountains, but not as high. Most have rounded slopes.

Not all landforms have slopes. A *plain* is a large, flat landform with little relief. *Relief* is the difference in elevation between high and low places. In the middle of the United States is a very large plain known as the Great Plains. Plains form in different ways, but all plains have the same topography. Right Mitten is flat on top, but the top is small and elevated, so it's not a plain.

Hills are lower than mountains and have gentle slopes. ▶

MAIN IDEA AND DETAILS List details that describe mountains, hills, and plains.

▲ Mount Etna, a volcano on the island of Sicily, is a single mountain.

Landforms from Ice

Look at the landforms shown below. They look different from each other, but they have one thing in common—they were both formed by glaciers. A **glacier** is a large, thick sheet of ice. As glaciers move, they change the land around and beneath them. For example, *moraines* (muh•RAYNZ) are long, low hills formed by materials carried by a glacier. As moving ice scrapes the land beneath it, rocks and other materials are picked up and carried along. This material is deposited when the glacier melts.

How can you tell a moraine from an ordinary hill? A moraine contains rocks, sand, and clay. If you dig into a moraine, you find these things deposited together. You do not find them together in most hills. There are many moraines in the northern part of the United States. Some are more than 200 km (120 mi) long!

Other landforms produced by glaciers are *glacial grooves*. These features form when a glacier scrapes and scratches the rock beneath it. As the glacier melts, grooves can be seen in the rock.

 MAIN IDEA AND DETAILS What detail tells you how a moraine is different from an ordinary hill?

In this glacier, you can see a moraine between ice flows. ▼

These glacial grooves on Kelley's Island, in Ohio, formed when ice scarred the rock. ▼

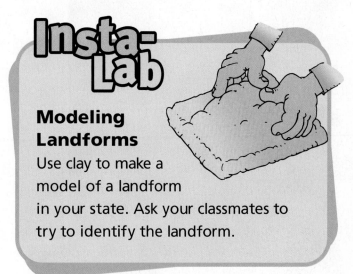

▲ Captiva is a barrier island on Florida's west coast. Because of currents, many shells wash up on the island's beaches in winter.

◀ Sand dunes form where the wind is strong and the sand deposits are plentiful. These sand dunes are in the Oregon Dunes Recreation Area.

Landforms of Sand

Some landforms are made of sand and small bits of rock. These landforms move and are shaped by both wind and water. Landforms of sand are more easily changed than landforms of rock.

A **sand dune** is a sand hill that is made and shaped by wind. As wind blows over a dune, the sand moves. This can change the dune's shape or even move the whole dune. Some dunes move as much as 30 m (100 ft) a year.

Like wind, water can also move sand. Water waves and currents reshape beaches, forming barrier islands and sand spits extending out into the water from the ends of many islands. *Sand spits* and *barrier islands* are long, narrow piles of sand that help protect the mainland from wave erosion. They are found all along the Atlantic coast and the Gulf of Mexico.

Rivers, too, can make sand landforms. Rivers carry sand from the land they flow through. When the flow of a river slows, the sand settles. This makes a landform called a *sandbar*. The Pacific coast has many sandbars where rivers flow into the ocean.

 MAIN IDEA AND DETAILS What details about sand dunes make them different from moraines?

Insta-Lab

Modeling Landforms
Use clay to make a model of a landform in your state. Ask your classmates to try to identify the landform.

This is the Grand Canyon, in Arizona. Canyons form wherever there is running water and land that is being uplifted.

Landforms from Water

The topography of the southwestern United States is beautiful and varied. There you will find landforms such as Mesa Verde (green mesa). A *mesa* is a tall, flat-topped rock feature. *Mesa* is a Spanish word meaning "table." A mesa forms as running water erodes the surrounding rock. The Southwest is also home to many canyons and unusual rock formations, like those in Monument Valley.

Canyons are deep valleys with steep sides. They are found throughout the Southwest. The Grand Canyon, in Arizona, is the largest land canyon in the world. The rushing water of the Colorado River carved through many layers of rock to make this mile-deep canyon. Much of the topography of the Southwest resulted from erosion by the Colorado River and streams that flow into it.

Not all landforms made by water are as dramatic as those in the Southwest. However, landforms that water has made are found almost everywhere in the world.

MAIN IDEA AND DETAILS What types of landforms in the Southwest were formed by running water?

▲ Monument Valley, along the Arizona-Utah border, was made by water and wind.

1. MAIN IDEA AND DETAILS Draw and complete the graphic organizer by listing details that describe each landform.

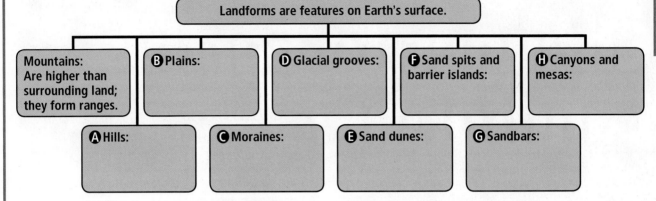

Landforms are features on Earth's surface.

Mountains: Are higher than surrounding land; they form ranges.

B **Plains:**

D **Glacial grooves:**

F **Sand spits and barrier islands:**

H **Canyons and mesas:**

A **Hills:**

C **Moraines:**

E **Sand dunes:**

G **Sandbars:**

2. SUMMARIZE Make an outline that summarizes the main idea and details of the lesson.

3. DRAW CONCLUSIONS How is the way a mesa forms similar to the way a canyon forms?

4. VOCABULARY Explain how the term *landform* is related to the term *topography*.

Test Prep

5. Critical Thinking Suppose you find a hill containing a jumble of small and large rocks. What kind of landform might it be? Explain.

6. What makes sand dunes and moraines similar?

   A. Both are formed by ice.
   B. Both are formed by rivers.
   C. Both are found in the Southwest.
   D. Both are kinds of hills.

Links

Writing

Expository Writing
Research the geography of your state. Use the information to write a **narration** for a tour of landforms in your state.

Math

Solve Problems
Suppose a sand dune travels 100 m in a year. At that rate, how long would it take for the dune to travel 1 km? How far would the dune travel in 15 years and 2 months?

Social Studies

Topographic Maps
Find a topographic map of your area, and compare it to your area's landforms. Record your observations about how various landforms are shown on the map.

 For more links and activities, go to **www.hspscience.com**

What Causes Changes to Earth's Landforms?

Fast Fact

Tons of Stuff The Mississippi River carries millions of metric tons of sediment into the Gulf of Mexico every year. These deposits collect at the mouth of the river. There is enough sediment to extend the coastline of Louisiana by more than 90 m (300 ft) every year. You can make a model to help you understand how this happens.

Rivers and Sand

Materials
- paint tray
- clay
- plastic cup
- clean sand
- water
- spoon
- kitchen baster

Procedure

1. Cover the slope of the paint tray with a thin layer of clay. Press and mold the clay to form a shoreline and a beach. Form a channel in the clay to model a riverbed.

2. Add equal amounts of sand and water to the cup. Stir the mixture so the sand becomes suspended in the water. Then fill the kitchen baster with the mixture.

3. Place the baster at the top of the river channel. Squeeze the bulb to release a flow of the sand-and-water mixture.

4. Release the mixture several times, changing the speed of the flow. Observe the behavior of the sand and water as the mixture runs down the channel.

Draw Conclusions

1. What happened to the sand when it reached the mouth of the river in your model?

2. How was the speed of the mixture related to the deposition of the sand?

3. **Inquiry Skill** Scientists learn by observing. You observed how sand is deposited in water. What does this tell you about the way water changes land?

Step 1

Step 3

Investigate Further

How do continuing deposits of sediment affect a river? Plan and conduct a simple investigation that answers this question.

VOCABULARY
delta p. 81
sinkhole p. 82

SCIENCE CONCEPTS
▶ what causes weathering, erosion, and deposition
▶ how wind, water, ice, and plants cause Earth's landforms to change

 READING FOCUS SKILL
CAUSE AND EFFECT Look for the causes of change in Earth's landforms, and their effects.

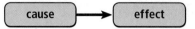

Changes Caused by Wind

Imagine yourself standing on a beach with your face to the wind. Sand hits your skin so hard that it begins to sting.

Now imagine this blowing sand hitting a rock. Over time, the sand wears away the rock by breaking it into smaller pieces. Recall from an earlier chapter that the process of wearing away rocks by natural means is known as weathering.

The weathered pieces of rock, some as large as sand grains, are carried away by the wind. The pieces keep moving as long as the wind is blowing. But when the wind slows down, the large pieces fall to the ground.

Over a long time, the wind leaves small piles of sand in some areas. These piles grow as more and more sand is blown into the pile. Slowly, they become sand dunes.

Sand dunes are found in many places, such as in deserts, at beaches, and on lakeshores. Some desert dunes are as high as a 30-story building! Many beaches along the Atlantic coast have long lines of dunes. These dunes help protect the land during storms. But they can also damage nearby buildings and roads as they move inland, pushed by strong winds from the ocean.

◄ A mushroom rock, like the one shown here, has this shape because the wind blew sand around the bottom of the rock, wearing it away.

CAUSE AND EFFECT
How can wind change landforms?

Changes Caused by Moving Water

Suppose your hands are dirty after working in the garden. Rinsing your hands removes most of the soil. The water flows over your hands, picks up the soil, and carries it away. In a similar way, moving water can change Earth's surface by carrying soil and small pieces of rock away from landforms.

Water is an important cause of change for Earth's landforms. Moving water can dig a mile-deep canyon or change the path of a river.

For example, a rapidly flowing river erodes its banks and its bottom. Eroding the banks makes the river wider. Eroding the bottom makes the river deeper. The moving water then carries sediment downstream. When the flow of water slows down, sediment is deposited. Deposits on a river's banks make it narrower. Deposits on the bottom make the river shallower.

 CAUSE AND EFFECT How can water cause a river's banks to change?

Canyons along the Colorado River are examples of changes made by moving water. For millions of years, the river has been wearing away rocks and carrying sediment downstream. The river has carved deeper and deeper into the landforms of the Southwest.

Erosion and Deposition

Moving wind or water has energy, which enables it to move sediment. The faster the wind or water moves, the more energy it has. Fast water, with a lot of energy, can erode a lot of sediment. Slow water, with little energy, can erode only a small amount of sediment. But all moving water, even a gentle rain, can erode some sediment.

Rain doesn't seem very powerful, but it can cause erosion. When rain falls on a bare hill or mountain, it splashes away soil. As it runs downhill, the water increases its speed and gains energy. The moving water carries away sediment. Over time, water erosion may leave gullies, or ditches, in the ground.

Ocean waves also cause erosion. Constant wave action can change sloping shorelines into cliffs. Waves crashing against the shore carry away broken bits of rock. Piece by piece, the cliffs get steeper. In many places, there is so much erosion that the top of a cliff overhangs the bottom. When this happens, the entire cliff can collapse into

▲ The channels and gullies in this hillside were caused by rain.

the ocean. Then waves begin eroding the collapsed rock and forming new cliffs.

Ocean waves change landforms in another way, too. If you stand on a beach and watch the waves, you see that each wave brings more sand onto the beach. Remember, the process by which sediment drops out of water is called deposition.

Why does deposition occur? You've read that sediment is carried in water as long as the water flows fast. Fast-flowing water has a lot of energy.

Crashing waves can change the face of a cliff.

New Orleans

Mississippi River Delta

▲ Floods deposit nutrient-rich soil on the flood plain.

◀ When the Mississippi River enters the Gulf of Mexico, the water slows down. Sediment is deposited, and the delta grows.

When water slows down, it loses energy. Larger pieces of sediment drop out of the water first and settle to the bottom. As the water slows down more, smaller and smaller particles sink to the bottom.

A river often deposits sediment at its *mouth,* the place where it empties into the ocean. The flow of water slows as a river reaches the ocean. As a result, much of the sediment the river carries is deposited, forming a delta. A **delta** is an area of new land at the mouth of a river.

Flooding can deposit sediment near a river. During heavy rains, a flooding river sends water over its banks. When the rains end, the water slowly returns to the river, but the sediment it carried is deposited on the land. This sediment is rich in nutrients that plants need. As a result, *flood plains,* as these areas are called, are usually good for

farming. But living on a flood plain can be dangerous. Rapidly flowing water can move houses as well as sediment.

 CAUSE AND EFFECT What causes a delta to form?

Insta-Lab

Settle Down
You'll need a clear container, some water, and a mixture of soil and sand. Fill the container half full of water. Put the mixture in your hand, and slowly drop it into the container. How does the mixture settle out of the water?

Sinkholes and Landslides

Water can change not only landforms on Earth's surface but also features underground. For example, groundwater can weather and erode soft rocks. Underground erosion causes caves to form. Often, the roof of a cave collapses due to the weight of material above it. If the cave is near the surface, a large hole, called a **sinkhole**, may open suddenly. Most sinkholes are found where limestone is common, such as in Florida.

As you learned, water isn't the only factor that causes erosion and deposition. Gravity can also cause these land-changing processes to happen. Gravity can make soil, mud, and rocks move quickly down a slope. This form of erosion is called a *landslide*. Landslides can happen suddenly, especially after heavy rains or earthquakes.

 CAUSE AND EFFECT What causes a sinkhole to form?

This mudflow in California was the result of heavy rains in the nearby hills. ▶

This sinkhole opened up suddenly in Winter Park, Florida, in 1981. It swallowed a city block. ▼

The Columbia ice field, in Canada, includes many glaciers.

▲ Glaciers carve deep U-shaped valleys as they flow slowly down a mountain.

Ice

Ice can change landforms in several ways. One way is by weathering rocks. The surfaces of most rocks have tiny cracks and holes that fill with water when it rains. If the weather is cold, the water turns to ice. As the water freezes, it expands, making the cracks bigger. The next time it rains, more water gets in, and the process continues. Over time, the rocks break into smaller and smaller pieces, until there is little more than a pile of sand.

Ice can change landforms in other ways, too. As you read in Lesson 1, glaciers can shape landforms by erosion and deposition. Glaciers often follow a river valley down a mountain. As they move, they change the V-shaped valley eroded by the river into a U-shaped valley.

Glaciers deposit their loads of sediment as they begin to melt. The result can be a huge moraine, such as Long Island in New York. Glacier deposits can also form small, round hills.

Focus Skill **CAUSE AND EFFECT** What changes to landforms can ice cause?

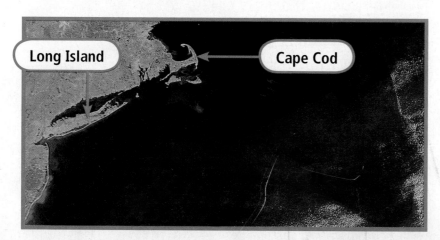

Long Island

Cape Cod

◀ Long Island, NY, and Cape Cod, MA, are huge moraines left by glaciers that once covered most of the northeastern United States.

Plants

Plants can also cause weathering and erosion. When a seed germinates on a rocky slope, it sends roots into tiny cracks or holes in the rock. The roots grow and may eventually become large enough to break the rock into smaller pieces. Some plants also release chemicals into the soil. These chemicals help weather rock by dissolving certain minerals.

Plants don't just weather rock. They also help preserve and protect Earth's landforms. Plant roots hold soil and sand in place. This helps prevent erosion by wind and water.

Farmers often plant clover or other *cover crops* in fields they aren't using to grow food crops. Cover crops help return nutrients to the soil and help prevent erosion. In some areas, farmers plant rows of trees to slow wind erosion of nearby fields.

This protection works naturally as well. Along many beaches, plants grow on dunes. The roots of these plants help hold the sand in place when the wind blows. That's why people should always use beach crossovers instead of walking across the dunes and damaging the plants.

 CAUSE AND EFFECT How do plants affect Earth's landforms?

Plant roots help hold sand in place. This preserves dunes that might otherwise blow away. ▼

▲ **The growth of plant roots can weather rock.**

1. CAUSE AND EFFECT Draw and complete the graphic organizers.

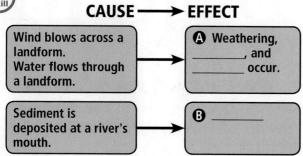

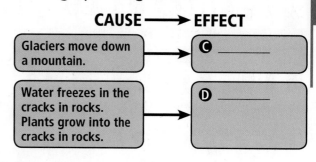

CAUSE ⟶ EFFECT

Wind blows across a landform.
Water flows through a landform.

Ⓐ Weathering, _____, and _____ occur.

Sediment is deposited at a river's mouth.

Ⓑ _____

CAUSE ⟶ EFFECT

Glaciers move down a mountain.

Ⓒ _____

Water freezes in the cracks in rocks.
Plants grow into the cracks in rocks.

Ⓓ _____

2. SUMMARIZE Write a short paragraph summarizing the factors that change Earth's surface.

3. DRAW CONCLUSIONS How are wind erosion and water erosion alike?

4. VOCABULARY Describe the formation of deltas and of sinkholes.

Test Prep

5. Critical Thinking Tell how snowdrifts and sand dunes are formed in similar ways. Then describe differences in how they are formed.

6. A 3-kg (7-lb) rock is placed on a hill. What do you hypothesize will happen to the rock in 100 years?

   A. will get heavier due to deposition

   B. will get lighter due to weathering

   C. will disappear completely

   D. will become a different rock

Links

Writing

Narrative Writing

Write a **description** of the events that made a landform look the way it does. You might tell about a mesa, a sand dune, or a moraine.

Math

Use Mental Math

Suppose a weathered rock breaks into two pieces. Then each piece breaks in two. How many pieces will there be? How many pieces will there be if the process occurs five more times?

Social Studies

Map Works

Draw a map showing places in the United States where you might find sand dunes, moraines, and deltas. On your map, color these places differently and include a key.

 For more links and activities, go to **www.hspscience.com**

How Do Movements of the Crust Change Earth?

No End in Sight Since 1823, Kīlauea, a volcano on the island of Hawai`i, has erupted 59 times. On January 3, 1983, Kīlauea began erupting again, and it hasn't stopped since. That's more than 20 years of continuous eruption! In the Investigate, you can make a model to help you understand volcanoes like Kīlauea.

Modeling a Volcanic Eruption

Materials
- newspaper
- pie pan
- safety goggles
- plastic gloves
- film canister with lid
- effervescent antacid
- teaspoon
- potting soil
- red food coloring
- light maple syrup

Procedure

1. Cover your workspace with newspaper, and place the pie pan on the paper. **CAUTION: Put on the safety goggles and the plastic gloves.**

2. Fill the film canister halfway with antacid.

3. Add some potting soil to the canister. Put the lid on, and shake the canister.

4. Open the canister, and add 10 drops of food coloring to the mixture.

5. Put the canister in the center of the pan. Add several handfuls of clean potting soil to the pan. Heap the soil against the canister to model the sides of a volcano.

6. Add some corn syrup to the canister. Observe what happens. It may take a few moments for the "lava" to start flowing.

Step 2

Step 6

Draw Conclusions

1. Did you observe clear paths in the lava flow? Explain.

2. **Inquiry Skill** Scientists use models to help them understand the dangers of certain natural processes. How might your model help communicate the potential danger of living near volcanoes?

Investigate Further

To protect against lava flows, people often construct barriers. Hypothesize how a barrier might help protect a community.

Reading in Science

VOCABULARY

plate p. 89
earthquake p. 90
epicenter p. 90
fault p. 91
magma p. 92
lava p. 92
volcano p. 92

SCIENCE CONCEPTS

▶ how movements of Earth's crust change the surface

▶ how quickly Earth's landforms can change

READING FOCUS SKILL

CAUSE AND EFFECT Look for what causes earthquakes, volcanoes, and mountains.

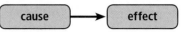

Earth's Structure

Imagine you're a miner digging for gold or gems. You dig deep into Earth, maybe 2 or 3 km (1 or 2 mi) down. But even at this depth, you've barely scratched Earth's surface. You'd need to dig down about 6000 km (4000 mi) to reach the center of Earth! What do you think you'd find at the center? Rock? The whole Earth seems to be rock, but it isn't.

Earth has four layers—the crust, the mantle, the outer core, and the inner core. If you could dig a hole to the center of Earth, you'd find that the layers are different from one another. The thin *crust* is solid rock. So is most of the next layer, the *mantle*. But some rock within the mantle is soft, like melted candy.

If you continued toward the center, the deeper you'd go, the hotter things would

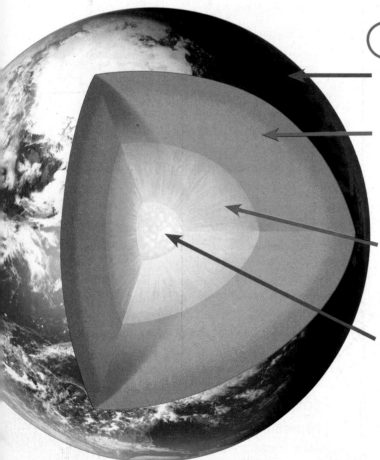

Earth's Layers

Crust 5–70 km (3–43 mi)
The crust is the surface layer of Earth.

Mantle 2885 km (1790 mi)
The mantle has two parts: The upper mantle and the lower mantle. Most of the mantle is solid rock, but some mantle rock is soft.

Outer Core 2270 km (1410 mi)
The hot outer core is liquid iron.

Inner Core 1210 km (750 mi)
The inner core is iron and nickel. Even though the core is very hot, great pressure at the center of Earth keeps the inner core solid.

Quick and Easy Project

Make a Topographic Map

Materials
- paint tray
- modeling clay
- ruler
- water
- sheet of paper
- pencil

Procedure

1. Use modeling clay to make several landforms at the bottom of the paint tray. You may want to include mountains, valleys, hills, and so on.

2. Using the ruler, mark centimeters on an inner side of the paint tray, starting from the bottom.

3. Pour enough water into the tray to reach the 1-cm mark.

4. Look at where the water line hits the landforms. Draw an outline of these water lines, viewed from above, on your paper.

5. Repeat Steps 3 and 4 for each higher centimeter mark until the water reaches the top of all the landforms.

Draw Conclusions

How does your topographic map show the landforms you made? What do the lines you drew on your paper represent? Do any of the lines cross each other?

Design Your Own Investigation

A Change in the Neighborhood

Find a place in your neighborhood to observe changes that might be taking place due to weathering or erosion. Decide how to keep a record of the changes. Draw conclusions about what may be causing the changes. Present your findings at a school science fair or community event.

Review and Test Preparation

Vocabulary Review

Use the terms below to complete the sentences. The page numbers tell you where to look in the chapter if you need help.

landform p. 70	**sinkhole** p. 82
topography p. 70	**earthquake** p. 90
glacier p. 72	**fault** p. 91
sand dune p. 73	**magma** p. 92
delta p. 81	**volcano** p. 92

1. A natural shape or feature of Earth's surface is a _____.

2. A _____ is a sheet of ice.

3. Molten rock beneath Earth's surface is _____.

4. The collapse of an underground cave may produce a _____.

5. A movement of the ground, caused by the sudden release of energy in Earth's crust, is an _____.

6. The landform of sand and other material deposited at the mouth of a river is called a _____.

7. A sand hill formed and shaped by wind is a _____.

8. A mountain made of lava and ash is a _____.

9. _____ is all the kinds of landforms in a certain place.

10. A break in Earth's crust is called a _____.

Check Understanding

Write the letter of the best choice.

11. In which order are the processes listed below most likely to occur?
    - **A.** erosion—deposition—weathering
    - **B.** deposition—erosion—weathering
    - **C.** weathering—deposition—erosion
    - **D.** weathering—erosion—deposition

12. **CAUSE AND EFFECT** Samantha made a display about changes on Earth. She made labels for a cause-and-effect table. Her brother tried placing the labels. These are his results.

Cause	Effect
Volcano	Sand Dune
Earthquake	Delta
Mountain	Deposition
Glacier	Moraine

Which of the causes is correctly paired with its effect?
    - **F.** earthquake
    - **G.** glacier
    - **H.** mountain
    - **J.** volcano

13. Which landform is most likely to be produced by windblown sand?
    - **A.** canyon
    - **C.** mesa
    - **B.** delta
    - **D.** sand dune

14. MAIN IDEA AND DETAILS Rita made this sketch of Echo Canyon. Which of the following most likely formed the canyon?

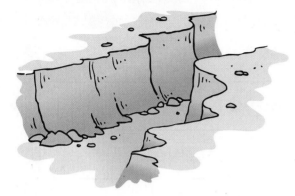

   F. lava   **H.** water erosion

   G. ice erosion   **J.** wind erosion

15. Look at the picture below. How were these landforms most likely produced?

   A. earthquake   **C.** water erosion

   B. ice erosion   **D.** wind erosion

16. If you wanted to make a model of how a delta forms, which of the following materials might be useful?

   F. a pile of cornflakes and a fan

   G. ice with dirt frozen inside

   H. mud and a bicycle pump

   J. water and fine sand in a bottle

Inquiry Skills

17. What can you **observe** about these pieces of rock that shows one was probably weathered by water?

18. How would you **make a model** of an earthquake?

Critical Thinking

19. Martin wants to put his pictures of landforms in order by how quickly the landforms were produced, from slowest to fastest. He has pictures of a fault after an earthquake, a cinder cone volcano, and a canyon. In what order should he put his pictures?

20. Rocks that form from ash are very light and can almost float in water. Rocks that form from lava are heavy. Terry and her class take a trip to a volcano that no longer erupts. She wants to know what kind of volcano it is. She collects some rocks and finds a mixture of light rocks and heavy rocks.

Part A What kind of volcano has Terry visited?

Part B How can she use the rocks to support her conclusion in class?

UNIT 3

Food and Nutrition

HEALTH

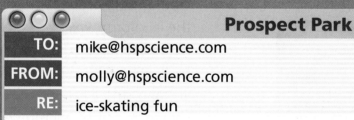

Prospect Park

TO: mike@hspscience.com

FROM: molly@hspscience.com

RE: ice-skating fun

Dear Uncle Mike,

I went to Prospect Park in Brooklyn, New York with Mom and Dad this weekend. We went ice-skating on the ice-skating rink. Mom said I could take skating lessons this winter. What fun! Mom, Dad, and I go to the park to exercise and stay healthy. Sometimes we bring our bikes and go bike riding. Other times we go horse-back riding. We always bring a healthful lunch so we will have energy to do the things we love to do in the park.

See you soon,

Molly

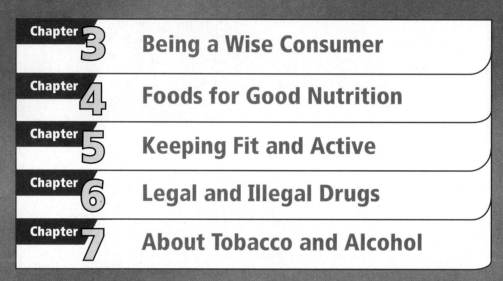

Shands Teaching Hospital

TO: corey@hspscience.com

FROM: constance@hspscience.com

RE: being a doctor

Dear Corey,

My cousin is going to the University of Florida and is studying to become a nurse. She gave me a tour of the Shands Teaching Hospital. She listened to me breathe with her stethoscope and let me listen to my own heartbeat. I think I want to be a doctor when I grow up!

Talk to you soon,

Constance

Experiment!

Lung Capacity No two people are exactly the same. One difference among people is lung capacity, or the amount of air the lungs can hold. Are the lungs of males the same size as the lungs of females? Do your lungs get larger as you get taller? Plan and conduct an experiment to find out.

Being a Wise Consumer

DRAW CONCLUSIONS When you draw conclusions, you use what you know and what you read. Use the Reading in Science Handbook on pages R19–R27 and this graphic organizer to help you read the health facts in this chapter.

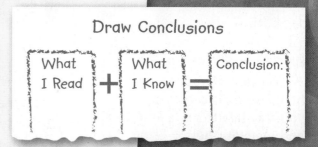

Draw Conclusions

| What I Read | + | What I Know | = | Conclusion: |

Health Graph

INTERPRET DATA Although most dental cavities can be prevented, the graph shows that as children grow older, the number of cavities increases. How does the average number of cavities for twelve-year-olds compare with the number for seventeen-year-olds? What do you think could reduce the difference?

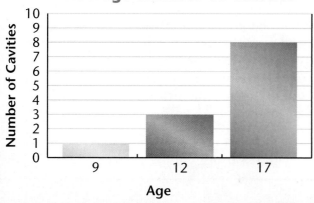

Average Number of Cavities

Daily Physical Activity

One of the easiest ways to take care of your body is to be sure to include some physical activity every day.

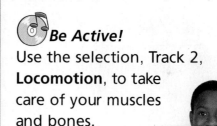*Be Active!*
Use the selection, Track 2, **Locomotion**, to take care of your muscles and bones.

Healthy Skin, Hair, and Nails

Lesson Focus

Taking care of your skin, hair, and nails can help you stay healthy and look and feel your best.

Why Learn This?

Learning about skin, hair, and nails can help you make wise choices about caring for them.

Vocabulary

ultraviolet rays
SPF
hair follicle
oil gland

Caring for Your Skin

You may think of your skin as just a covering for your body. But it's much more than that. Your skin is an organ that protects you from diseases and helps keep body tissues from drying out. Keeping your skin healthy is important. Showering or bathing regularly with soap and water helps remove dirt, germs, dead skin cells, and excess oil from your skin. Use a mild soap to help keep your skin from drying out. You may want to use lotion if you have dry skin.

Wash your hands often to stop the spread of germs that cause illness. Always wash your hands before you prepare food or eat and after you use the bathroom. Wash your hands after you touch items that may have germs on them, such as trash or an animal. If you cough or sneeze into your hands, wash them before you touch anything.

DRAW CONCLUSIONS **Why should you wash your hands after sneezing into them?**

◀ Wash your hands carefully. Using soap and warm water, rub your hands together for about twenty seconds. Then rinse your hands well and dry them with a clean cloth or towel.

Sun Dangers

The sun can be more dangerous for your skin than dirt and germs are. The sun gives off invisible waves of energy called **ultraviolet rays** (uhl•truh•vy•uh•lit), or UV rays. These rays cause sunburn and tanning, which are signs that the skin has been harmed. Years of being in the sun can damage your skin, causing wrinkles, loss of stretchiness, and dark spots. Over time, skin damage may lead to skin cancer. If some skin cancers aren't treated early, they can cause death.

It is important to find skin cancer in its early stages. A change in the appearance of a mole or birthmark may be an early indication of skin cancer. Know the simple ABCD rules for possible signs of skin cancer. If you find any of these signs, see a health-care professional.

CAUSE AND EFFECT **What is the effect if the cause is "I spend hours in the sun"?**

Did You Know?

If you are like most kids, you'll spend more time in the sun before you're eighteen years old than you will for the rest of your life. By protecting your skin now, you can greatly reduce your chances of developing skin cancer as an adult.

ABCD Rules for Signs of Skin Cancer

- **Asymmetry** One-half of a mole doesn't match the other half.

- **Border** The edges of a mole are irregular, ragged, uneven, or blurred.

- **Color** The color of the mole isn't the same all over but may have differing shades of brown or black. Sometimes the spot will have patches of red, white, or blue.

- **Diameter** The diameter of the mole is larger than $\frac{1}{4}$ inch or is growing larger.

People with fair skin sunburn especially easily. ▶

Consumer Activity

Make Buying Decisions
Jana is standing in front of the sunscreens at the store. Write what Jana should look for on the labels when making a buying decision.

Sunscreen Protection

When you go outside, it's important that you protect yourself from the sun. Following these precautions will help you stay safe in the sun.

- Cover up. Wear shirts and pants that cover and protect as much of your skin as possible.
- Use a sunscreen with an **SPF**, sun protection factor, of at least 30. Apply the sunscreen 30 minutes before going outside. Be generous when applying the sunscreen to your body. Reapply sunscreen every two hours if you are swimming or sweating. Use lip balm with sunscreen to protect your lips.
- Wear a hat to protect your face, neck, and ears.
- Wear sunglasses to protect your eyes from harmful UV rays.
- Limit your sun exposure. Stay out of the sun between 10 A.M. and 4 P.M., when UV rays are strongest.

Quick Activity

Choose Sun Protection
Do you need a different sunscreen for an afternoon at the beach than you do for bike riding? Write down other items you need for sun protection for both activities.

Sunscreen Protection

SPF	Amount of Protection
0–14	Offers little or no protection from the sun. Not recommended for UV-ray protection.
15–30	Provides some UV-ray protection. The higher the SPF, the more protection. An SPF of at least 30 is recommended.
30+	Recommended for high UV-ray exposure, as in high altitudes and on or near water, sand, or snow.

SUMMARIZE Tell what you should do to protect your body from UV rays when you're outdoors.

Caring for Your Nails

Your nails protect the tips of your fingers and toes. Like hair, nails grow from your skin. Keeping your nails trimmed is important for their appearance and health.

Long nails can break or tear easily, exposing living skin. Dirt and germs can get under your nails even when they are neatly trimmed. To prevent the spread of germs, clean your nails at least once a day. Use warm, soapy water and a nail brush to remove the dirt and germs. Watch for changes in your nails. A change can be a sign of illness.

Don't bite your nails. Doing so can spread germs from your nails to your mouth. Use nail clippers or manicure scissors to cut your toenails and fingernails. Don't cut your nails too short. Making them too short can expose living skin or cause the nail to grow into the skin. Exposing the living skin around a nail can lead to infection. Cut each toenail straight across, just beyond the tip of your toe.

MAIN IDEA AND DETAILS Give two details to support this statement: Keeping your nails trimmed to the right length is important.

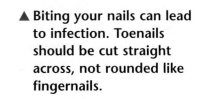

▲ Biting your nails can lead to infection. Toenails should be cut straight across, not rounded like fingernails.

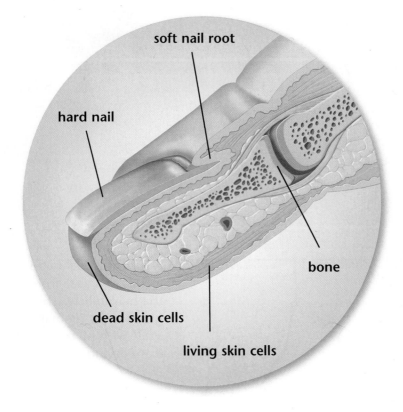

soft nail root

hard nail

bone

dead skin cells

living skin cells

◀ The fingernails you can see are dead cells that grow from living skin cells in the soft nail root.

Personal Health Plan ▶

Real-Life Situation
Combing or brushing your hair is important for looking your best. Suppose a person in your gym class asks to borrow your comb or brush.
Real-Life Plan
Write down what you would say to politely refuse to lend your comb or brush.

Caring for Your Hair

Much of your body is covered with hair. Each hair grows from a pitlike area called a **hair follicle** (FAHL•ih•kuhl). Special cells in the follicle grow to form hair. These cells grow, die, and then harden. The dead cells are forced out of the hair follicle as new cells form. The dead cells stack up, one on top of another, in a long column that makes up the hair shaft. An **oil gland** in each follicle makes oil that coats the hair and spreads over the surface of your skin. The oil makes your hair and skin soft and smooth and keeps it from drying out.

There are about 200,000 hairs on your head. They help protect your scalp from the sun. They also keep you warm in cold weather. Each hair grows from four to seven years and then falls out.

To keep hair looking neat, brush or comb it each day. Brushing gets rid of tangles and spreads oil over the hair shafts. Brushing once a day is usually enough to keep your hair healthy. Comb your hair often throughout the day to keep it looking neat.

Grooming is important, but don't share combs or

Although it may appear healthy, the part of the hair that you can see is actually dead. Only the hair follicle is alive. ▼

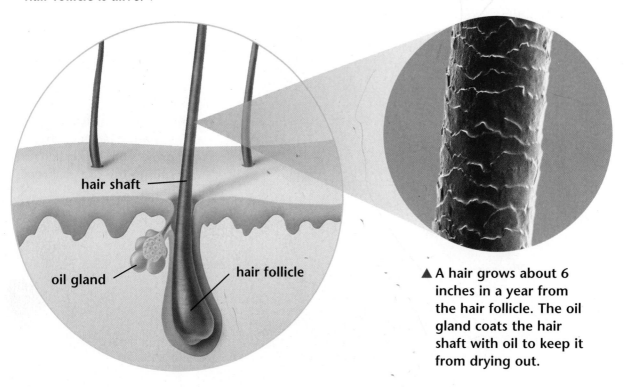

hair shaft

oil gland

hair follicle

▲ A hair grows about 6 inches in a year from the hair follicle. The oil gland coats the hair shaft with oil to keep it from drying out.

brushes with friends. Head lice can be passed from person to person by sharing items that are used on the head.

Shampooing your hair keeps it clean. Talk with a parent about how often to wash your hair. If your hair is naturally oily, you may need to wash it every day. If your hair is dry, you can wash it less often. A parent can help you find a shampoo that works well with your hair type.

Comb your hair gently after shampooing. Gentle combing helps keep wet hair from being damaged. Unless your hair is very curly, let it dry a little before combing. To make your hair easier to comb, use a small amount of conditioner to coat the hair shafts.

Letting your hair dry naturally is best. Electric dryers can make your hair brittle, causing it to break. Curling irons, hot rollers, and hot combs damage hair, too. If you want to dry and style your hair, use a blow-dryer on a warm setting. Brush your hair gently as you blow-dry it.

CAUSE AND EFFECT
What might happen if you blow-dry your hair every day?

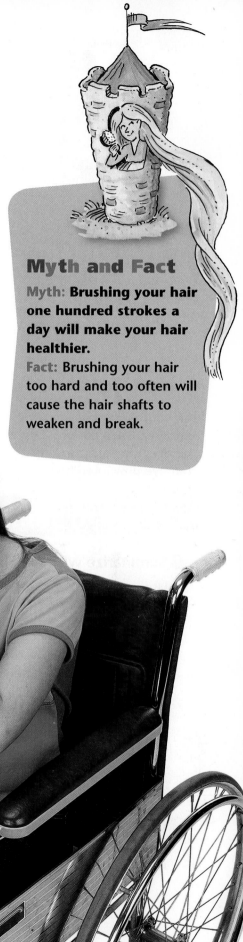

Myth and Fact

Myth: Brushing your hair one hundred strokes a day will make your hair healthier.

Fact: Brushing your hair too hard and too often will cause the hair shafts to weaken and break.

About 200,000 hairs grow on your head. They protect your scalp from the sun and cold weather. ▶

Personal Hygiene

Before and during puberty, hormones will cause changes in your body. For example, your oil glands will release more oil, which may cause pimples called *acne*.

Acne forms when a pore becomes clogged with oil, dead skin cells, and bacteria. The bacteria grow in the blocked pore. The pore may swell and become red, forming a pimple. To remove excess oil and control acne, wash your face often with soap and water. If you do get acne, it's not your fault. Acne develops because of changes caused by hormones.

You may also notice that you sweat more than you did when you were younger and that the sweat has an odor. These changes are normal and are also caused by hormones. Daily bathing and using a deodorant or an antiperspirant can help control body odor and excess sweating.

SEQUENCE Tell how a pimple forms.

▲ Hormone changes may cause coarse hair to grow on your body during puberty. Ask a parent before using a razor to remove unwanted hair.

Lesson 1 Summary and Review

❶ Summarize with Vocabulary

Use vocabulary and other terms from this lesson to complete these statements.

The sun gives off _____, which can damage your skin. Sunscreen with a(n) _____ of 30 is recommended for all skin types. Hair grows from a pit in the skin called a(n) _____. Your skin and hair are protected from water loss by oil from _____. _____ and _____ control body odor and excess sweating.

❷ Why do you need your skin?

❸ Critical Thinking What should you do if a mole on your body is growing larger and its border is irregular?

❹ (Focus Skill) DRAW CONCLUSIONS Complete this graphic organizer to draw a conclusion about the importance of washing your hands.

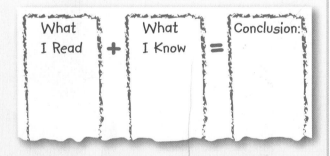

| What I Read | + | What I Know | = | Conclusion: |

❺ Write to Inform—Explanation

Some classmates are making fun of a boy who has acne. Write a paragraph to explain why the acne isn't the boy's fault.

Respect

Develop Self-Confidence

Almost everyone would like to have the same self-confidence that many of their favorite celebrities have. But for some people, being confident isn't easy, especially when they're in front of others. To be confident, you must respect yourself. Here are some tips to help you respect yourself and develop self-confidence:

- **Always look your best. The extra time you spend on grooming will boost your confidence.**
- **Use antiperspirant or deodorant to control sweating and body odor.**
- **Keep your hair clean and neatly combed.**
- **Take care of your teeth and gums to prevent cavities, gum disease, and tooth loss.**
- **Wash your face with soap and water to control acne. See your doctor for acne cleansers and creams, if necessary.**
- **If you are asked to speak in front of an audience, prepare notes about what you're going to say. Practice giving your presentation in front of a mirror, making eye contact with a pretend audience. Avoid reading to the audience from your notes.**

Activity

Speaking in front of an audience can be frightening. Ask your teacher if you may read your favorite short story aloud to the class. Practice the tips above to help yourself gain confidence.

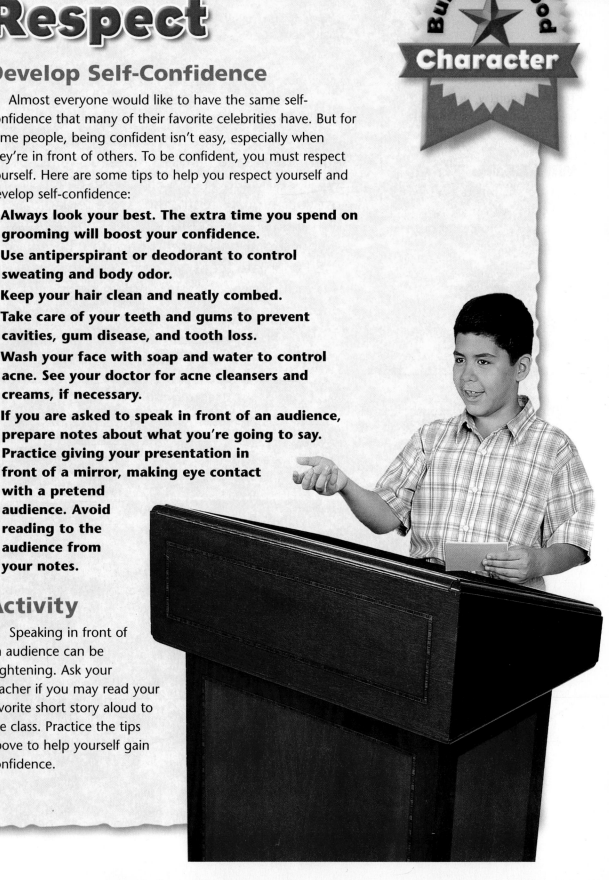

Building Good Character

Healthy Teeth and Gums

Kinds of Teeth

Taking care of your teeth is important to your smile and to your health. Your first teeth started coming in when you were a baby. These teeth, called primary teeth, continued to come in during childhood. As you lost your primary teeth, they were replaced by permanent teeth. Permanent teeth have to last the rest of your life. If one is lost, no tooth will replace it.

By your late teens, you will have thirty-two teeth. This includes four " extra" molars in the back of your mouth. These molars are sometimes called wisdom teeth. Your wisdom teeth may not appear until you are an adult, or maybe not at all.

 DRAW CONCLUSIONS Why is taking care of your permanent teeth important?

The shape of each tooth is well suited to its function. *Incisors* have sharp edges for cutting food. The pointed *cuspids* are good for tearing food. *Molars* and *bicuspids* have flat surfaces for grinding food. ▶

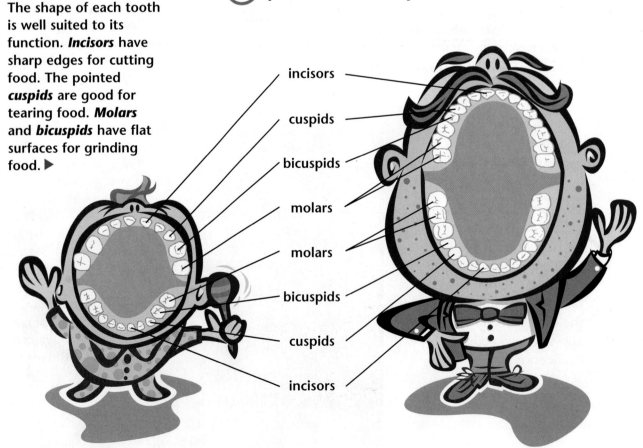

incisors
cuspids
bicuspids
molars
molars
bicuspids
cuspids
incisors

Caring for Your Teeth and Gums

Teeth are made up of three layers. Each tooth has a hard, protective *crown* made of *enamel*. Under the crown is a softer material called *dentin*. Dentin makes up most of the tooth. The *pulp* contains blood vessels that nourish the tooth. It also contains nerves that sense pain and temperature. The *root* anchors the tooth in the jaw. The teeth are surrounded by soft tissue—the gums.

Brushing and flossing remove food and bacteria from teeth and gums. Floss your teeth at least once a day before brushing. Brush your teeth at least twice a day after eating. Use a soft-bristled toothbrush and toothpaste that contains fluoride. *Fluoride* is a mineral that helps protect teeth. Your toothbrush and toothpaste should have the American Dental Association (ADA) seal.

SEQUENCE **Name the layers of a tooth in order, starting with the outermost layer.**

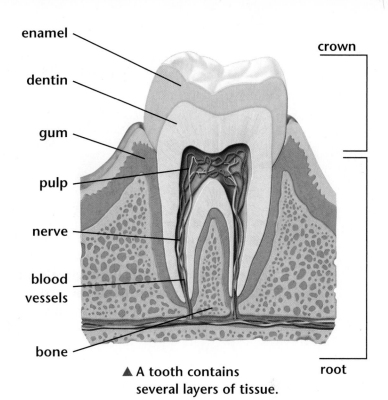

▲ A tooth contains several layers of tissue.

enamel
dentin
gum
pulp
nerve
blood vessels
bone
crown
root

Brushing and Flossing

Brush using short, back-and-forth strokes. To brush along the gumline and the inner surfaces of your back teeth, angle the toothbrush. To clean the inner surfaces of your front teeth, use the tip of the toothbrush. Also brush your tongue.

Cut a piece of floss about 18 inches long. Wrap it around your middle fingers. Insert the floss between two teeth. Gently rub the side of each tooth, moving away from the gumline, with up-and-down motions. Unwind a clean piece of floss, and repeat to clean between all teeth.

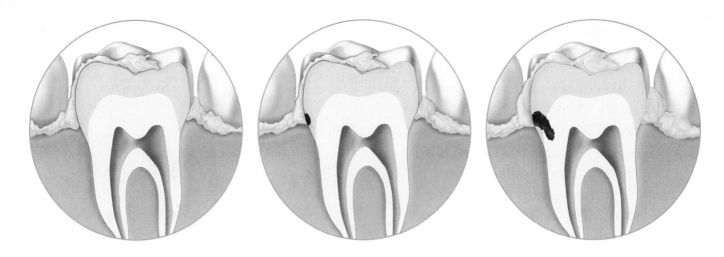

▲ Regular visits to the dentist can catch dental problems. The tooth at the left is covered with plaque. The center tooth shows the beginning of a small cavity. The tooth at the right has a large cavity. See page 390 for what to do in a dental emergency.

See page 390 for what to do in a dental emergency.

Dental Problems

Everyone—including you—has bacteria in his or her mouth. These bacteria make a sticky substance called **plaque** (PLAK), which coats your teeth. When the bacteria in plaque break down sugars in the foods you eat, acids form. These acids make holes, called cavities, in your tooth enamel. If a cavity isn't treated, the hole spreads through the dentin to the pulp and then to the root. A dentist treats a cavity by removing the damaged portion of the tooth. The dentist then fills the hole with a hard material, and the tooth is saved.

Plaque can cause other problems, too. If plaque is allowed to remain on the teeth, it forms a hardened material. This material can cause **gingivitis** (jin•juh•VYT•is), a gum disease in which the gums become red and swollen. Untreated gingivitis can develop into a more severe form of gum disease, in which the gums weaken and pull back from the teeth. Teeth may then fall out. Brushing and flossing can stop gingivitis in its early stages.

CAUSE AND EFFECT Tell how plaque can affect your teeth.

Health & Technology

Computer-Enhanced X Rays Dentists use computer-enhanced X rays to find cavities that are just beginning to form. When a cavity is found early, there is little tooth damage. A small cavity can be repaired without removing a large portion of the tooth.

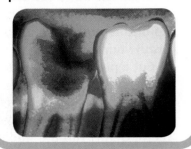

Orthodontia

You may know someone who wears a *dental appliance*—a device that straightens crooked teeth. Some people wear braces, usually for several years, to straighten teeth. After the braces are removed, a person may wear another dental appliance, called a retainer, at night. The retainer keeps the teeth from moving out of place.

The straightening of crooked teeth is called **orthodontia** (awr·thuh·DAHN·shuh). Straightening teeth makes them easier to clean and helps prevent cavities and gum diseases. Straightening can also prevent uneven wear of the teeth. Orthodontia helps ensure that your teeth will last a lifetime.

COMPARE AND CONTRAST
Tell how braces and a retainer are alike and different.

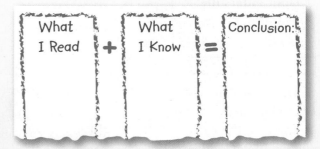

◀ Cleaning the teeth carefully while wearing braces is very important.

ACTIVITY

Life Skills

Make Responsible Decisions
Anna is hungry for a snack but knows she won't be able to brush her teeth right away. At a food stand, she sees caramel corn, ice cream, taffy, and fresh fruit. Help Anna decide which snack is best. Write your choice based on what you know about dental care.

Lesson 2 Summary and Review

❶ Summarize with Vocabulary

Use vocabulary and other terms from this lesson to complete the statements.

Babies have _____ teeth. Older children and adults have _____ teeth. Bacteria cause a sticky substance called _____ to form on your teeth. When acids attack the teeth, _____ form. Crooked teeth can be corrected by_____.

❷ Why is taking care of your teeth and gums important?

❸ Critical Thinking Why should you floss before you brush?

❹ (Focus Skill) **DRAW CONCLUSIONS** Complete this graphic organizer to draw a conclusion about taking care of your teeth.

What I Read	+	What I Know	=	Conclusion:

❺ Write to Inform—How-To

In your own words, tell how to floss and brush your teeth.

Care of Your Eyes and Ears

Lesson Focus
Vision and hearing are important senses that tell you about the world.

Why Learn This?
Knowing how your eyes and ears work can help you protect your vision and hearing.

Vocabulary
farsighted
nearsighted
astigmatism
decibels

How You See

When you wake up in the morning, the first thing you probably do is open your eyes and look around. Your eyes are organs that sense light and let you see the world around you.

When you look in a mirror, you can see several parts of your eye. The *cornea* (KAWR•nee•uh) is a clear covering that protects the eye. The black-looking *pupil* in the center of your eye is surrounded by the colored *iris* (EYE•ris). Muscles in the iris control the size of the pupil. This determines how much light enters your eye. Using the diagram below, trace the path of light through your eye.

Your body has several built-in ways to protect your eyes. The bones of your skull protect the eyes from injury. Eyelashes keep out dust and other particles. Your eyelids close if anything comes near your eyes. And tears flush away particles that enter the eye.

Focus Skill **DRAW CONCLUSIONS** **How does the iris control the amount of light that enters the eye?**

1 The *cornea* protects the eye and helps focus light entering the eye.

2 Light enters the eye through the *pupil*.

3 The *iris* adjusts the amount of light entering the eye.

4 The *lens* bends light rays so that images focus on the retina.

5 Light-sensing cells in the *retina* change light into nerve signals.

6 The *optic nerve* carries messages from the eye to the brain.

Vision Problems

Many people don't have perfect vision. A **farsighted** person can see things that are far away, but things that are nearby look blurry. For other people the opposite is true. A **nearsighted** person can see things nearby, but objects far away are blurry. For people with **astigmatism** (uh•STIG•muh•tiz•uhm), the cornea or lens of the eye is curved unevenly. Everything looks blurry to people with astigmatism.

Eye exams are important to ensure that your eyes are healthy and working well. Be sure to cooperate with vision checks at school. If you wear glasses, it's important to have your eyes rechecked every two years; more often if there is a family history of eye disease or if you wear contact lenses. Also, have a parent take you to an eye doctor anytime you have a problem seeing.

CAUSE AND EFFECT **What may be the cause if everything you see on the chalkboard appears blurry?**

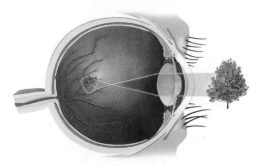

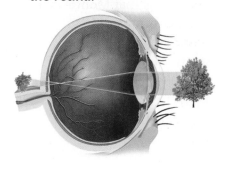

If you are nearsighted (above), the image will focus in front of the retina. If you are farsighted (below), the image will focus behind the retina.

If your eyes feel tired or you get headaches when using a computer, tell a parent. You may need to see an eye doctor. ▶

Protecting Your Vision

Although your body has ways to protect them, your eyes can still be damaged. If you play sports, fast-moving objects can hit your eyes. You should wear safety goggles for protection. You should also wear them when you work with sharp objects, hot liquids, or household cleaners. All of these things can seriously damage your eyes. If you're around someone who is cutting grass, sanding wood, or pounding nails, wear safety goggles to protect your eyes from dust and flying objects.

The UV rays that damage your skin can damage your eyes, too. Even on partly cloudy days, wear sunglasses to protect your eyes. The darkness of the tint is not a good indicator of UV protection. Look for sunglasses with a label stating that they block all UV rays.

SUMMARIZE Name five situations in which you should wear safety goggles.

People mowing their lawns should protect their eyes, ears, and skin by wearing safety goggles (below), ear plugs, a hat, and sunscreen. ▶

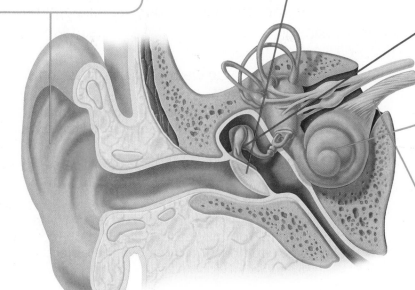

1 The outer ear directs sound waves into the *ear canal.*

2 Sound waves cause the *eardrum* to vibrate.

3 Vibrations cause the *hammer* to move the *anvil*, which moves the *stirrup.*

4 The moving stirrup causes fluid in the *cochlea* to vibrate. Hairlike cells lining the cochlea move, changing the vibrations into nerve signals.

5 The *auditory nerve* carries the signals to the brain, where they are interpreted as sound.

How You Hear

Your ears collect sound waves, process them, and send nerve messages to your brain. This enables you to hear sounds. The outer ear collects sound waves and directs them into the ear canal. There, sound waves make the eardrum vibrate. The vibrations are passed to three small bones in the middle ear. As the bones move, fluid in the inner ear vibrates. Tiny hairlike cells turn the vibrations into nerve signals. These signals are carried to the brain, where they are interpreted as sound. Trace the path of sound in the diagram above.

Like your eyes, your ears have some built-in protection. Most of the ear is within the skull and so is protected by bone. In the ear canal, glands produce a waxy material that traps dirt before it can reach the internal ear parts.

Tubes lead from your middle ear to your throat. These tubes drain fluid that collects in your ears and help keep air pressure the same on both sides of the eardrum. This protects the delicate eardrum and keeps your ears working well.

SEQUENCE Describe the path, as a series of ordered steps, that sound takes through the ear.

Did You Know?

Did you ever feel your ears "pop" when you were riding in an airplane or in an elevator? This feeling was caused by pressure building up in your ears. The popping occurred when the tubes that run between your ears and your throat opened up to relieve the pressure. This is your body's way to prevent ear damage.

▲ Earmuffs and earplugs can reduce the sound level that reaches your ears. You should use ear protection when you're around loud noises.

Protecting Your Hearing

Like your eyes, your ears are delicate organs. Follow these guidelines to take care of your ears and protect your hearing.

- Be careful when you wash your ears. Wash only the outside of your ears.
- Never put anything into your ear canals. Small objects, including cotton swabs, can damage your ears.
- Ask a parent if you think your ear canals need to be cleaned. You may need an appointment with a doctor or nurse to clean them.
- If something gets stuck in your ear, don't try to get it out yourself. You may push the object deeper into your ear. A doctor should remove the object.

Loud sounds can harm your ears by damaging the tiny hairlike cells in the cochlea. If these cells are damaged, you could lose part of your hearing. The body can't replace these cells, so the damage may be permanent. The best way to protect your hearing is to avoid loud sounds as much as possible. Keep your television, stereo, and other sources of sound at a reasonable volume. You should also cooperate during hearing tests at school.

Health & Technology

Audiometry Many schools conduct hearing tests to measure a student's ability to hear the sounds of human speech. Sounds differ in pitch—highness or lowness. An audiometer measures your ability to hear sounds (tones) of different pitches. During the test, you wear headphones. The person conducting the test will check both ears. When the test is complete, you'll know if you can hear speech the way you should.

Hearing tests can determine if you have a hearing loss. A doctor can prescribe a hearing aid if there is a serious hearing loss.

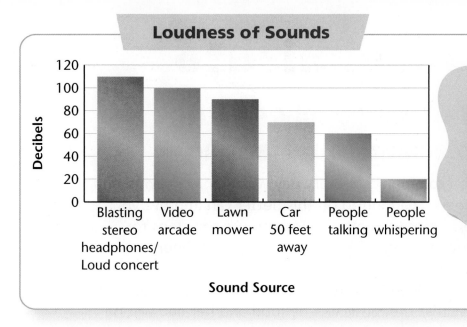

Loudness of Sounds

Decibels vs. Sound Source

Quick Activity

Based on the graph, list three sounds that could damage your hearing. What can you do to prevent damage in each example you list?

The loudness of sounds is measured in units called **decibels** (DEHS•uh•buhlz). Over time, any continuous sound at or above 85 decibels can damage your ears.

 DRAW CONCLUSIONS Name two things you do for which you should wear ear protection.

Lesson 3 Summary and Review

❶ Summarize with Vocabulary

Use vocabulary and other terms from this lesson to complete these statements.

A person who is _____ clearly sees things that are far away, but nearby things look blurry. A person who is _____ clearly sees things that are nearby, but faraway things look blurry. Everything looks blurry to a person who has_____. The loudness of sound is measured in _____. Cells in your eye that sense light are in the _____.

❷ How can you protect your eyes from UV rays?

❸ Critical Thinking Name three things that would appear blurry to you if you were farsighted.

❹ **DRAW CONCLUSIONS** Complete this graphic organizer to draw a conclusion about taking care of your ears.

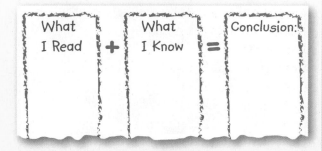

| What I Read | + | What I Know | = | Conclusion: |

❺ Write to Express— Solution to a Problem

Write how you would solve the problem of your brother playing music too loudly.

Communicate

with Your Family About Protecting Your Hearing

You communicate every day with family, friends, and strangers. Learning to do this better can improve your relationships with others. You can use the steps for **Communicating** to help you communicate more effectively.

Kayla has won front-row tickets to a rock concert. She knows that the music will be loud and her dad will be concerned about protecting her hearing. How can Kayla communicate with her dad about the concert?

1 Understand your audience.

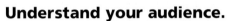

"Wow! Great tickets!" thinks Kayla. But she wonders how she'll tell her dad that they're sitting in the front row. He'll tell her it's bad for her hearing.

2 Give a clear message. Use a respectful tone of voice.

I've never had tickets for the front row before. What if we wear earplugs?

Kayla calmly and respectfully explains to her dad why she wants to sit in the front row. Then she makes a suggestion.

3 Listen carefully, and answer any questions.

"That's a good idea, but if it's still too loud, will you agree to leave?"

"Yes."

Kayla listens to her dad telling her about leaving if the music is still too loud.

4 Gather feedback.

"Enjoying the concert, Kayla?"

Kayla asks her dad how the earplugs are working for him. "They're working great," he replies. "They make the concert enjoyable."

 ## Problem Solving

A Roberto shares a room with his older brother. His brother likes to play loud music in their room. Roberto's ears ring after he leaves the bedroom when his brother is playing his music.

- Use the steps for **Communicating** to help Roberto work out this problem with his brother.

B When Susie's dad mows the lawn, the noise is very loud. Susie is afraid that the noise will damage her dad's hearing.

- Explain how Susie can respectfully share her concerns with her dad. Describe solutions she might suggest.

Being a Health Consumer

Lesson Focus

As a consumer you make choices about products and services that can affect your health.

Why Learn This?

Learning to read labels carefully and to analyze advertisements can help you become a wise health consumer.

Vocabulary

health consumer
ingredients

Sources of Health Information

Do you help choose your own brand of health-care products, such as soap, shampoo, and toothpaste? If you do, you are a health consumer, a person who buys and uses health products or services. Getting good information about products is an important step in making good choices as a health consumer. You also need to know how to compare and evaluate products. Having these skills will help you choose the best products for you and avoid wasting money.

When you gather health information, it's important to choose information that is reliable. Some of the information available to you contains myths. Myths are ideas that are thought to be true by some people but are actually false. Advertising can be one source of health myths.

Your library has books and magazines with information about health. To get facts rather than myths, look for books written by health-care professionals. ▼

Books, posters, newsletters, videos, and magazines about health are sources that can contain reliable health information. ▶

Advertisements appear in many places, including on television, in magazines, on the Internet, on the radio, and in newspapers. Their purpose is to make you want to buy a product, whether it's the best one for you or not. The information in advertisements may be true, false, or misleading. It's important to use reliable sources to determine the truth. That way you can make wise buying choices.

In addition to the sources pictured on these pages, your family is a good source of health information. Health-care professionals are also good sources. Your doctor, dentist, pharmacist, and school nurse can give you and your parents reliable information for making wise consumer choices.

Other good sources of consumer information are magazines published by consumer groups. Consumer groups test and rate health products, such as soaps, hand lotions, shampoos, and sunscreens. Newsletters that are produced by health organizations sometimes rate health products, too.

DRAW CONCLUSIONS **Why might an article from a toothpaste company be a poor source of information about which toothpaste to buy?**

Information Alert!

Health information changes as new health studies and new medicines are introduced.

GO ONLINE For the most up-to-date information, visit The Learning Site. www.harcourtschool.com/ health

Organizations such as the American Heart Association and the American Cancer Society have pamphlets that contain reliable health information. ▼

127

Learning from Product Labels

Most health products have detailed labels. The label on the front of a product usually gives the product name, a brief explanation of what the product does, and the amount of product in the package. Since this front label shows on the store shelves, manufacturers often include advertising there. Remember to carefully evaluate the information presented in advertising. The toothpaste and shampoo labels on these pages show information that usually appears on the front of a product.

The label on the back of a product often includes additional information. That label includes a full explanation of what the product does. You should still be careful when reading the label on the back. It may also contain advertising that may or may not be true.

Also shown on labels is the list of **ingredients** (in·GREE·dee·uhnts), or the things that are in the product. Some products, such as toothpastes and dandruff shampoos, provide health benefits. The ingredients that provide the benefits are listed on the labels as active ingredients.

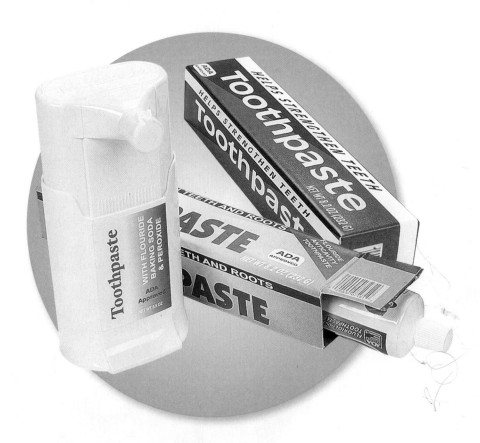

Toothpaste containing fluoride provides a health benefit. The ADA seal tells you the product is approved by the American Dental Association. ▶

128

Quick Activity

Analyze Labels Make a table with two columns. Label one column *Advertising Claims* and the other *Useful Information*. Analyze the labels on several bottles of shampoo. Then write information from the labels into the table.

Reading the list of ingredients can be important if you have allergies to soaps, perfumes, dyes, flavorings, or other materials. If you read the label, you can avoid using products with ingredients that may harm you.

Most labels give directions for using the products. You may not need directions for some products, such as shampoo. For other health products, such as medicines, it's important to follow the directions very carefully. Failing to follow the directions may be harmful to your health.

Some labels contain product warnings. The warnings contain information that may save your life. It's important to read and follow all product warning information carefully.

SUMMARIZE List the information that is included on health product labels.

Advertisers try to keep the names of their products in front of you as much as possible. That way, the products will be familiar to you and you might choose them when the time comes to buy. ▶

Analyzing Advertisements

Ads appear all around you—in magazines and newspapers, on radio and TV, on the Internet and billboards. You even see ads on T-shirts, backpacks, and drinking cups. Advertisers may use easy-to-remember songs to remind you of their products. They might use catchy logos or slogans to grab your attention. Advertising can have a strong influence on you. But if you know the tricks advertisers use to get your attention, you can make good buying choices.

One trick of advertisers is to try to convince you that everyone is using their products. The message is that you should use the products, too, if you want to be popular. Some advertisers use famous people to tell you why you should buy certain products. Advertisers hope that you'll trust the good things the famous people say about the products.

Another trick advertisers use is to make you think that their products are good buys. They may offer free gifts or tell you that buying their products will save you money. Don't be fooled by these tricks. Check what the advertisers are saying to see if the products really are bargains.

er White Toothpaste

Don't be fooled by advertising tricks. Use common sense to evaluate products. Consider a product's cost, features, quality, and safety, and listen to the advice of others. Before you buy something, ask yourself these questions: "Do I really need this product? Will it do what I want it to do? Is the price reasonable?" If you can answer *yes* to all of these questions, you're probably making a wise choice. If you answer *no* to any of the questions, you should think again before buying the product.

Parents and health-care professionals can help you decide whether you really need a product. They may suggest different products. They also may suggest stores that have lower prices for the products you are considering. By listening to the advice of informed consumers, such as your parents, and by using common sense, you can become a wise health consumer.

Advertisers use celebrities to promote their products. People trust celebrities because they feel they know them. This advertiser wants you to believe you can be a celebrity, too, if you visit Dr. Capps. ▼

I got my famous smile from Dr. Capps!

MAIN IDEA AND DETAILS Give three details to support this idea: Some advertisers use tricks to get consumers to buy their products.

New Sources of Health Information

The website of the CDC, or Centers for Disease Control and Prevention, has accurate health information. ▼

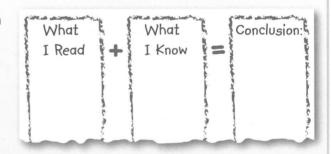

Today you can get reliable health information with the click of a mouse. The Internet enables you to quickly find the answers to many health questions. But anyone can put information on the Internet, so you must make sure that the source you use is reliable. Unreliable sources may give wrong or even dangerous health information. Websites hosted by the government and by hospitals, universities, and professional organizations are the most reliable.

Remember that even reliable sites aren't designed to answer all health questions. They can't replace the advice that you get from a parent, your doctor, or other health-care professional.

SUMMARIZE Tell why evaluating health information on the Internet is important.

Lesson 4 Summary and Review

❶ Summarize with Vocabulary

Use vocabulary and other terms from the lesson to complete the statements.

A _____ buys or uses health products or services. A person who is allergic to certain things should check the lists of _____ that are on the health-care products he or she uses. Ideas that are thought to be true by some people but are actually false are known as _____. Ingredients that provide medical benefits are known as _____.

❷ Why do you think some advertisers use misleading information instead of reliable health information?

❸ Critical Thinking What sources could you use to find reliable information about the benefits of adding fluoride to toothpaste?

❹ (Focus Skill) DRAW CONCLUSIONS Complete this graphic organizer to draw a conclusion about the importance of being a wise consumer.

What I Read	+	What I Know	=	Conclusion:

❺ Write to Entertain—Poem

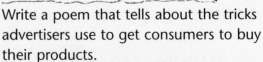

Write a poem that tells about the tricks advertisers use to get consumers to buy their products.

ACTIVITIES

 Math

Calculate Savings Your favorite shampoo is on sale in two different sizes. The 12-ounce bottle is $4.49, and the 8-ounce bottle is $3.19. Which size is less expensive per ounce? How much less?

 Science

Show How Sound Travels Research sound to find out how sound waves travel. Then make a visual display to show what you learn.

 Technology

Tell About Dental Lasers Dental lasers are replacing drills in some dentists' offices. Lasers can be used to treat cavities with less pain and noise than a drill. Lasers are used for gum surgery, too. Find more information about dental lasers. Then make a video, a slide presentation, a poster, or a brochure about this new technology.

GO ONLINE For more activities, visit The Learning Site. www. harcourtschool.com/health

 Home & Community

Identify Noise Pollution Make a list of loud noises that you hear in or around your home. Talk with your parents or, with your parent's approval, community leaders about possible ways to reduce any dangerously loud noise. If it can't be reduced, identify ways to protect your hearing from this noise pollution.

Career Link

Orthodontist Orthodontists are dentists who specialize in straightening teeth and correcting other problems of the mouth. Suppose you are an orthodontist. Make a brochure for your patients to explain the importance of orthodontia to good dental health. In the brochure, explain the importance of cleaning your teeth carefully while wearing braces.

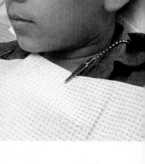

Reading Skill

DRAW CONCLUSIONS

Draw and then use this graphic organizer to answer questions 1–3.

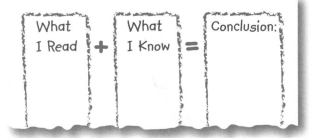

1 Write what you read in this chapter about the sun's effects on your body.

2 Write what you already knew about the sun's effects on your body.

3 Write a conclusion you can draw from this information.

Use Vocabulary

Use vocabulary and other terms from this chapter to complete the statements.

4 If left untreated, _____ can lead to serious gum disease that may cause tooth loss.

5 A sticky substance called _____ forms naturally on your teeth.

6 The correction of crooked teeth is called _____.

7 The loudness of sound is measured in units called _____.

8 All images are blurry for a person with _____.

9 A(n) _____ person can see things clearly that are far away.

10 Ideas thought to be true but which are actually false are called _____.

 Check Understanding

Choose the letter of the correct answer.

11 Which of the following would a health consumer purchase?
  A deodorant   **C** candy bar
  B compact disc   **D** ice-cream bar

12 Invisible rays given off by the sun are called _____.
  F sonic rays   **H** tanning rays
  G sound waves   **J** ultraviolet rays

13 The _____ release oil that coats your hair and your skin.
  A hair shafts   **C** hair follicles
  B hair surfaces **D** oil glands

14 Hair grows from pitlike areas in your skin, called _____.
  F hard nails   **H** hair follicles
  G bones   **J** retinas

15 The term *SPF* means _____.
  A sound protection factor
  B sun protection factor
  C silent protection factor
  D saving protection factor

16 Which of the following would **NOT** be used for sun protection?

F   **H**

G   **J**

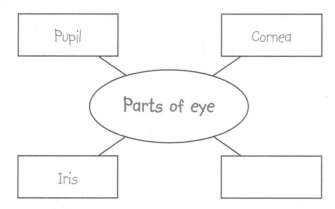

Pupil | Cornea

Parts of eye

Iris |

17 Which word or phrase is missing from the graphic organizer?

A follicle   **C** auditory nerve

B shaft   **D** retina

18 The top part of a tooth, as shown in the diagram, is called the _____.

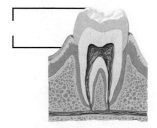

F root   **H** pulp
G dentin   **J** crown

19 Which of the following is **NOT** part of the ear?

A optic nerve
B auditory nerve
C cochlea
D hammer

20 The coiled tube in your inner ear is known as the _____.

F stirrup   **H** Eustachian tube
G anvil   **J** cochlea

Think Critically

21 Suppose your doctor tells you to use a face wash that contains benzoyl peroxide. At the drugstore, you see several face washes. How can you be certain that the one you choose contains benzoyl peroxide?

22 You want to floss your teeth every day, but you keep forgetting. What type of cue could you use to remind you to floss at the same time every day?

Apply Skills

23 **BUILDING GOOD CHARACTER**
Respect You have been asked by a youth group to give a presentation on skin care. Apply what you know about respect and developing self-confidence to tell how you would prepare for your presentation.

24 **LIFE SKILLS**
Communicate Your sister likes to listen to her favorite CDs with her headphones. The music is so loud that you can hear it across the room. How can you communicate a responsible way for her to listen to music?

Write About Health

25 **Write to Inform—Explain** Identify a variety of consumer influences, including advertising methods, that affect the buying habits of you and your classmates. Write a paragraph to explain how these influences affect your buying decisions.

CHAPTER 4

Foods for Good Nutrition

onions

kale

tomatoes

eggplant

pears

plum

COMPARE AND CONTRAST When you compare things, you tell how they are alike. When you contrast things, you tell how they are different. Use the Reading in Science Handbook on pages R19–R27 and this graphic organizer to help you read the health facts in this chapter.

Compare and Contrast
Topic:
Alike   Different

Health Graph

INTERPRET DATA Americans eat a lot of fruits and vegetables. At least $1\frac{1}{2}$ cups of fruit and 2-$2\frac{1}{2}$ cups of vegetables are recommended each day for good health. What is the difference in the percent of people who eat the least amount of fruits and vegetables and the people who eat the greatest amount?

Fruit and Vegetable Consumption

Number of Servings	Percent
Never or less than $\frac{1}{2}$ cup a day	~3
One cup a day	~34
Three cups a day	~39
Four or more cups a day	~23

Daily Physical Activity

Eating the right foods in the right amounts is one way to stay healthy. Being physically active is another way.

Be Active!
Use the selection, Track 3, **Late for Supper**, to use some food energy.

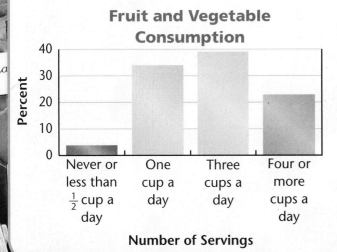

Food—Fuel for the Body

Food As Fuel

Your body is a little like a car. A car needs fuel to run, and so do you. While most cars use gasoline as fuel, the human body uses food. Burning fuel releases energy the car uses to run. A car doesn't need to change gasoline into another form in order to release this energy. Your body is different. It must *digest*, or break down, food before it can use the nutrients food contains.

Nutrients (NOO•tree•uhnts) are substances in food that provide your body with energy. Nutrients also provide building materials the body needs for growth, repair, and daily activities.

Breaking down food is your digestive system's main function. When your digestive system breaks down food, it releases several kinds of nutrients. These include carbohydrates, fats, and proteins.

 COMPARE AND CONTRAST How are your body and a car alike? How are they different?

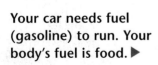 Your car needs fuel (gasoline) to run. Your body's fuel is food. ▶

Digestion

Let's follow a bite of a turkey sandwich to discover how your digestive system breaks down the sandwich into nutrients your body needs. Digestion begins in your mouth. Your teeth chew the bite into smaller pieces. Your saliva contains **enzymes** (EN•zymz), chemicals that help break down foods to release nutrients. Different enzymes are needed to digest different foods.

After you swallow, the food mass moves toward your stomach. There, the partly digested food is squeezed and churned. And more nutrients are released from your bite of sandwich.

Next, the food mass moves into the small intestine, where more enzymes finish the job of digestion. Now the nutrients are ready to move into your bloodstream and into your body cells. Anything that cannot be digested passes into your large intestine.

SEQUENCE List the parts of your digestive system in the order that food moves through them.

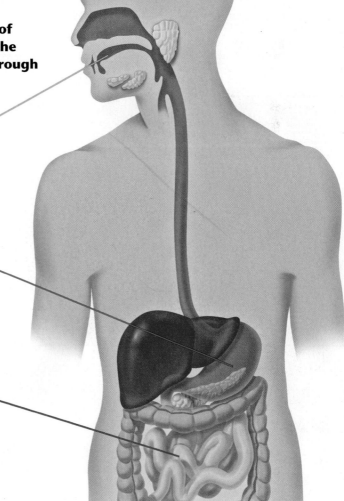

1 Enzymes in your saliva begin to break down starch in the bread.

2 In your stomach, acid begins to break down the meat in the sandwich.

3 Additional enzymes complete digestion in your small intestine. Then nutrients pass into your blood.

Carbohydrates and Fats

Most of the energy your body needs comes from nutrients called carbohydrates. The **carbohydrates** (kar•boh•HY•draytzs) we eat most are sugars and starches.

Some foods, such as syrup and hard candy, are nothing but sugar. Many other foods, including fruits, some vegetables, and milk, contain sugars along with other nutrients. Starches are made of many sugars linked together. Beans, breads, and pasta are all rich in starches. During digestion, your body breaks down starches into sugars.

The nutrients that contain the most energy are **fats**. Plants, animals, and people store excess energy as fats. Butter, margarine, and oils are mostly fats. Most *junk-food* snacks, such as chips, cookies, cakes, and chocolate, have lots of fat. Foods such as meats, nuts, and milk products also contain fats. But unlike junk food, these foods also contain other important nutrients.

DRAW CONCLUSIONS Which food would supply more energy—a handful of raisins or a handful of peanuts? Why?

◀ What nutrients give these kids the quick energy they need to play basketball?

▲ Which of these protein-rich foods do you like?

Proteins

You've certainly grown a lot since you were a baby. You can thank nutrients called proteins for most of this growth. **Proteins** (PROH•teenz) are the building blocks of your body. Your body uses proteins to build and repair cells.

Remember that your body can store extra energy in the form of fats. Your body cannot store extra protein. It needs a new supply every day. You get proteins just as you get carbohydrates and fats—from the foods you eat. Some foods have more proteins than others. Meat, fish, eggs, and milk products are all good protein sources. Dried beans and peas, nuts, and grains also contain proteins.

DRAW CONCLUSIONS Why do you think a child needs more protein than an adult?

Quick Activity

Research Fat Find out how the amount of fat in different kinds of milk is indicated on the milk bottle or carton. What do the numbers mean? Make a table comparing the number of fat grams in different kinds of milk.

Vitamins and Minerals

In addition to carbohydrates, fats, and proteins, there are other nutrients that your body needs in smaller amounts. **Vitamins** (VYT•uh•minz) are nutrients that help your body perform specific functions. They are essential to life. Some vitamins help your body use other nutrients. Other vitamins help keep parts of your body strong and healthy. Your body cannot make most vitamins. It has to get them from foods you eat.

(MIN•uhr•uhlz) are another kind of nutrient, helping your body to grow and work. Minerals help keep your bones and teeth strong, help your body release energy from food, and keep your cells working well. The photographs below show foods that are rich in different vitamins and minerals.

⭐ **Focus Skill** **COMPARE AND CONTRAST** **Name two ways in which calcium is similar to vitamin A and two ways it is different.**

Vitamin A keeps your skin and eyes healthy. It is found in yellow and orange vegetables, tomatoes, and leafy green vegetables.

Vitamin B_1 is needed to release energy from nutrients. It is found in meats, fish, whole-grain breads, and some beans.

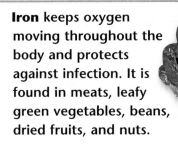

Vitamin C helps keep your blood, gums, and teeth healthy. It is found in citrus fruits, strawberries, and tomatoes.

Iron keeps oxygen moving throughout the body and protects against infection. It is found in meats, leafy green vegetables, beans, dried fruits, and nuts.

Calcium builds strong bones and teeth, helps muscles work, and helps blood clot. It can be found in milk, milk products, and broccoli.

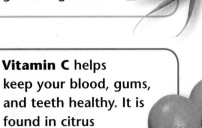

Phosphorus builds strong bones and teeth and helps cells function. It is found in meat, poultry, dried beans, nuts, milk, and milk products.

Water and Fiber

Water is the nutrient your body needs most. You need water to digest food, to transport nutrients to your cells, and to build new cells. Water helps keep your body temperature stable. It also helps remove carbon dioxide, salts, and other wastes from your body.

You get some water from the foods you eat, but you get most of the water you need from drinks like water, milk, and juice. To stay healthy, most people need six to eight glasses of water each day.

Fiber is another part of a healthful diet. Your body needs fiber to help move other foods through the digestive system. Fresh vegetables, fruits, and whole grains are all high in fiber.

MAIN IDEA AND DETAILS **What are two important things water does for your body?**

Whole-grain cereals, like shredded wheat, have more fiber than processed cereals. ▼

Lesson 1 Summary and Review

❶ Summarize with Vocabulary

Use vocabulary from this lesson to complete the statements.

Nutrients with a lot of energy are _____ and _____. Nutrients called _____ are used to build and repair cells in your body. Your body cannot make most _____. Your blood needs iron, a _____, to carry oxygen throughout your body.

❷ What are the main uses of nutrients in your body?

❸ Critical Thinking Why is water a nutrient, even though most of the water you take in doesn't come from food?

❹ (Focus Skill) COMPARE AND CONTRAST Draw and complete this graphic organizer to show how carbohydrates and proteins are alike and different.

Topic:

Alike	Different

❺ Write to Inform—How-To

Describe how a person could design a weekly menu that includes all the necessary nutrients every day.

MyPyramid

Lesson Focus

MyPyramid groups foods with similar nutrients and shows the amounts from each food group people should have each day.

Why Learn This?

You can use MyPyramid to help you plan a balanced diet.

Vocabulary

nutritionist
MyPyramid

Information Alert!

MyPyramid reminds you to eat a balanced diet and to be physically active every day. The amounts shown here are for children between the ages of 9 and 13.

GO ONLINE For the most up-to-date information, visit The Learning Site. www.harcourtschool.com/health

Grains
Eat 5–6 ounces every day

Vegetables
Eat 2–2 $\frac{1}{2}$ cups every day

MyPyramid

People who work in supermarkets arrange similar foods together so they are easy to find. Nutritionists do something very similar but for a different reason. A **nutritionist** is a scientist who studies nutrition and healthful diets. Look at **MyPyramid**, which is a tool to help you eat a balanced diet. It was prepared by nutritionists at the United States Department of Agriculture (USDA).

If you look carefully, you will see that the nutritionists grouped each food with other foods that have similar nutrients. The colored bands of MyPyramid represent the five food groups and oils. MyPyramid shows the portions you should eat from each food group. The bands can help you remember. Eat more foods from wider bands, and eat fewer foods from narrow bands.

MyPyramid also includes a person climbing steps. This is to remind you that you should be physically active every day. The more active you are, the more food you can eat from each group.

MAIN IDEA AND DETAILS **What two kinds of information does MyPyramid give you?**

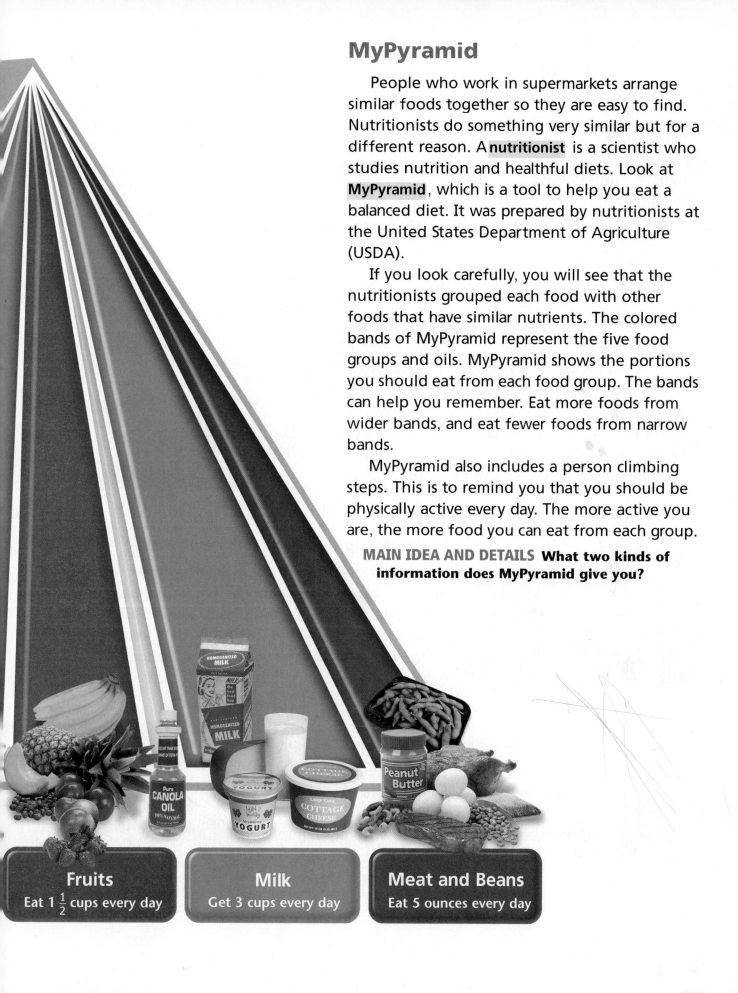

Fruits
Eat 1 $\frac{1}{2}$ cups every day

Milk
Get 3 cups every day

Meat and Beans
Eat 5 ounces every day

A Balanced Diet

Your body needs the right amounts of different nutrients each day to stay healthy. You get those nutrients by eating a balanced diet. The foods in each group of MyPyramid contain similar nutrients. That means you can substitute one food for another in the same group. For example, instead of meat, you could eat fish or eggs. You get many of the same nutrients in fish and eggs as you do in meat.

The number of servings from each food group are suggested for children ages 9–13.

Grains Group (Eat 5–6 ounces every day.)

Rice, bread, tortillas, pasta, and cereals are all made from grains. Grains contain carbohydrates, protein, fiber, minerals, and vitamins. Eat at least 3 ounces of whole grains every day. One ounce of grains is equivalent to 1 "mini" bagel, 1 slice of bread, 5 whole wheat crackers, $\frac{1}{2}$ English muffin, or 3 cups of popcorn.

Fruits Group (Eat 1–1 $\frac{1}{2}$ cups every day.)

Fruits contain carbohydrates, including sugar, fiber, vitamins, and minerals. Choose whole, canned, or dried fruit instead of fruit juice to reduce sugar and increase fiber. One cup of fruit equals 1 small apple, 1 medium grapefruit or pear, 1 large orange or peach, $\frac{1}{2}$ dried fruit, or 1 cup of 100% fruit juice.

Vegetables Group (Eat 2–2 $\frac{1}{2}$ cups every day.)

Vegetables contain many vitamins and minerals. Many also contain carbohydrates, such as fiber and starch. Eat lots of dark-green veggies such as broccoli and spinach and orange vegetables such as carrots and sweet potatoes. Pinto beans, kidney beans, and lentils also count as vegetables. One cup of vegetables equals 2 cups raw leafy greens, 1 cup cooked beans and peas, 1 cup corn, or 1 cup cabbage.

Meat & Beans Group (Eat 5 ounces every day.)

These foods contain protein, fats, vitamins, and minerals. One ounce of food from this group equals 1 ounce of lean beef, pork, or ham, 1 ounce fish, chicken or turkey without skin, 1 egg, $\frac{1}{4}$ cup cooked dry beans or peas, 1 tablespoon of peeanut butter, and $\frac{1}{4}$ cup tofu.

Milk Group (Get 3 cups every day.)

These foods are sometimes called dairy products, because they are made from milk. Dairy products contain a lot of carbohydrates, protein, fats, and minerals, especially calcium. Choose low-fat or fat-free dairy foods when possible. One cup equals 1 cup milk, 1 cup yogurt, $1\frac{1}{2}$ ounces hard cheeses, 2 cups cottage cheese, or $1\frac{1}{2}$ cups ice cream.

Oils (Eat no more than 5 teaspoons each day.)

Most people can get all the oils they need from the other foods they eat. For example, $\frac{1}{2}$ avocado provides $3\frac{1}{2}$ teaspoons of oil. If you do eat oils, liquid oils such as corn oil, soybean oil, and olive oil are best. Try to limit solid fats such as butter or solid margarine.

By eating a variety of foods from each food group every day, you will be eating a balanced diet. You will be giving yourself the nutrients you need for energy and for your body to grow and repair itself.

SUMMARIZE Name the five food groups, and give examples of at least two foods from each group.

Personal Health Plan ▶

Real-Life Situation
You're going to a restaurant, and you want to make sure you choose healthful foods.

Real-Life Plan
List two things you can do to make sure you choose healthful foods from a menu.

Life Skills

Make Responsible Decisions

Using MyPyramid, review the types and amounts of foods people should eat each day. Use the guidelines to write a menu of meals for yourself for one day. Remember to include foods that you like, and leave out those that you are not allowed to eat.

Planning Meals

You can use MyPyramid to plan a healthful snack when you get home from school. A healthful snack would include foods from several of the food groups.

When planning your snack menu, think about what you ate for breakfast and lunch. Think about what you might eat for dinner. Check the amounts of food recommended for each group of the pyramid. Design your snack so that it gives you more of the foods you might not get enough of during the rest of the day.

The menu below shows what Keya's mother has planned for dinner each night. Which food groups are represented in the menu? Which food groups are missing?

COMPARE AND CONTRAST Suppose you aren't allowed to eat the same foods for your after-school snack two days in a row. What menu could you make up so that your snack on Tuesday includes the same food groups as your snack on Monday?

Planning meals helps you eat a balanced diet. ▼

Weekly Menu

Monday	baked chicken, green beans, mashed potato
Tuesday	fish, chips, corn, tomatoes
Wednesday	chicken salad, carrots, bread
Thursday	meatloaf, salad, peas, bread
Friday	soup and salad, lima beans
Saturday	pasta with meat sauce, spinach, bread
Sunday	turkey, mashed potatoes, beets

Jennie's friend is coming for lunch. What if she can't eat what Jennie has chosen? ▶

Lunch menu The lunch Jennie prepared for herself and a friend included a peanut butter sandwich made with whole-wheat bread. But her friend is allergic to peanuts. What kind of sandwich could Jennie substitute for the peanut butter one?

Lesson 2 Summary and Review

1 Summarize with Vocabulary

Use vocabulary and other terms from this lesson to complete the statements.

_____ was prepared by USDA _____ to show how a person might plan a balanced _____. It tells how much food from each group people should eat every day.

2 Which foods on MyPyramid should you choose in the smallest amounts or not at all?

3 Critical Thinking What foods could you substitute for a friend who doesn't eat meat?

4 **COMPARE AND CONTRAST** Draw and complete this graphic organizer to show how the Vegetables group and the Grains group are alike and different in terms of nutrients.

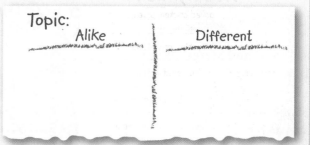

Topic:
Alike   Different

5 Write to Inform—Explanation

List the foods you like to eat, and explain whether they make a balanced diet or not.

149

Eating Healthfully

Lesson Focus

To stay healthy, a person needs to eat only as much food as his or her body needs each day.

Why Learn This?

Eating more or less than your body needs can be unhealthful.

Vocabulary

portion control
anorexia
calories
energy balance

Portion Control

Almost everyone who eats in a fast-food restaurant has been asked this question: " Do you want to supersize that?" Supersizing means adding more food—sometimes a lot more—for a little extra money. Every time you supersize a meal, you are eating two or three or more additional servings of food. The items that are most often supersized are those that you should be eating less of, such as fries, soft drinks, and shakes. These often lack important nutrients.

You need to eat a variety of foods to get all the nutrients your body needs. But you also need to control the size of the portions you eat. **Portion control** means limiting the amount of food you eat at each meal. Without portion control, you may gain more weight than is healthy. In the United States, more than 15 percent of preteens are greatly overweight. Being greatly overweight as an adult is called *obesity*. Obesity can double the chances of getting diseases such as diabetes and heart disease.

Did You Know?

In the United States, about 16 percent of ten-year-olds are overweight. In Italy, about 30 percent are overweight.

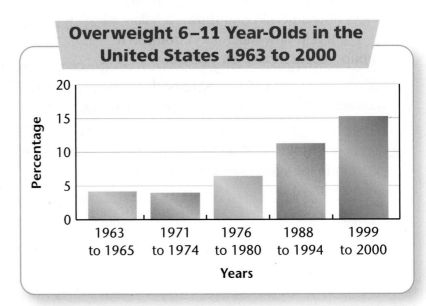

Overweight 6–11 Year-Olds in the United States 1963 to 2000

▲ Low self-esteem
sometimes causes
young women to
"see" themselves as
overweight, even
when they are not.

Obesity isn't the only problem related to portion control. As they grow, many teenage girls think they are overweight, whether they really are or not. To avoid gaining weight, some eat less food than their bodies need to stay healthy.

About 5 percent of young women develop a serious eating disorder called anorexia (an•uh•REKS•ee•uh). Anorexia is excessive dieting and, at times, *self-starvation*. Starvation means not eating at all. Anorexia causes poor general health, low blood pressure, heart problems, bone weakness, and even death.

 COMPARE AND CONTRAST **How are serving size and portion control alike? How are they different?**

All the foods we eat provide calories for daily activities. ▼

Energy Balance

To keep your body at a healthy weight, you must balance the calories you take in with the calories you use up. **Calories** are a measure of the amount of energy in a food. All three nutrient groups—carbohydrates, fats, and proteins—contain calories. Your body can use these nutrients for energy. Carbohydrates and proteins have the same number of calories—about 4 per gram of food eaten. Fat has about 9 calories per gram.

When you take in more calories per day than you need, your body changes the excess calories into fat, and you gain weight. If you use more calories per day than you take in, your body uses stored fat for energy, and you lose weight. The ideal, called **energy balance**, is to take in the same number of calories as you use. Energy balance keeps you from gaining weight or losing weight. The best way to keep your body at a healthy weight is to combine good eating habits with regular exercise. You will learn more about the benefits of exercise in Chapter 5.

Chicken Soup

Calories Used per Hour

Activity	Calories Used
Walking	155
Swimming	345
Basketball	430
Running	455

SUMMARIZE What is the best way to keep your weight the same as it is now?

Athletes can usually eat a lot because they use more calories than the average person. ▶

Quick Activity

Calorie Intake and Energy Use Your body burns calories all the time, but some activities use more calories than others. The table shows how many calories a 100-pound person uses doing a variety of activities. Suppose you eat a 750-calorie dessert. Calculate how long you would have to walk or swim to use up those extra calories.

Lesson 3 Summary and Review

❶ Summarize with Vocabulary

Use vocabulary from this lesson to complete the statements.

The amount of energy in food is measured in _____. Taking in and using the same amount of food energy is called _____. Gaining or losing weight is often the result of poor _____. Supersizing meals can cause weight gain, which can lead to health problems. Excessive dieting, or _____, is also unhealthful.

❷ Why is portion control important?

❸ Critical Thinking What might happen to your muscles if you exercise a lot but don't take in enough calories?

❹ (Focus Skill) COMPARE AND CONTRAST Draw and complete this graphic organizer to show how obesity and anorexia are alike and different.

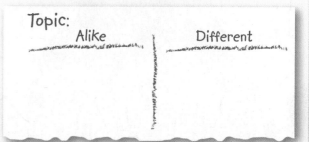

Topic:

Alike	Different

❺ Write to Inform—Explanation

Research, then explain why someone shouldn't gain or lose weight too quickly.

Influences on Food Choices

Family, Friends, and Culture Affect Food Choices

The United States is full of people who came here from other countries and brought their foods with them. The cultures of your parents and grandparents influence your food choices the most. How can the country where your family came from influence what you eat?

Family members can influence the foods you eat, too. Suppose you have an older brother whom you admire. You might want to imitate his food choices. Or, if you don't get along with him, you might choose foods that are different from those he chooses. The same is true of your classmates. The way you feel about them might make you go along with or reject their food choices. No matter what kinds of foods you choose, you should make sure they are healthful.

Many restaurants offer foods of different countries. Which kinds of foods do you like? Why? ▶

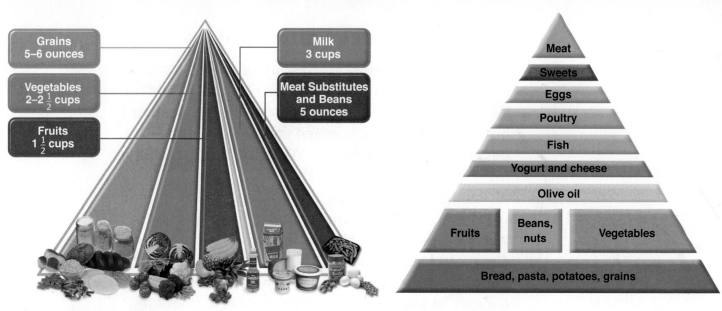

Grains
5–6 ounces

Vegetables
2–2 $\frac{1}{2}$ cups

Fruits
1 $\frac{1}{2}$ cups

Milk
3 cups

Meat Substitutes
and Beans
5 ounces

Meat

Sweets

Eggs

Poultry

Fish

Yogurt and cheese

Olive oil

Fruits

Beans,
nuts

Vegetables

Bread, pasta, potatoes, grains

▲ People who don't eat meat can still have a healthful diet. A *vegetarian food pyramid* includes foods such as beans that replace meats, poultry, and fish.

▲ The *Mediterranean food pyramid* reflects foods eaten in countries like Spain, Italy, and Greece. It has more fish than meat.

People's diets are also influenced by their environments. In some places, people eat the wild plants and animals that live in the area. Some people eat the crops they grow and the meat of the animals they raise. People who live in coastal areas tend to eat more seafood than people who live far from the sea. How does the place where you live influence what you eat?

A person's values can also influence what he or she eats. For example, vegetarians choose not to eat meat. Some people don't eat meat because they are against the killing of animals or because of their religious beliefs. How do your personal values affect what you eat?

MAIN IDEA AND DETAILS Give two reasons why one person's diet might be different from another's.

Quick Activity

Compare Pyramids Compare sources of protein and daily amounts in MyPyramid and one of the pyramids above. Colors show similar food groupings. Then make a table of any differences.

Seasons Affect Food Choices

Do you like a hot bowl of soup or maybe a cup of hot chocolate on a cold winter day? A cool salad and an ice-cold glass of milk might be better if the weather is hot and humid. People often eat different foods depending on the weather. What foods do you like in different kinds of weather?

People used to eat different things during different seasons, too. Your parents and grandparents had to wait for late summer to find fresh corn in the market. They could buy canned or frozen corn in the winter, but not fresh. Some foods, like apples and potatoes, are easy to keep fresh. But strawberries, blueberries, tomatoes, and peppers spoil easily. So why can we find all these fruits and vegetables in most supermarkets all year? Look carefully at the labels on these foods and you will find the answer.

Many of these foods are grown in countries like Mexico, Panama, and Brazil, where it's warm all year.

SUMMARIZE Why don't seasons influence a person's choice of foods much anymore?

When the weather is cold, you probably choose hot foods, like soup. ▼

When the weather is hot, you might eat fresh fruits and vegetables that don't need to be heated. ▶

156

Freezing, drying, canning, vacuum-packing, smoking, and salting are methods of preserving food. ▼

Food Packaging We can eat certain foods all year because of preservation methods such as canning and freezing. Food irradiation is a method of preserving food and killing germs that cause spoilage and disease. This helps some fresh fruits, meats, and vegetables last longer and be safer to eat. The technology for this process was developed to treat foods eaten by astronauts on early space missions.

Cost and Unit Price Affect Food Choices

Foods imported from other parts of the world usually cost more than those produced locally. This may influence what people eat. For example, peaches grown in Chile may be available in February, but they may be too expensive for most families. So, they may buy frozen or canned peaches instead.

Unit price, or the cost of a certain amount of a food, may also influence choice. Suppose a 10-oz can of Brand A peas costs $0.60, while a 12-oz can of Brand B costs $0.66. Which is the better buy? The unit price of Brand A is $0.06/oz, while the unit price of Brand B is $0.055/oz. Brand B is more economical and may be the choice of many shoppers.

Unit pricing also allows shoppers to choose the most economically sized package of the same brand. Buying a half-gallon of juice, for example, is usually less expensive per ounce than buying two quarts.

DRAW CONCLUSIONS Which is more economical—a 6-oz box of cereal for $2.49 or a 12-oz bag of the same cereal for $4.89?

Unit pricing enables shoppers to choose foods and other products that are more economical. ▼

41.5¢ per ounce Unit price

Retail Price

$2.49

pint of Strawberries

096253

6 ounces net weight

Emotions Affect Food Choices

Personal Health Plan ▶

Real-Life Situation
Suppose you're feeling upset about something and don't feel like eating.
Real-Life Plan
Make a menu of well-balanced meals for days when you aren't feeling well. Use your plan when you need it.

Often, people who feel stress or who are upset are likely to eat unhealthful foods. Some people eat large amounts of food or they eat junk food, like chips, cookies, and ice cream when they are upset. These kinds of foods are sometimes called *comfort foods*, because people think eating them makes them feel better. Other people stop eating altogether when they are upset or stressed.

Unfortunately, it won't help your feelings to eat lots of food, to eat junk food, or to eat nothing at all. Eating a balanced diet is more likely to make you feel better. The nutrients provided by the right amounts of healthful foods help you deal with stressful situations.

Even when you're feeling fine, you might choose foods because of some emotion. For example, if your grandma always makes pizza when you visit, you might enjoy having pizza with your friends because it reminds you of the fun you have at your grandma's.

Focus Skill **COMPARE AND CONTRAST** **What two opposite changes in eating habits can occur when a person is upset?**

▼ What foods do you eat when you're having fun?

Health Concerns Affect Food Choices

Your food choices can be affected by how your body reacts to certain foods. If you have a food allergy, you probably become ill if you eat the food you are allergic to. A **food allergy** (AL•er•jee) is a bad reaction to a food that most other people can eat. Food allergies can give people rashes, upset stomachs, and headaches. Sometimes food allergies interfere with breathing. People who have severe allergic reactions to certain foods can even die.

Some foods contain chemicals that change the way the body functions. For example, caffeine is a chemical that speeds up body activity. It can make you jittery and keep you awake at night. Caffeine is found in coffee, tea, chocolate, and many soft drinks. You should either avoid foods that have caffeine or limit the amount you eat or drink.

Illnesses can also influence people's food choices. For example, people with diabetes must keep track of the carbohydrates they eat. People with heart disease should limit the amount of fats they eat. And people with high blood pressure should avoid salty foods.

A number of different foods, including peanuts, strawberries, shellfish, and milk, may cause allergies. If you discover that you are allergic to certain foods, you should avoid those foods.

If you are already healthy and want to stay that way, you should eat a healthful diet. Eat a wide variety of foods so you get all the nutrients you need. Avoid foods high in sugar, fat, and salt. Be aware of the amounts of food you eat, too. Too much of a good thing can still be bad for you. Follow portion size guidelines. However, don't cut out something altogether unless you are allergic to it. You still need carbohydrates, fats, and proteins—just not in large amounts.

CAUSE AND EFFECT Identify three possible effects of caffeine on a person's body.

▲ Strawberries and peanuts can cause food allergies.

Lesson 4 Summary and Review

❶ Summarize with Vocabulary

Use vocabulary and other terms from this lesson to complete the statements.

If you break out in a rash after eating a certain food, you may have a _____. _____ is a chemical found in some foods and drinks that can make you jittery. People who have _____ should limit the amount of carbohydrates they eat.

❷ Give an example that shows how unit price can influence a person's choice of foods.

❸ Critical Thinking Why is it a bad idea to eat large amounts of healthful foods?

❹ (Focus Skill) COMPARE AND CONTRAST

Choose two countries whose foods you eat. Draw and complete this graphic organizer to show how the foods of these countries are alike and different.

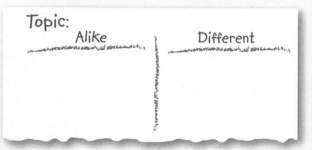

❺ Write to Inform—Explanation

Describe how your family influences your food choices.

Responsibility

Self-Control

As you grow older, you must take more and more responsibility for your health. This includes choosing healthful foods. It also includes practicing self-control. With self-control you can choose portion sizes that are right for you.

When you look at three popcorn containers at a theater refreshment stand, you might be tempted to get the biggest one. Even if you aren't very hungry, the smell may be tempting you. Or maybe it's the price—the biggest one might cost only a little more than the medium size.

But is the biggest container the most healthful for you? Popcorn is made mostly of carbohydrate. On its own, popcorn is a healthful snack. But at most theaters, popcorn is cooked in fatty oil and covered with butter and salt. Too much carbohydrate, oil, butter, and salt are not good for you.

Activity

Suppose you are the person at the theater refreshment stand. What should you do? You can ask for the popcorn without butter and salt, or you can have just a little of each. You can buy the small container or you can share the larger one with a friend. Write about and explain a healthful choice.

Food Labels and Advertising

Lesson Focus
Food labels and advertising can influence the choices you make when you are selecting foods.

Why Learn This?
Reading food labels and analyzing advertisements can help you make healthful food choices.

Vocabulary
ingredients
additives
preservatives

Quick Activity

Analyze Food Labels Study the food labels on the boxes of two different dry cereals. Make a table comparing the nutritional values of the two cereals. Which cereal gives you more fiber? Less sugar? More calories? More protein?

Food Labels Provide Information About Nutrition

What's in a box of macaroni and cheese? You might think it's just macaroni and cheese. In fact, even something as simple as macaroni and cheese is made up of many different ingredients. **Ingredients** (in•GREE•dee•uhnts) are all the things that make up a food. What are the ingredients in macaroni and cheese? Look at the label on the following page to find out.

On every box of macaroni and cheese—and on every packaged food—there is a Nutrition Facts label. It tells you how big a serving size is and how many servings are in each package. It also tells you how many calories a serving contains and the nutrients that are in every serving. The label even tells you how much of each day's recommended nutrients one serving provides.

You can learn a lot about what you are eating by reading the Nutrition Facts labels on packaged foods. ▶

Nutrition Facts

Serving Size 2.5 oz
(70g/about 1/3 Box)
(Makes about 1 cup)
Servings Per Container about 3

Amount Per Serving	In Box	Prep*
Calories	260	410
Calories from Fat	25	170

	%Daily Value***	
Total Fat 2.5g**	4%	28%
Saturated Fat 1.5g	8%	23%
Cholesterol 10mg	3%	3%
Sodium 560mg	23%	31%
Total Carbohydrate 48g	16%	16%
Dietary Fiber 1g	4%	4%
Sugars 7g		
Protein 11g		

Vitamin A	0%	15%
Vitamin C	0%	0%
Calcium	10%	15%
Iron	15%	15%

*Prepared with Margarine and 2% Reduced Fat Milk.

**Amount in Box. When prepared, one serving (about 1 cup) contains an additional 1g total fat (3.5g sat. fat), 190mg sodium and 1g total carbohydrate (1g sugars).

***Percent Daily Values are based on a 2,000 calorie diet. Your daily values may be higher or lower depending on your calorie needs:

	Calories:	2,000	2,500
Total Fat	Less than	65g	80g
Sat Fat	Less than	20g	25g
Cholest	Less than	300mg	300mg
Sodium	Less than	2,400mg	2,400mg
Total Carb		300g	375g
Dietary Fiber		25g	30g

INGREDIENTS: ENRICHED MACARONI PRODUCT (WHEAT FLOUR, NIACIN, FERROUS SULFATE [IRON], THIAMIN MONONITRATE [VITAMIN B1], RIBOFLAVIN [VITAMIN B2], FOLIC ACID), CHEESE SAUCE MIX (WHEY, WHEY PROTEIN CONCENTRATE, MILKFAT, MILK PROTEIN CONCENTRATE, SALT, SODIUM TRIPOLYPHOSPHATE, CITRIC ACID, SODIUM PHOSPHATE, LACTIC ACID, CALCIUM PHOSPHATE, YELLOW 5, YELLOW 6, ENZYMES, CHEESE CULTURE)

Serving Size tells you how much to eat to get the calories and nutrients listed.

Servings per Container is equal to the total amount of food in the package, divided by the serving size.

Calories tells you how much energy you get from eating one serving.

Lists amounts of protein, fats, carbohydrates, sodium, sugar, cholesterol, and fiber per serving.

Percent Daily Value shows how much of an adult's daily need for a nutrient is met by one serving.

Lists vitamins and minerals in the food, including those in the food naturally and those that are added.

Ingredients includes the main ingredients as well as any additives and preservatives.

The Nutrition Facts label also tells you what nutrients are in the food. Many of the ingredients in the macaroni and cheese, such as wheat and milk, are on MyPyramid. Some, like calcium and vitamin D, are also nutrients. Other ingredients are additives and preservatives.

Additives (AD•uh•tivz) are things food manufacturers add to foods. Some additives, such as sugar, are nutrients. Other additives, such as salt and food coloring, change the way a food tastes or looks. Manufacturers sometimes add vitamins and minerals to restore the nutritional value of a processed food.

Preservatives (pree•ZERV•uh•tivz) are chemicals added to foods to keep them from spoiling. By law, additives and preservatives must be listed as ingredients on food labels.

You can use the information on food labels to compare different foods or to compare different brands of the same food. You can also use it to decide how much of a food you should eat at one time. It is important to read the label if you are on a special diet or are allergic to any foods. Nutrition Facts and ingredients lists can help you choose foods that are good for you.

SUMMARIZE What kinds of information are shown on food labels?

▲ Ads make you more aware of products. However, they may not give you much information about the products.

Advertisements Influence Food Choices

Do you watch television, read magazines, or look at billboards along the highways? If so, you've probably seen ads for foods. Have you ever seen a food ad and then really wanted that food? If so, the ad did its job.

Many ads appeal to your emotions. They try to make you think that eating certain foods will make you feel good. An ad could show a group of children having fun while eating pizza. A movie star might tell you how good a hamburger tastes. Or a sports star might suggest that drinking a certain juice will make you more like him or her. Some food products have prizes inside the packages. People may buy the product just to get the prize. Advertisers use these "tricks" to get you to buy.

Some ads make claims about the healthfulness of a food. An ad might say the food is low in fat, high in fiber, or sugar-free. While it is against the law to lie in an advertisement, ads can still be misleading. For example, many foods labeled "low-fat" are still high in calories if they contain extra sugar in place of some of the fat. Food packages can also claim to offer health benefits that have not been proved.

If you prefer to eat foods without additives or preservatives, you might choose products labeled " all natural." But be careful. Having no additives or preservatives doesn't mean that a food is good for you. For example, some potato chips are labeled " 100 percent natural." But the potatoes are still fried in oil and contain a lot of fat and salt. It's true that salt and oil are natural. But too much salt in your diet can increase your blood pressure, and too much fat can lead to heart disease.

Just remember that food ads and food packages are designed to make you want to buy the foods. If you look carefully at the Nutrition Facts labels, you can decide for yourself what foods are healthful if eaten in the proper amounts.

MAIN IDEA AND DETAILS **What is an ad designed to do, and how does it do it?**

Lesson 5 Summary and Review

❶ Summarize with Vocabulary

Use vocabulary and other terms from this lesson to complete the statements.

The _____ in a package of food are written on the _____ label. Sometimes, manufacturers put things in foods to improve how the foods look or taste. These things are called _____. To keep a food from spoiling, a food manufacturer might add one or more _____.

❷ On a Nutrition Facts label, what does the information under Percent Daily Value tell you?

❸ Critical Thinking Why might the label "100 percent natural" on a packaged food be misleading?

❹ COMPARE AND CONTRAST Draw and complete this graphic organizer to show how the food labels of two cereals can be alike and different.

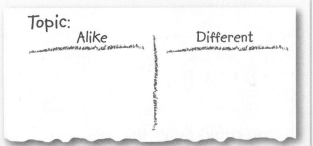

Topic:

Alike   Different

❺ Write to Inform—Description

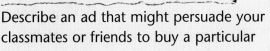

Describe an ad that might persuade your classmates or friends to buy a particular food product.

Make Responsible Decisions

About Fast Food

Suppose you're at a fast-food restaurant for dinner. You got up too late to eat breakfast this morning. Then you had pizza and a cola for lunch. Now you want to order the supersized double cheeseburger special. Follow the steps for **Making Responsible Decisions** about eating a more healthful dinner.

1 **Find out about the choices you could make.**

2 **Eliminate any choices that will make you sick or are against your family rules.**

You could order the special—double cheeseburger, fries, and large cola. Or, you could order a grilled chicken sandwich, a green salad, and a banana smoothie.

You like cola, but you have already had one today. Fries are your favorite, but your parents allow you to have only one portion per week.

3 Imagine the possible results of each choice.

The cheeseburger and fries are high in fat and the cola contains sugar. The chicken has less fat, there are vegetables in the salad, and fruit in the smoothie.

4 Make the decision that is right for you.

You order the grilled chicken sandwich, salad, and smoothie.

 # Problem Solving

A. Joanna needs a lot of energy for track practice, but she isn't sure what she should eat at the coffee shop.
  - Use what you know about the steps for **Making Responsible Decisions** to help her choose healthful foods.

B. Jerry's mom prepares three healthful meals every day. She gives him fruits and raw vegetables for snacks. This afternoon Jerry wants to go to the Burger House with his friends.
  - What should Jerry order to show that he is trustworthy when eating away from home?

LESSON 6

Food Preparation and Safety

Lesson Focus
Foods must be stored and prepared properly in order to be safe.

Why Learn This?
You can use what you learn to safely store and prepare foods in your home and to avoid food poisoning.

Vocabulary
food poisoning

Food Poisoning

You probably wouldn't think of eating uncooked chicken or eggs. They just don't taste good. But there are more important reasons for not eating uncooked foods. Eating certain uncooked or undercooked foods can cause food poisoning. **Food poisoning** is an illness caused by eating foods containing harmful germs.

Germs get into foods from soil, water, air, and people who haven't washed their hands. Germs also spread from one food to another. Suppose you use a knife to cut some uncooked chicken. Then you use the same knife to cut a sandwich. You could transfer germs from the chicken to the sandwich.

Food poisoning can cause stomach cramps, nausea, and diarrhea. Some forms of food poisoning are very dangerous and can even cause death.

CAUSE AND EFFECT **How can someone working in a kitchen spread germs to the food?**

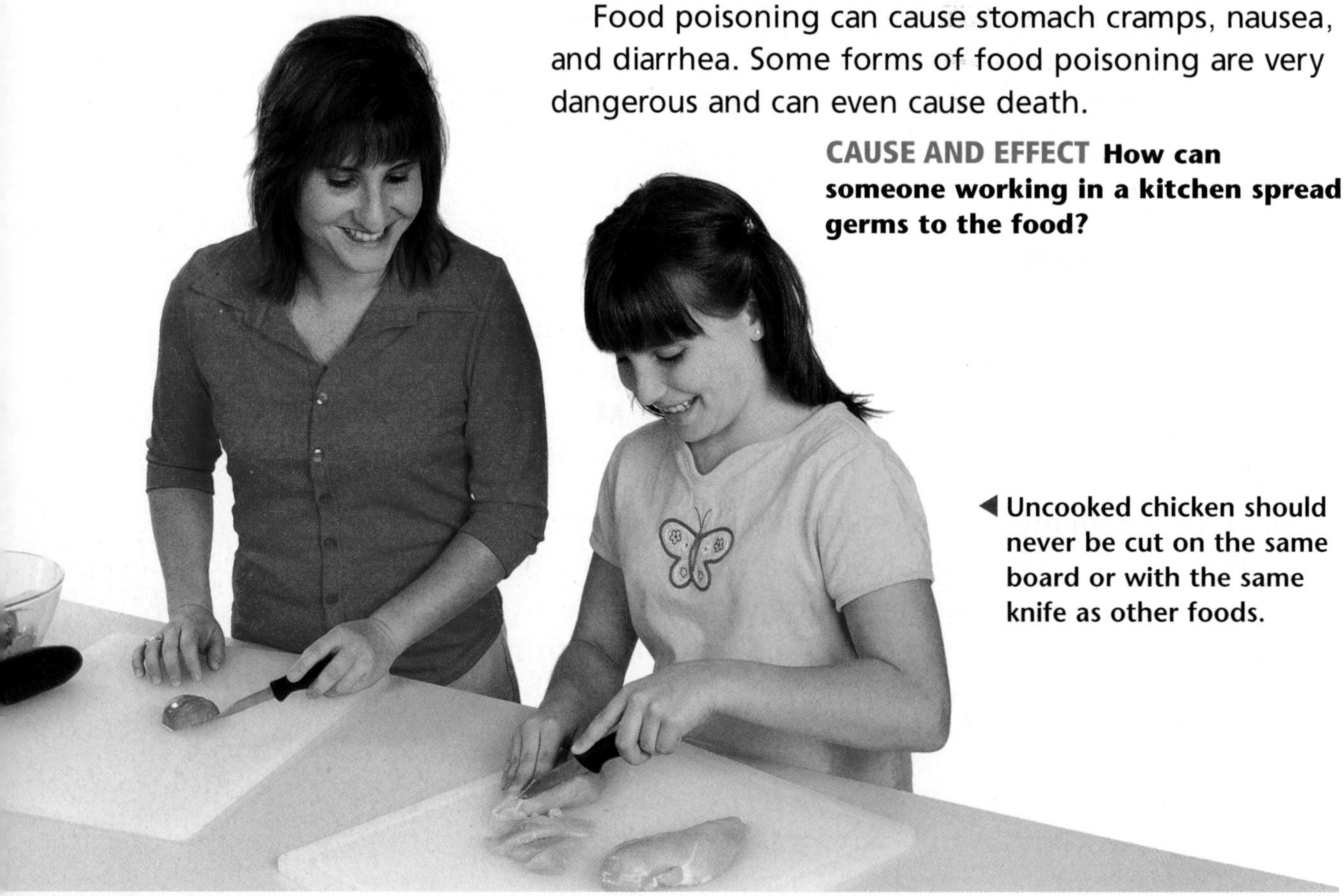

◀ Uncooked chicken should never be cut on the same board or with the same knife as other foods.

Proper Storage Keeps Foods Safe

Germs are everywhere. You can't get rid of them all. The important thing is not to let germs multiply. When germs in food multiply, the food starts to look odd, smell unusual, and taste bad. It has spoiled. The way to keep foods from spoiling is to store them correctly.

Germs multiply rapidly at room temperature but more slowly at low temperature. That's why it's important to store cooked foods and all meats, milk, and eggs in a refrigerator. Covering foods like breads and cereals by wrapping them or putting them in containers can help keep them from spoiling. Although vegetables and fruits don't spoil quickly, storing them in a refrigerator keeps them fresh.

Different foods spoil at different rates. Even in a refrigerator, uncooked meat spoils in a few days. Milk will last for about a week, and cheeses and eggs last for several weeks. Juices, vegetables, and most fruits will last much longer. Freezing foods keeps them safe much longer.

COMPARE AND CONTRAST (Focus Skill) **What foods spoil the fastest in the refrigerator? The slowest?**

▼ **Different foods need to be stored in different parts of the refrigerator.**

Store cooked foods in plastic containers or wrapped in plastic.

Keep meat, poultry, and fish in the coldest part of the refrigerator. Store them wrapped.

Store eggs and milk in their original cartons. Throw away any cracked eggs. Don't keep eggs or milk on the refrigerator door.

Store fruits and vegetables in a vegetable crisper or in unsealed plastic bags.

Prepare a Safe Meal

Think about everything you've touched today. Think about all the other hands that have touched those things. There are hundreds of places you could have picked up germs. To prevent food poisoning when you prepare food, remember these four rules:

- Clean, clean, clean!
- Separate—don't contaminate!
- Refrigerate properly!
- Cook thoroughly!

Clean, clean, clean!

The first and most important thing to do before you prepare a meal is to wash your hands. Do this before you touch anything. Use warm water and plenty of soap, and scrub for twenty seconds. Make sure to clean under your fingernails and between your fingers. After you wash your hands, dry them with a clean towel. Make sure countertops are clean and dry.

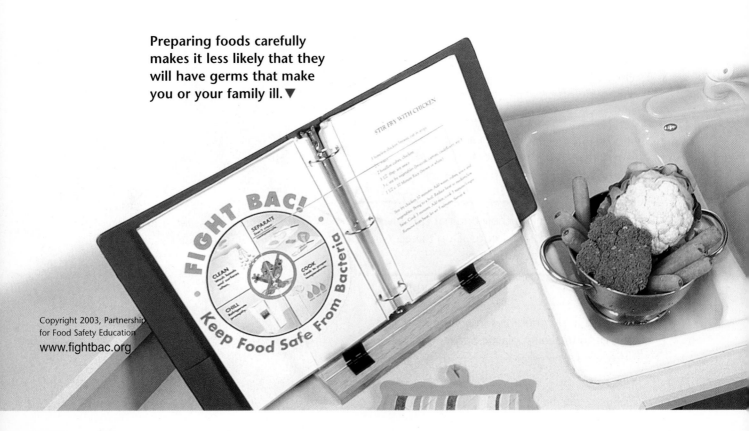

Preparing foods carefully makes it less likely that they will have germs that make you or your family ill. ▼

Before preparing or eating fresh fruits or vegetables, wash them thoroughly. This will help get rid of germs as well as any chemicals that were used to kill insect pests. After eating, wash dishes and set them out to dry. If you use towels to dry dishes, always use clean ones.

Separate—don't contaminate!

Raw meat, poultry, seafood, and eggs are the foods most likely to carry harmful germs. After you handle these foods, wash your cutting board and utensils thoroughly with hot water and soap. *Never* cut fruits or vegetables on a surface where you have had raw meat, poultry, seafood, or eggs.

Refrigerate properly!

Keep cold foods cold until you use them. If you are going to cook a food that is frozen, thaw the food in a refrigerator or in a microwave, not on a countertop.

Never leave food that needs to be refrigerated sitting at room temperature for more than two hours.

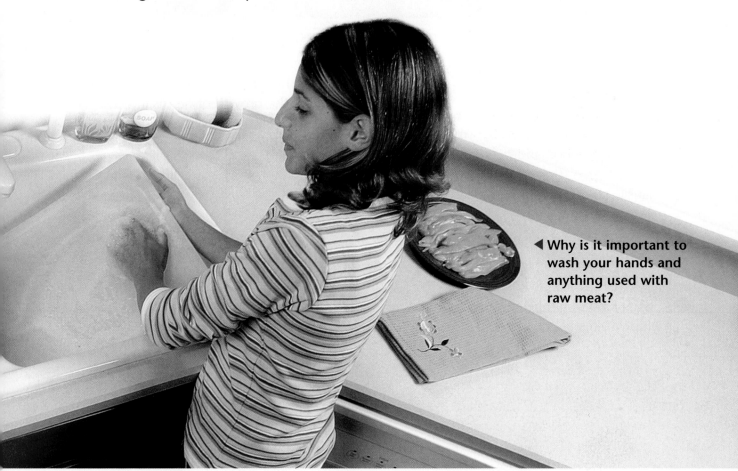

◀ Why is it important to wash your hands and anything used with raw meat?

▲ Cooking foods completely will reduce the risk of getting food poisoning. Most germs are killed by heat.

Cook thoroughly!

Cooking kills most harmful germs in food. But foods that are not cooked all the way through can still cause food poisoning. To be safe, cook eggs until the yolks are hard. Cook meat and poultry until they are no longer pink inside.

Finally, remember that your eyes, nose, and taste buds are there to protect you. If something looks odd, smells unusual, or tastes bad, throw it out. If you follow these guidelines, you will reduce the chances of getting or causing food poisoning.

 COMPARE AND CONTRAST How do high and low temperatures fight food poisoning in different ways?

Lesson 6 Summary and Review

❶ Summarize with Vocabulary

Use vocabulary and other terms from this lesson to complete the statements.

Pains in your stomach with cramps, _____, and _____ might be signs that you have _____. Refrigeration and freezing slow the growth of _____ that can make foods spoil, while sitting out at room temperature speeds up their growth.

❷ Critical Thinking What is the worst thing that can happen to a person who gets food poisoning?

❸ At what kind of temperature do germs multiply fastest?

❹ **COMPARE AND CONTRAST**
Complete this graphic organizer to show how high and low temperatures affect the growth of germs in ways that are alike and different.

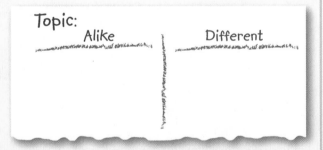

Topic:

| Alike | Different |

❺ Write to Inform—How-To
Describe a method to prevent germs from spreading from a piece of uncooked chicken to a piece of cooked chicken.

ACTIVITIES

Physical Education

Carbo-Loading Athletes prepare in many ways for long-distance races called *marathons*. The winner will run for more than two hours without stopping. In addition to training, a marathon runner may do something before a race called carbo-loading. Find out what carbo-loading is, and write a paragraph explaining it.

Science

In the Body Use a sheet of poster board to make an outline of a body. Then cut out photos or drawings from magazines and newspapers of foods that represent the six nutrient groups. Paste these on the poster board, and write a short caption explaining the ways in which each nutrient helps the body.

Technology Project

Compare Nutrients Different foods contain different amounts of nutrients. Nutrients and their amounts are listed on the nutrition labels. Using a computer, make a table that compares the nutrients of three similar foods. If a computer is not available, make a poster.

 For more activities, visit The Learning Site.
www.harcourtschool.com/health

Home & Community

At School Many school cafeterias provide menus in advance. Study next week's menu for your school cafeteria. If a menu isn't available, keep a journal of what is served each day for one week. Look at MyPyramid on pages 144–145. Add up the number of lunch foods that fit into each group. Then describe ways the foods can be used as part of a balanced diet.

Career Link

School Dietitian School dietitians plan meals for school lunches. They prepare nutritious menus for schoolchildren, making sure students get a balance of the nutrients they need. Suppose you are the dietitian for your school. Prepare a series of menus for one week of school lunches. Be sure to use the information you have learned in this chapter as you prepare your menu.

Focus Skill Reading Skill

COMPARE AND CONTRAST

Draw and then use this graphic organizer to answer questions 1 and 2.

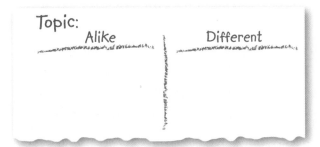

1 Write at least two ways in which a piece of whole-wheat bread and a lump of sugar are alike.

2 Write at least two ways in which a piece of bread and a lump of sugar are different.

ABC Use Vocabulary

Match each term in Column B with its description in Column A.

Column A	Column B
3 A nutrient such as calcium or iron	**A** calorie
	B preservative
4 A measure of the energy in food	**C** additive
	D mineral
5 A condition resulting from extreme dieting	**E** oils
	F anorexia
6 Something added to a food to keep it from spoiling	
7 Something put in food to make it more nutritious	
8 Yellow bar in MyPyramid	

? Check Understanding

Choose the letter of the correct answer.

9 An enzyme ____.
 A holds energy needed by your body
 B is a carbohydrate
 C helps release energy from food
 D causes food poisoning

10 Digestion begins in the ____.
 F stomach   H small intestine
 G esophagus   J mouth

11 If calcium is missing in a person's diet, the person might ____.
 A have difficulty seeing at night
 B have soft bones
 C have swollen gums
 D have digestion problems

12. Which list of foods belongs in the Grains group?
 F broccoli, carrots, lentils
 G milk, cheese, yogurt
 H breads, cereals, rice, and pasta
 J chicken, nuts, peas

13 Which of these foods would your grandparents **NOT** have found in a supermarket in winter?
 A apples   C steak
 B fresh corn on   D fish
    the cob

14 If you were trying to add protein to your diet, which of these foods would be the best to eat?

F   H

G   J

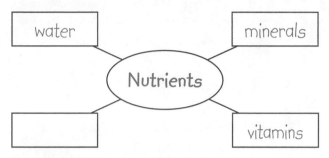

water

minerals

Nutrients

vitamins

15 Which nutrient is missing from the graphic organizer?

A fats

C carbohydrates

B proteins

D all of these

16 Which of the following will you **NOT** find on a Nutrition Facts label?

F protein content

H carbohydrate content

G fat content

J water content

17 At which of the following temperatures will germs grow fastest?

A 5°F (freezer)

C 68°F (room)

B 40°F (refrigerator)

D 150°F (dishwasher)

18 Eat chicken only if it is cooked so thoroughly that the inside is no longer _____.

F red

H white

G pink

J orange

19 In a refrigerator, which of the following foods spoils fastest?

A uncooked meat

C milk

B hard cheese

D pasteurized juice

Think Critically

20 You slice a peach, a piece of chicken, and a tomato, in that order, with the same knife without washing it. Only the people who eat the chicken, the tomato, or both get food poisoning. Explain how this could happen.

21 Your doctor says your bones are too soft. What question about your diet might your doctor ask? Why? What might he or she suggest you do to make your bones stronger?

22 You see a TV commercial advertising a breakfast cereal. Your favorite basketball player is shown in the background dunking the ball into the basket. How would this affect the way you think about the cereal? Would you be more tempted to buy it? Why or why not?

Apply Skills

23 **BUILDING GOOD CHARACTER**

Respect You are invited to dinner at a friend's home. You and your friend have the chore of cleaning up after dinner. You notice that a plate of leftover meat is sitting on the countertop. Your friend suggests you play some games now and leave the meat where it is. How can you show good self-control in this situation?

24 **LIFE SKILLS**

Make Responsible Decisions You learn from some friends about a new diet. It's supposed to make you lose 10 pounds in a week. Do you decide to try it? Why or why not?

Write About Health

25 **Write to Inform—Explanation** Explain why reading Nutrition Facts labels is important to your health.

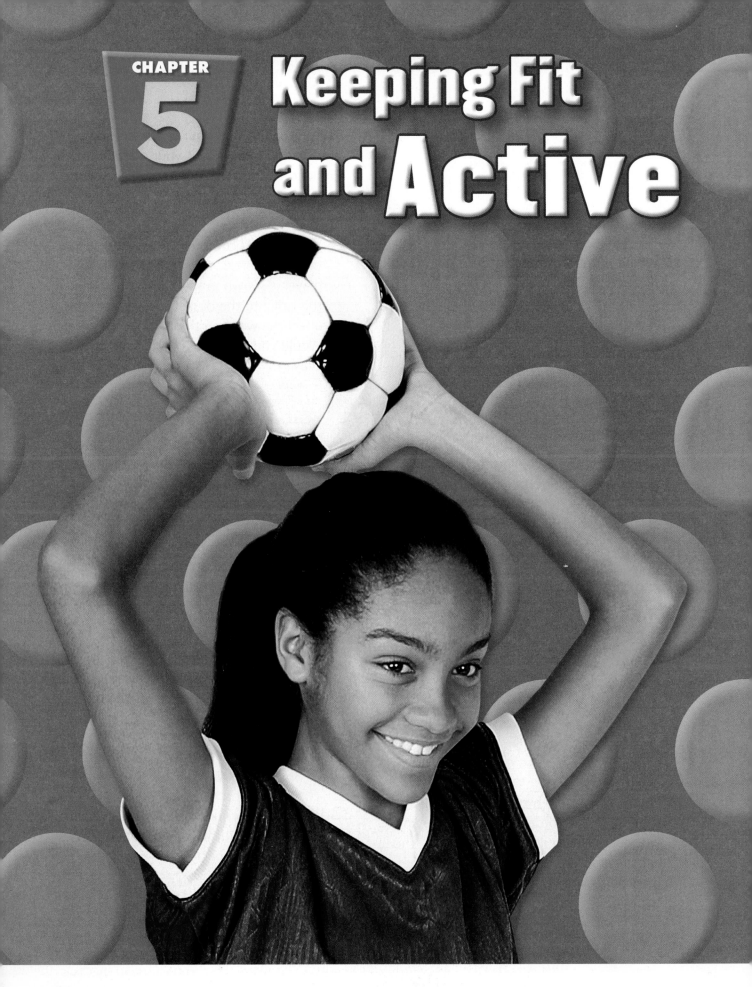

CHAPTER 5

Keeping Fit and Active

Reading Skill

IDENTIFY MAIN IDEA AND DETAILS
The main idea is the most important thought in a passage. Details tell about the main idea. They tell *who*, *what*, *when*, *where*, *why*, and *how*. Details help you understand the main idea. Use the Reading in Science Handbook on pages R19–R27 to help you read the health facts in this chapter.

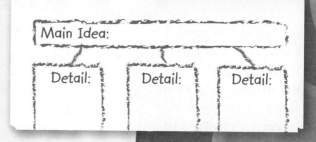

Main Idea:

Detail: | Detail: | Detail:

Health Graph

INTERPRET DATA These are the results of a recent study that looked at the relationship between physical activity and body weight. Based on the graph, list three facts about physical activity, eating, and weight. Do you think the trends shown will change in the near future? Why or why not?

Health Behaviors and Obesity in Teenagers

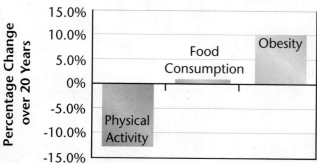

Percentage Change over 20 Years

15.0%
10.0%
5.0%
0%
-5.0%
-10.0%
-15.0%

Food Consumption

Obesity

Physical Activity

Daily Physical Activity

Along with good food choices, some physical activity every day will help keep your muscles, bones, and heart healthy.

 Be Active!

Use the selection, Track 4, **Jam and Jive**, to give your heart a workout.

LESSON 1 Being Active and Fit

Lesson Focus
Young people who get the proper amount of Sleep, participate in physical Activity, and make healthful Food choices Every day (SAFE) will enjoy good health.

Why Learn This?
You can use what you learn for making healthful choices about sleep, activity, and food.

Vocabulary
physical activity

Sleep, Activity, and Food

Have you ever thought about things that keep you healthy and fit? Tanisha was interested in how sleep, activity, and food help keep people fit. She went to her teacher with an article on healthful lifestyles. The article said that a healthful lifestyle should include a proper amount of sleep, physical activity that is fun and is done most days of the week, and wise food choices. Tanisha asked if her class could form a group she called the SAFE club to promote good health and physical fitness. *S* stands for *Sleep*, *A* stands for *Activity*, *F* stands for *Food choices* that are healthful, and *E* stands for *Every day*. Her teacher thought it was a great idea.

Your body needs all parts of the SAFE routine. The first part, sleep, is important in several ways. When you sleep, body tissues work to build new cells, repair old cells, and help fight infections.

Healthful foods provide energy to help you do activities longer. ▶

178

▲ These girls and their dogs help one another stay physically active.

PERSONAL HEALTH PLAN ▶

Real-Life Situation
Studies show that fifth graders do best in school if they get nine hours of sleep each night. Suppose because of soccer practice, homework, and TV, you sleep only seven hours.
Real-Life Plan
Write a plan for changing your schedule so you can get more sleep.

A lack of sleep can cause you to have trouble thinking clearly. It also can make you feel tired. A wise choice is to get plenty of rest before school, because sleep helps you do your best.

To be healthy and fit, your body needs physical activity. **Physical activity** is using your muscles to move your body. There are many reasons why physical activity can improve health. Activities such as walking, biking, swimming, and running can help keep your bones, muscles, and heart healthy and help you maintain a healthful weight.

Your body also needs good food. Good food choices are important decisions to learn to make. The foods you choose can affect your weight and your energy level.

Remember: To be physically fit and healthy, your body needs these things—sleep, activity, and good food every day. Healthful living should be a habit. It needs to be part of your daily life.

 MAIN IDEA AND DETAILS List the main ways you can become fit. Include three things you can do to maintain your health.

Did You Know?

A person who has trouble sleeping can go to a sleep clinic for help. The person sleeps there for a night or two as part of a test to determine why he or she does not sleep normally.

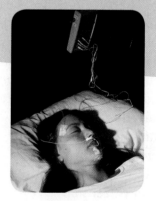

▲ Hiking with your family is a fun way to stay physically active.

The Benefits of Physical Activity

Being physically active has many benefits. Suzanne joined the SAFE club. She thought she was watching too much television and playing too many video games. She made a personal health plan that included biking, inline skating, and keeping a journal to record her TV watching.

For one month, Suzanne exercised and watched less TV. Then she made a list of the benefits to her of being physically active. At the next meeting of the SAFE club, she shared the list.

- Being physically active helped me reach a healthy weight.
- I feel that exercise has helped me build stronger muscles and bones. It's also helped me do physical activities for a longer period of time.
- Exercise has improved my self-esteem because I can do things I couldn't do before.
- I feel more relaxed and can better handle stressful situations at home and at school.

CAUSE AND EFFECT **What changes did Suzanne see in herself after she joined the SAFE club?**

Consumer Activity

Equipment You don't need to spend a lot of money to be fit or to have fun. Many activities require little more than comfortable shoes and loose-fitting clothes. List the things people actually need for some physical activities.

Quick Activity

List Safety Needs Pick an activity you like to do. List the safety equipment you need for it. Also list the rules you need to follow to stay safe.

▼ Boating is a fun activity you can do with friends. Many communities rent small boats and offer instruction on how to use them.

Overcoming Barriers to Physical Activity

Some people can't do some physical activities because they face physical challenges. But everyone can be active. People just may need to make a change in their activities so they can do them.

For example, Saul couldn't run with his friends because he was in a wheelchair. Saul talked to his physical education teacher. His teacher encouraged him to become more active using his wheelchair. He also suggested that Saul and his friends try swimming together. Saul found several new activities to enjoy with his friends and to help him stay fit.

DRAW CONCLUSIONS Saul stayed fit by using his wheelchair and by swimming. What conclusion can you draw about fitness and physical challenges?

◀ List some of the barriers this person has overcome to do this activity.

Lesson 1 Summary and Review

❶ Summarize with Vocabulary

Use vocabulary from this lesson to complete the statement.

_____ is using your muscles to move your body.

❷ Why is sleep important to your health? About how many hours of sleep does a person your age need each night?

❸ Critical Thinking How can making good food choices be an important part of your plan for keeping physically fit?

❹ **MAIN IDEA AND DETAILS** Draw and complete this graphic organizer to show some benefits of physical activity.

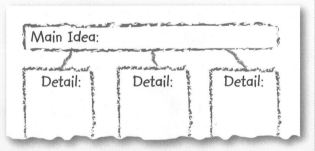

Main Idea:

Detail: Detail: Detail:

❺ Write to Inform—Description

Make up a story about Phil Fit, a boy in the SAFE club at his school. Write about a day in the life of Phil. Include sleep, physical activities, and good food choices.

Fairness

Play by the Rules

Any game or activity is more fun when all the players respect each other and follow all the rules. When players cheat, the game becomes pointless and players lose respect for each other.

Here are some rules to follow when you play any game:

- **Always listen for instructions when you receive the signal to stop. This may be the most important rule to ensure a fun game.**
- **If you're not familiar with the rules of a game, ask questions or ask for an explanation.**
- **Show respect for other players by not fighting or arguing. Players receive penalties for those behaviors.**
- **When someone breaks a rule, politely tell him or her or your coach.**
- **Understand the consequences of breaking a rule.**
- **If a rule is broken, team members should discuss the problem so it won't happen again.**
- **Learn how to properly care for equipment.**

Activity

Make a list of the important rules for your soccer team. Ask your teacher or coach to help you rank the rules in order of importance. Then list the rules in order of how often they are broken. Show the list to the soccer team. At the end of the season, compare your lists.

It's important to be fair and play by the rules at all times. ▶

How Exercise Helps Your Body Systems

Lesson Focus

Being physically active makes you stronger, helps you feel good, and improves your self-image.

Why Learn This?

Learning about the benefits of physical activity can help you exercise regularly.

Vocabulary

cardiovascular fitness
aerobic exercise
anaerobic exercise

Exercise Helps Your Respiratory System

Regular exercise, such as swimming and biking, helps your entire respiratory system. Your respiratory system includes all the parts of your body that work to get oxygen into your blood and carbon dioxide out of it. Look at a diagram of the respiratory system. Find the *diaphragm* (DY•uh•fram). It is a large, flat muscle that separates your lungs from the organs in the lower part of your body. When you breathe in, your diaphragm contracts and moves down. This pulls air in through your nose, down your *trachea*, and into your lungs. When you breathe out, your diaphragm relaxes and moves up. This pushes air out of your lungs.

The diaphragm does most of the work of breathing. The rest is done by your ribs and the muscles around them. As you breathe in, muscles move your ribs up and out to the side. Then, as you breathe out, your ribs

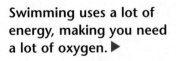

Swimming uses a lot of energy, making you need a lot of oxygen. ▶

move back down and in. Like all muscles, your diaphragm and the muscles around your ribs get stronger with regular exercise.

When air enters your lungs, it goes into *alveoli*. In those tiny sacs oxygen enters your blood. Your blood then carries the oxygen to all the cells of your body. Body cells use oxygen to convert the nutrients from the food you eat into energy. During that process body cells produce carbon dioxide. This waste gas travels to your lungs. Then it is breathed out.

When you exercise, your body needs a lot of energy and produces a lot of waste. Your lungs need to take in more oxygen and get rid of more carbon dioxide, so you breathe more deeply and more often. As you take deep breaths, the alveoli open up. When you exercise regularly, the alveoli stay open most of the time. This makes your lungs take in extra oxygen each time you breathe.

SEQUENCE **Write the steps by which oxygen gets into the blood.**

Personal Health Plan ▶

Real-Life Situation
The more you do a physical activity, the easier it becomes. Suppose you sign up to run in a 5-kilometer (5K) race to be held in three months.
Real-Life Plan
After talking with your physical education teacher, write a step-by-step plan for training that would enable you to complete the race.

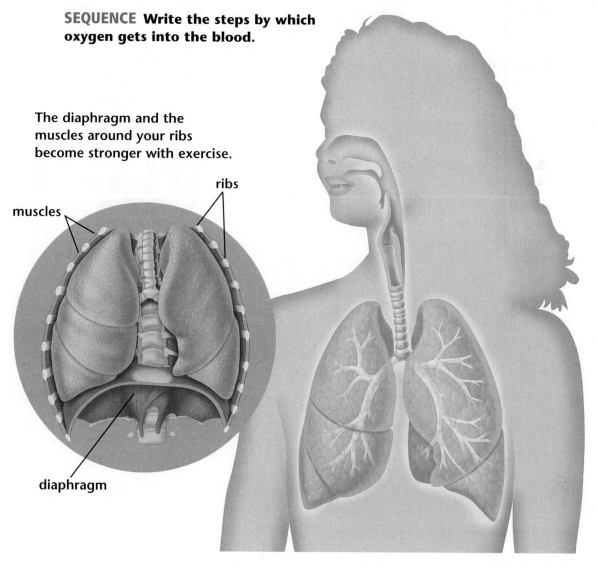

The diaphragm and the muscles around your ribs become stronger with exercise.

muscles

ribs

diaphragm

Exercise Helps Your Circulatory System

Exercising regularly helps your circulatory system stay healthy. Exercise strengthens your heart, a muscle that pumps blood to all the cells of your body. When you exercise, your heart beats faster. More oxygen and nutrients are carried to your body's cells.

Regular exercise also reduces the amount of fat in your blood. Fat can build up on the inner walls of arteries. This reduces the flow of blood to body organs. It can also cause serious problems in the circulatory system, such as heart attacks and strokes.

Cardiovascular fitness (kar•dee•oh•VAS•kyoo•ler) is the good health of the circulatory system, including a strong heart. When your heart is strong, you can be active for a long time without getting tired. A strong heart pumps more blood with each beat. When you are resting, it beats more slowly, pausing longer between beats.

Notice the differences between a healthy artery (above) and one clogged with fat (below).

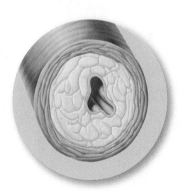

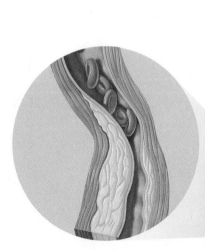

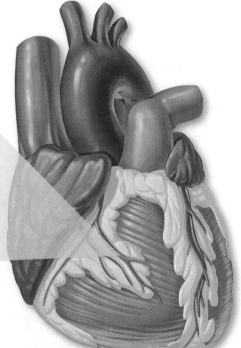

Clogged arteries in the heart can cause chest pains and heart attacks.

Aerobic exercise (air•OH•bik) increases your heartbeat rate for a period of time. This helps build cardiovascular fitness. Aerobic exercise includes bicycling, jogging, and swimming. As you do this kind of exercise, you also breathe harder and faster. Your muscles receive all the oxygen they need to keep working. You should do aerobic exercise at least three times a week for at least twenty minutes at a time. Aerobic exercise also can reduce stress. If you feel angry, sad, or bored, aerobic exercise can help lift your mood.

Not all types of exercise build cardiovascular fitness. In anaerobic exercise (an•er•OH•bik), the muscles work hard for a short time. They use the oxygen they already have faster than it can be replaced. Sprinting and rowing as fast as you can are examples of anaerobic exercise. Anaerobic exercise builds muscle strength.

COMPARE AND CONTRAST **How are aerobic exercise and anaerobic exercise different? What does each help build?**

Myth and Fact

Myth: More children are overweight now than in the past because kids today eat more.
Fact: Over the last twenty years, young people have been eating only 1 percent more food but have become 13 percent less active physically.

◄ Working together is important in a relay race. Think of other physical activities in which you work with others as a team.

The Activity Pyramid

The activity pyramid gives guidelines for ways to build fitness. Some activities build skill-related fitness. These help you improve your performance in a sport. Other activities promote health-related fitness. These help you improve your overall health and fitness. You can use the pyramid to plan physical activities based on the goals you want to achieve.

Sitting Still Watching TV; playing computer games **small amounts of time**

Light Exercise Playtime; yardwork; softball **2–3 times a week**

Strength and Flexibility Exercises Weight training, dancing, pullups **2–3 times a week**

Aerobic Exercises Biking; running; soccer; hiking **30 + minutes, 2–3 times a week**

Regular Activities Walking to school; taking the stairs; helping with housework **everyday**

If you are just beginning to exercise, you could do the following:

- Increase participation in everyday activities, like walking, whenever you can.
- Decrease the amount of time you spend watching television and playing video and computer games.

If you already exercise, you could use the activity pyramid to do the following:

- In the middle of the pyramid, find activities that you enjoy, and do them more often.
- Set up a plan to do your favorite activities more often.
- Explore new activities.

DRAW CONCLUSIONS Write down the activities you do in a typical day. At which level on the pyramid is most of your activity? What types of activities do you need to add to your routine?

Did You Know?

One video-arcade game is actually good for your health. Using background music as a guide, you follow lighted arrows with your feet. Young people report they really work up a sweat and it's fun, too!

Lesson 2 Summary and Review

1 Summarize with Vocabulary

Use vocabulary from this lesson to complete the statements.

Exercise that makes the heart work hard builds _____. Exercise that increases the heartbeat rate is called _____. Exercise that works your muscles hard for a short time, such as sprinting, is called _____.

2 Critical Thinking How can following the activity pyramid improve physical fitness?

3 How does exercise benefit the respiratory system?

4 **MAIN IDEA AND DETAILS** Draw and complete this graphic organizer to show ways that exercise helps your body.

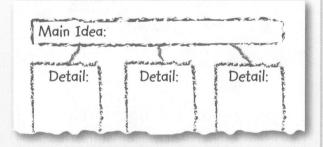

Main Idea:

Detail: Detail: Detail:

5 Write to Inform—How-To

Write a description of how to use the activity pyramid to begin an exercise program.

189

Set Goals

About Family Fitness

To stay healthy and fit, you need to keep active. Because our lives are so busy, it's often hard to find time for physical activities. Using the steps for **Setting Goals** can help you build a successful exercise plan.

At the dinner table one evening, Marco's mother says she thinks the family doesn't get enough physical activity. She feels that if the family members do physical activities together, they'll be more physically fit. What should Marco's family do?

1 **Choose a goal.**

We should do things together!

Marco's mother suggests that the family do physical activities together. Marco decides to use goal setting to help his parents plan the activities.

2 **Plan steps to meet the goal, and determine whether you need help.**

Marco meets with his father to plan some activities. Marco knows that Mom likes biking and the whole family likes to cross-country ski in the winter.

3 Check your progress as you work toward the goal.

Marco writes the planned activities on a calendar. He checks them off as the family finishes each one.

4 Reflect on and evaluate your progress toward the goal.

Marco is proud that his family is working together to reach a fitness goal.

Problem Solving

A. Serena's goal is to be able to run a mile without stopping.
  • How can she use the steps for **Setting Goals** to help her reach this endurance goal?

B. Juan lives a block away from a park and wants to shoot 300 baskets each day during the summer.
  • How might Juan reach his goal while keeping up his responsibility to help with family chores?

Ways to Exercise

Exercise Safely

Is exercise a part of your daily life? Exercising can include skill-related activities, such as basketball, tennis, or dancing. However, ordinary chores can provide health-related activity, too. These include walking the dog, raking the lawn, or vacuuming the carpet. To increase your level of physical fitness, try adding new activities to those you already do.

To help prevent injuries when you exercise, always begin with a *warm-up*. A warm-up is exercise that prepares your muscles—including your heart—to work hard. Always warm up your muscles gradually before harder exercise and before stretching.

Some stretching exercises help upper-body muscles.

Other stretching exercises help lower-body muscles. Always warm up before stretching.

One way to warm up is to do a slower version of your main activity. The warm-up might be easy pedaling if you are cycling, or jogging in place before running. Be sure to warm up for at least five minutes. After a warm-up, your body is prepared to stretch and exercise hard without harming muscles, joints, or your heart.

After exercising, do a *cool-down*. A cool-down includes doing your main exercise at a slower pace. That gives your heartbeat rate time to return to normal. Then stretch the muscles you used during your main exercise. Spend five to ten minutes cooling down.

▲ Wear the proper safety gear for the sport you're playing. What safety equipment is used in baseball?

Wearing the proper clothing for your activity and for the weather can help keep you safe. Wear loose, comfortable clothing that lets air move through. Choose cotton or other fabrics that allow sweat to evaporate. Use layers of clothing to keep warm in cold weather.

To prevent injury, wear shoes that provide support for your ankles and a cushion for your heels. The shoes must fit well and give you the traction you need. Also to prevent injury, always use the right safety gear. This may include a mouth guard, a helmet, shin guards, elbow pads, and kneepads.

MAIN IDEA AND DETAILS Focus Skill **To prevent injuries, what should you do before and after exercising?**

Quick Activity

Keeping Safe Talk with a parent about the physical activities he or she liked to do at your age. What safety equipment do people use now that was not used in the past for some of those activities?

Leg stretches increase your flexibility. ▼

▲ Chin-ups develop muscular strength.

Kinds of Exercise

Aerobic exercises mostly strengthen your heart and lungs. They build cardiovascular fitness. Anaerobic exercises mostly strengthen your muscles. Many exercises help improve strength, flexibility, and endurance.

Strength: Exercises that build muscular strength make your muscles stronger. Several types of anaerobic exercises build strength. Walking up steps strengthens leg muscles. Crunches strengthen stomach muscles. Pull-ups and push-ups strengthen arm muscles.

Flexibility (flek·suh·BIL·uh·tee): Exercises that increase flexibility help your body bend and move comfortably. Stretching helps you become more flexible. Dancing is also good for flexibility.

194

Endurance: Exercises that build **muscular endurance** enable you to use your muscles for long periods without getting tired. Aerobic exercises build endurance. Hiking with the family, swimming, and biking are a few examples.

Include endurance exercises in your fitness plans. For these exercises, set both short-term and long-term goals. Suppose you want to be able to run a mile without stopping. Your short-term goal might be to run half a mile. When you can do that, add 100 yards several times until you reach your final goal.

SUMMARIZE **What kinds of exercises build strength, flexibility, and endurance?**

Did You Know?

A wearable heart monitor gives you immediate feedback about your heartbeat rate as you exercise. You can use a monitor to keep your heartbeat rate within a safe range. Some schools use monitors in physical education classes.

◀ Running builds muscular endurance and cardiovascular fitness.

Fitness Testing

You can measure your fitness by taking some simple tests. These tests will help you determine your fitness level and decide what you can do to improve. **Caution:** Don't take these tests if your doctor has limited your physical activity for any reason. To take the test for endurance, you need to have been doing aerobic exercises for at least eight weeks.

- Try doing at least 36 abdominal crunches in 2 minutes. This measures muscular strength.

- Try doing the sit-and-reach at 9 inches or farther. Using a box and a ruler, stretch as far as you can with your knees straight, toes up, and one hand over the other. This measures flexibility.

- Try jogging 1 mile on a measured track. If you are a girl, try to jog the mile in 12 minutes or less. If you are a boy, aim for 11 minutes or less. This measures muscular endurance and cardiovascular fitness.

DRAW CONCLUSIONS **After practicing, try all three of these fitness tests. What do the results tell you about your level of fitness?**

Meeting the Standards: Fifth-Grade Fitness Results

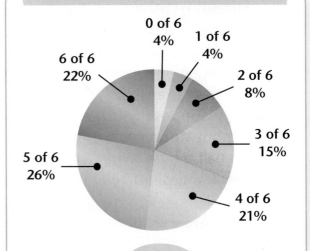

0 of 6 4%
1 of 6 4%
2 of 6 8%
3 of 6 15%
4 of 6 21%
5 of 6 26%
6 of 6 22%

Quick Activity

Analyze Graphs
On tests of six fitness standards, a group of fifth graders scored as shown on the graph. What total percentage of the students met at least four of the standards?

The sit-and-reach is a test of flexibility, while sit-ups test muscular strength.

Jumping rope is fun and a stress reliever. ▶

▲ Playing catch with a flying disk is fun. It also provides you with several different types of physical activity.

Fitness Is Fun

Many of the activities that improve your physical fitness are lots of fun. You can make up games with your friends, go on bike trips or hikes with your family, or swim at a local pool. Physical activities also help reduce stress. If you feel angry, sad, or just bored, exercising can lift your mood. Exercising can even give you a lift if you're feeling tired.

ACTIVITY

Life Skills

Make Responsible Decisions
Coach Jones wants you to try out for the soccer team next year. You've already committed to taking piano lessons and playing in the band. Make a list of the pros and the cons of being on the soccer team.

197

Try some physical activities with your family to enjoy different seasons of the year.

- Ice-skate, ski, or build snow sculptures in the winter.
- Fly kites, walk in the woods, or bicycle in the spring.
- Play beach volleyball, go canoeing, or go swimming in the summer.
- Take hikes, chop wood, or pick apples in the fall.

DRAW CONCLUSIONS Survey the members of your family about the activities they like to do. Then draw a conclusion about two activities your family would most enjoy doing together.

Playing ball is an activity that is easy and fun for people of all ages. ▶

Lesson 3 Summary and Review

1 Summarize with Vocabulary

Use vocabulary from this lesson to complete the following statements.

Jogging is an example of an activity that builds _____.

The sit-and-reach measures _____.

Weight lifting has become a popular activity because it builds _____.

2 How long should your cool-down last after you have been running for 15 minutes?

3 Critical Thinking When buying shoes, what are two important features to look for so you can exercise comfortably?

4 **MAIN IDEA AND DETAILS**

Complete this graphic organizer by starting with muscular strength as the main idea.

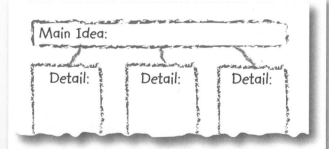

Main Idea:

Detail: Detail: Detail:

5 Write to Inform—Narration

Write a story about the types of physical activities you like and the benefits you see in them. You might name your favorite activity and tell why you like it.

ACTIVITIES

 Math

Add Up Activity Time Make a table of all the physical activities you do each week. Give yourself a point for each ten-minute period you spend doing each activity. Then make a bar graph that shows four weeks of each activity.

 Science

Measure Time Differences Run the 100-meter dash on three trials, and find the differences in your times. First, measure a 100-meter distance, or use the markings on a track. Then run your three trials, with a 2-minute rest between runs. Your teacher or a partner can help you time them. Tell whether your times increased, decreased, or stayed the same. Find the size of each increase or decrease.

 **Technology Project**

Based on the main ideas in this chapter, make a list of reasons to get SAFE—plenty of Sleep, Activity, and healthful Food choices, Every day. Make a computer slide show or a poster that shows examples of each of the four parts of SAFE.

GO ONLINE For more activities, visit The Learning Site. www. harcourtschool.com/health

 Home & Community

Pro-Fitness Postage Stamp Make a postage stamp that promotes positive physical activity. The stamp should be labeled "Fitness Is Fun" and should show people doing fun activities or exercises.

Career Link

Physical Education Instructor
Suppose that you work as a physical education instructor at your school. Write out a lesson plan for one day. It should include aerobic and anaerobic activities. Make sure you indicate the length of time for each class and that you include warm-up and cool-down activities.

Reading Skill

IDENTIFY MAIN IDEA AND DETAILS

Draw and then use this graphic organizer to answer questions 1 and 2.

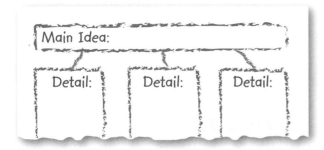

1 Using exercise as the main idea, write down details related to warm-ups.
2 Using physical fitness as the main idea, write down details that show how to measure muscular endurance.

 Use Vocabulary

Match each term in Column B with its meaning in Column A.

Column A	Column B
3 What pull-ups can help build	A aerobic exercises
4 Should be done after hard exercise	B anaerobic exercises
5 Exercise that increases heartbeat rate	C activity pyramid
	D cool-down
6 Should be done before exercise	E muscular strength
7 Exercises that work your muscles hard for a short time	F warm-up
8 Diagram that shows guidelines for activity	

Check Understanding

Choose the letter of the correct answer.

9 The letter *S* in the acronym SAFE stands for _____.

A Stretch C Sleep
B Stress D Serving size

10 Sleep has been found to help _____ old cells.

F destroy H repair
G feed J change

11 Which of these behaviors is a poor health habit?

A walking to school each day
B playing video games for three hours
C eating an apple each day
D watching no more than one hour of TV

12 When you are starting a new physical activity, it's important to develop a ____ to help you reach your fitness goal.

F plan H menu
G label J report

13 Being _____ helps you and others have fun and gain respect.

A fair C fast
B strong D first

14 Which of the following is the **BEST** example of anaerobic exercise?

F   G

H   J

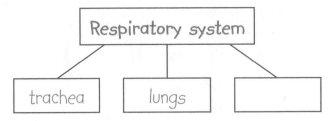

Respiratory system
- trachea
- lungs
- [blank]

15 Which detail is missing from the list of the parts of the respiratory system?

A leg muscles   **C** heart

B liver   **D** alveoli

16 On the activity pyramid, the activities that build flexibility are located at the _____.

F bottom   **H** center

G middle   **J** top

17 If you are following the activity pyramid to improve fitness, which section of the pyramid do you use least?

A bottom   **C** center

B middle   **D** top

18 Regular exercise reduces the amount of _____ in your blood.

F oxygen   **H** fat

G protein   **J** cells

19 Which of the following is the correct order for exercising safely?

A cool down, warm up, exercise

B warm up, cool down, exercise

C warm up, exercise, cool down

D exercise, warm up, cool down

Think Critically

20 You are planning a long-distance hike and want to bring along the best beverage. What would you choose? Why?

21 Suppose you stayed up late studying for your math test and slept only six hours. How might this affect your ability to do well on the test?

22 You are telling others about the health benefits of the SAFE club. What are some of the benefits you would tell about?

Apply Skills

23 **BUILDING GOOD CHARACTER**
Fairness You are asked to fill in on a friend's soccer team. You notice that one of the rules is being broken. Apply what you know about fairness to help correct the problem.

24 **LIFE SKILLS**
Set Goals Your SAFE club is planning a game day for the school. Use what you know about setting goals to plan this activity.

Write About Health

25 **Write to Inform—Explanation** Explain how following a fitness plan can help you meet a goal.

CHAPTER 6
Legal and Illegal Drugs

Reading Skill

IDENTIFY CAUSE AND EFFECT An effect is what happens. A cause is the reason, or why, it happens. Use the Reading in Science Handbook on pages R19–R27 and this graphic organizer to help you read the health facts in this chapter.

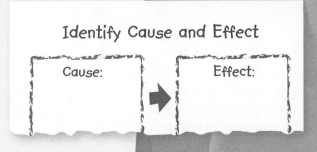

Identify Cause and Effect

Cause: → Effect:

Health Graph

INTERPRET DATA Anabolic steroids are prescription medicines, but some people abuse them—that is, they use them for a purpose other than what was intended. About what percentage of high school students have used anabolic steroids?

Illegal Drug Use by High School Students

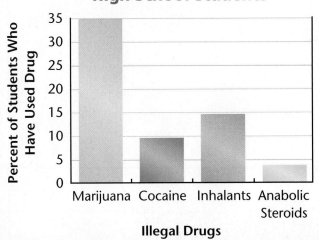

Percent of Students Who Have Used Drug

Marijuana Cocaine Inhalants Anabolic Steroids

Illegal Drugs

Daily Physical Activity

Staying away from illegal drugs is a good way to stay healthy. So is getting some physical activity every day.

 Be Active!

Use the selection, Track 8, **Jumping and Pumping**, to make your body feel better.

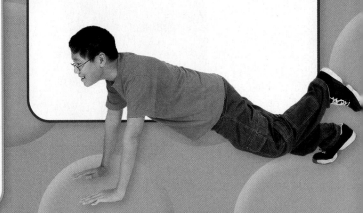

How Medicines Help the Body

Lesson Focus

Medicines can help you stay healthy if they are used correctly. They can be harmful if they are used incorrectly.

Why Learn This?

Learning how to use medicines safely will help you stay healthy.

Vocabulary

drug
medicine
prescription medicines
over-the-counter
  medicines
side effects

Drugs and Medicines

Everyone becomes ill or gets hurt. Harmful bacteria in food can give you an upset stomach. An allergy can make you sneeze, and a scraped knee can be painful. Sometimes a medicine, which is a kind of drug, can help you feel better or heal you more quickly, but only if it is used the right way.

A **drug** is a substance, other than food, that affects the way your body or mind works. A **medicine** is a drug used to prevent, treat, or cure an illness. Illegal drugs, such as cocaine and marijuana, also cause changes in the body. But unlike medicines, illegal drugs cause changes that do not improve your health. Illegal drugs are harmful to use and can even be deadly.

Many medicines come from plants like these that live in rain forests. ▶

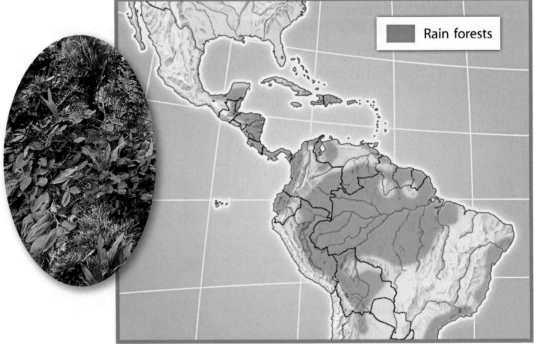

Rain forests

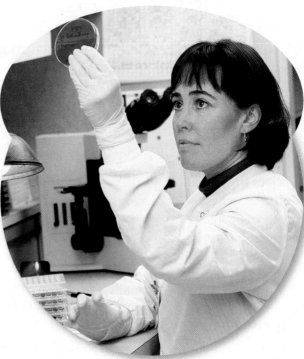

▼ Today, many medicines are made in laboratories.

▲ Some rainforest plants have been used to treat illnesses for many years.

Different medicines improve health in different ways. Vaccines help prevent diseases such as polio, measles, and chicken pox. Antibiotics kill organisms that cause infections, such as strep throat. Pain relievers help reduce aches and pains. Some people take medicines to control health problems such as allergies, asthma, diabetes, and high blood pressure.

Scientists working for drug companies are always developing new, more effective medicines. They make many new medicines in laboratories by using chemicals. They also find new medicines in plants, animals, and minerals. Before a new medicine can be sold, however, the government must approve it. Scientists who work for the government test every new medicine to make sure it is safe and effective. It often takes years of testing before a new medicine can be sold.

Focus Skill

CAUSE AND EFFECT What effect does an antibiotic have on an infection, like strep throat?

A prescription medicine has a label that may also have special directions, such as "Take with food" or "Do not take with other medicines." ▼

Prescription Medicines

Suppose you go to the doctor about a sore throat. The doctor examines you, decides what's wrong, and prescribes a medicine. Following the doctor's orders, a pharmacy prepares a prescription medicine for you.

Prescription medicines are medicines that can be bought only with a doctor's order. They are strong and can be harmful if not used correctly. That's why you should always have a parent or other trusted adult give you any prescription medicine.

A doctor considers many things before writing a prescription. These include the patient's symptoms, age, weight, other medicines being taken, and any allergies.

Your doctor writes your prescription for you only. It's dangerous to take a medicine prescribed for someone else, even if both of you have the same health problem.

SUMMARIZE Why is it important to take medicines prescribed for you only?

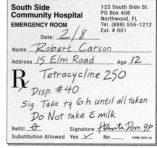

South Side
Community Hospital
EMERGENCY ROOM

123 South Side St.
PO Box 456
Northwood, FL
Tel. (888) 555-1212
Ext. # 001

Date: 2/8
Name Robert Carson
Address 15 Elm Road   Age 12
R Tetracycline 250
Disp. #40
Sig. Take tq 6h until all taken
Do Not take ē milk
Refill 0   Signature Hunti Dom gp
Substitution Allowed Yes ✓ No ___   FORM 2003-04

206

◄ Pharmacies and supermarkets sell many OTC medicines, such as pain relievers, nasal sprays, eye drops, cough syrups, and acne creams.

Over-the-Counter Medicines

If you have a slight headache, you probably don't need to see a doctor. Instead, your parent can give you an over-the-counter pain reliever.

Over-the-counter (OTC) medicines are medicines that can be bought without prescriptions. OTC medicines usually treat minor health problems. They are for short-term use. Some cough medicines, nasal sprays, and pain relievers are OTC medicines.

Like prescription medicines, OTC medicines can be harmful if not used correctly. That's why it's important to always have a parent or other trusted adult help you with an OTC medicine.

The label on an OTC medicine tells what the medicine treats and how it should be taken. The label also tells the length of time to take the medicine. In addition, it lists warnings for people who should not take the medicine. For example, an aspirin label might say, " Children and teens should not use this medicine for flu symptoms."

COMPARE AND CONTRAST **What are the similarities and differences between prescription medicines and OTC medicines?**

Did You Know?

Hundreds of OTC medicines were once prescription medicines. After a prescription medicine has been used safely for many years, the government may reclassify it as an OTC medicine.

How Medicines Affect the Body

Medicines come in many forms. Some are creams rubbed on the skin. Others are drops placed in the eyes, ears, or nose. Most medicines are pills or liquids that are swallowed. From the small intestine, a medicine enters the bloodstream and is carried to all parts of the body.

Different medicines have different side effects. **Side effects** are unwanted effects of a medicine. For example, an allergy medicine might make you sleepy. Most side effects are not serious. But if you ever feel strange after taking a medicine, tell a parent or other trusted adult right away.

You should also avoid taking two or more different medicines at the same time without your doctor's directions. This can cause side effects that are different from those listed on either medicine's label. These effects can be very dangerous. That's why it's important for your parent to ask your doctor or pharmacist before giving you more than one medicine at a time.

SEQUENCE After you swallow a pill, how does the medicine reach different parts of your body?

Myth and Fact

Myth: All medicines made with "natural" ingredients are safe.

Fact: "Natural" does not always mean "safe." Always consult a doctor before using natural medicines. For example, ephedra, or ma huang, is a dangerous herbal drug that can cause heart attacks and strokes.

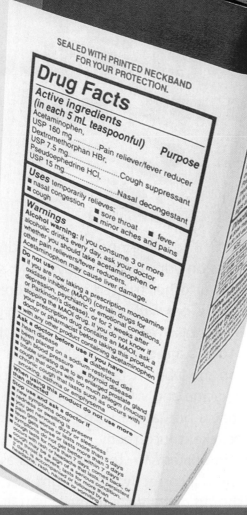

SEALED WITH PRINTED NECKBAND
FOR YOUR PROTECTION.

Drug Facts

Active ingredients
(in each 5 mL teaspoonful)   **Purpose**
Acetaminophen,
USP 160 mg ....Pain reliever/fever reducer
Dextromethorphan HBr.
USP 7.5 mg....................Cough suppressant
Pseudoephedrine HCl,
USP 15 mg.....................Nasal decongestant

Uses temporarily relieves:
■ nasal congestion   ■ sore throat   ■ fever
■ cough   ■ minor aches and pains

Warnings
Alcohol warning: If you consume 3 or more
alcoholic drinks every day, ask your doctor
whether you should take acetaminophen or
other pain relievers/fever reducers.
Acetaminophen may cause liver damage.
Do not use
■ if you are now taking a prescription monoamine
oxidase inhibitor (MAOI) (certain drugs for
depression, psychiatric or emotional conditions,
or Parkinson's disease), or for 2 weeks after
stopping the MAOI drug. If you do not know if
your prescription drug contains an MAOI, ask a
doctor or pharmacist before taking this product.
■ with any other product containing acetaminophen
Ask a doctor before use if you have
■ heart disease
■ been placed on a sodium-restricted diet
■ high blood pressure   ■ diabetes
■ trouble urinating due to an enlarged prostate gland
■ cough that occurs with too much phlegm (mucus)
■ chronic cough that lasts such as occurs with
smoking, asthma or emphysema
When using this product do not use more
than directed
Stop use and ask a doctor if
■ new symptoms occur
■ pain or nervousness or sleepless
■ you get nervous, dizzy or sleepless
■ fever gets worse or lasts more than 3 days
■ redness or swelling is present
■ cough gets worse or lasts more than 5 days
■ cough lasts for more than 7 days, comes back, or
occurs with fever, rash or headache. A persistent
cough may be a sign of a serious condition.
2 a headache, that lasts for more than
7 days is accompanied or followed by fever.

Read Labels The OTC medicine shown here has important information printed on the side of its box. It's important to read this information before taking the medicine. Use the information on this box to write a dialogue between a pharmacist and a patient who has questions about this medicine.

Lesson 1 Summary and Review

❶ Summarize with Vocabulary

Use vocabulary from this lesson to complete these statements.

A _____ is a _____ that is used to treat an illness. Some medicines are _____ medicines, and others are _____, both of which can cause _____, such as sleepiness.

❷ What is the difference between over-the-counter medicines and prescription medicines?

❸ Critical Thinking How do medicines benefit people, and how can they harm people?

❹ (Focus Skill) CAUSE AND EFFECT Draw and complete this graphic organizer to show the effects of antibiotics on the body.

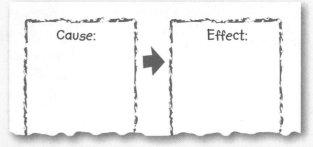

| Cause: | | Effect: |

❺ Write to Inform—Description

Write a paragraph describing some effects of helpful drugs and harmful drugs.

Medicine Use, Misuse, and Abuse

Lesson Focus

Medicines can be abused if they are not taken correctly.

Why Learn This?

Learning the dangers of medicine abuse will help you use medicines safely.

Vocabulary

dosage
expiration date
self-medication
medicine abuse
addiction
anabolic steroids

Use Medicines Safely

It's important to remember that medicines can have strong effects on your body. Always make sure you talk with a parent or other trusted adult before taking any medicine. Medicines will help you only if you use them correctly. If you take medicines incorrectly, they can harm you. To use a medicine safely, always read the directions on the label. It tells you when and how to take the medicine and when not to take it. Never use a medicine that is not labeled. You might take the wrong medicine or take it incorrectly.

It is also important to store medicines as directed. If you store them incorrectly, they might not work the way they should or they could make you ill.

Most medicines should be kept in a cool, dark place, away from moisture. Some medicines must be kept in the refrigerator. Check medicine labels for storage directions.

Never take any medicine without the direction of a parent or other trusted adult. ▶

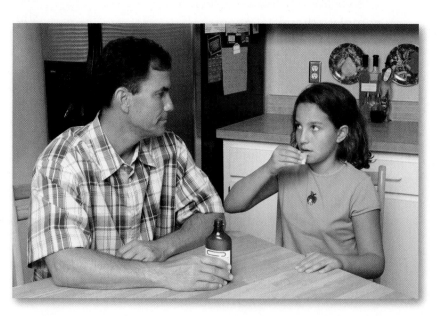

1 Patient's name

A doctor writes a prescription for one patient. The doctor considers the symptoms, age, weight, and allergies of the patient. Never take someone else's medicine or give your medicine to someone else.

2 Directions

Follow the directions that come with your medicine. Be sure to take it at the right time and in the right dosage. The **dosage** is the amount of medicine to take.

3 Warnings

Pay attention to the warnings and cautions printed on the label. This can help you avoid some side effects of a medicine. It also helps ensure that the medicine is stored and given correctly.

4 Refills

This tells you if you can get more of the medicine without getting a new prescription.

5 Date

This is the date the prescription was filled. The label might include an **expiration date**, the last date the medicine should be used.

TOWN DRUG
49 HARDING RD. PHONE 555-8531 SPRINGFIELD, OH 46203
Federal law prohibits transfer of this drug to any person other than patient for whom prescribed.

1 57146   Dr. Greg Hardy
ADA SPRINGER 21-OCT-03   3   Q: 20 ORG: 21-OCY-30
ERYTHROMYCIN 500mg
EXPIRES: 21-NOV-03   5   **MAY CAUSE DROWSINESS**

2 DIRECTIONS: Take 1 tablet orally four times daily. Finish all medication

4 REFILL: NONE

To use prescription medicines safely, always read the information on the label.

You must also be careful about the foods you eat when taking some medicines. Some foods stop medicines from working. For example, some antibiotics shouldn't be taken with fruit juice. The acid in the juice reduces the ability of the antibiotics to kill bacteria.

Using medicines safely requires a great deal of care and caution. That's why it's important never to make decisions on your own about medicines. A parent or other trusted adult should always help you use medicines.

MAIN IDEA AND DETAILS Make a list of rules you can follow to always use medicines safely.

ACTIVITY

Life Skills

Communicate

Christina has a prescription for a new medicine. Her mother isn't sure how often Christina should take it or what side effects to expect. What could Christina's mother do to learn more about the medicine?

Medicine Misuse and Abuse

Jason's head hurts and he feels warm. He finds some aspirin in the medicine cabinet. The label says, "Relieves pain and fever." What should he do?

Jason should NOT take the aspirin. Doing so would be self-medication. **Self-medication** is deciding on your own what medicine to take. Children and teens should never take asprin unless a doctor orders it.

If Jason took the aspirin, he would also be misusing a medicine. **Medicine misuse** is taking a medicine without following the directions. The directions warn that children and teens should never take aspirin unless a doctor says it's all right. Aspirin can cause Reye's syndrome, a serious condition that can lead to brain damage and even death. Using leftover prescription medicines or taking too much of a medicine are also examples of medicine misuse.

Some people abuse medicines. **Medicine abuse** is taking medicine for some reason other than treating an illness. The medicines people abuse most are those that cause changes in the brain and nervous system. People who abuse medicines can even develop an addiction. An **addiction** is the constant need for and use of a drug, even though it is not medically necessary. People addicted to drugs sometimes feel they need the drugs, much as other people need food and sleep. Addiction is dangerous. It can lead to serious illness or death.

◄ Sometimes you don't really need medicine. Sarah has a stomachache from eating too many snacks. She thinks she needs some medicine to feel better. However, her mother has her lie down with a warm water bottle, and soon she is feeling well again. ▶

Some OTC medicines can be abused. Prescription medicines, especially those for pain, can also be abused. **Anabolic steroids** are prescription medicines that are used to treat certain health problems. But they are also abused by some people. Anabolic steroids have unpleasant and dangerous side effects. These include hair loss, irritability, depression, fatigue, severe acne, and violent behavior. Longtime use of anabolic steroids can cause liver and heart disease and kidney failure.

DRAW CONCLUSIONS Why are anabolic steroids dangerous?

Personal Health Plan

Real-Life Situation
Exercise can help you in several ways. Suppose you want to be stronger.
Real-Life Plan
Make a list of exercises you enjoy that can increase your strength.

This man is gaining muscle strength the proper way—by exercising, not by taking drugs. ▶

Lesson 2 Summary and Review

❶ Summarize with Vocabulary

Use vocabulary and other terms from this lesson to complete the statements.

Children and teenagers should never _____ because they can easily _____ medicine by taking the wrong _____. When a person starts using medicines for a reason other than treating an illness, he or she is _____ medicine. This can lead to _____. One commonly abused medicine is _____.

❷ What are three things you can do to make sure you use medicine safely?

❸ **Critical Thinking** What is the difference between medicine misuse and medicine abuse?

❹ (Focus Skill) IDENTIFY CAUSE AND EFFECT

Draw and complete this graphic organizer to show the effects of medicine abuse and addiction.

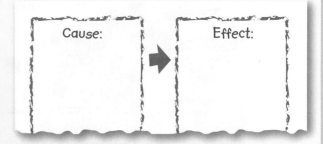

Cause: → Effect:

❺ Write to Entertain—Short Story

Write a story describing a person who has started abusing medicines. Include in your description the consequences of the abuse.

Illegal Drugs

Illegal Drugs Harm the Body

Medicines are legal drugs if they are used correctly. But some drugs should never be used. They are **illegal drugs**—drugs that are not medicines and that are against the law to sell, buy, have, or use.

People who break the law by using or selling illegal drugs may be sent to prison. But even more serious than going to prison are the harmful effects that illegal drugs have on the body. Some illegal drugs can damage the body or even kill a person. Some illegal drugs can make the heart beat so fast that the user can have a heart attack and die. They can also make blood vessels burst in the brain and cause a stroke.

Illegal drugs also have long-term effects. For example, smoking one illegal drug can lead to memory loss, asthma, and lung cancer. Sniffing another illegal drug can damage the nose, causing sores to form

One of the jobs of the United States Coast Guard is to stop illegal drugs from coming into the country. Each year, the coast guard seizes billions of dollars' worth of illegal drugs. ▼

inside. It can even break down the septum, the wall that separates the nostrils.

Long-term illegal drug users often do not eat as they should. They may become thin and weak. They are also ill more often than people who don't use drugs. Using an illegal drug during pregnancy can cause birth defects or cause the baby to be born addicted to drugs.

Using some illegal drugs can lead to *tolerance*—the need to use more and more of a drug. A user's body gets used to a drug, and the user needs more of the drug to feel the same effect as before. As tolerance increases, so does the risk of an overdose. An **overdose** is a dangerously large dose of a drug. It can cause severe illness or even death.

The use of illegal drugs has serious effects on a person's life. Users of illegal drugs often become drug addicts. Drug addicts' lives are ruled by drugs. Addicts may no longer care about school or work, family, or friends. They care only about getting more drugs. They can't stop taking drugs because their bodies need the drugs. If the drugs are taken away, the users experience withdrawal. **Withdrawal** is the painful reaction that occurs when someone suddenly stops using a drug. Symptoms can include vomiting, shaking, seeing and hearing things that aren't there, seizures, and even death. Drug addicts usually need medical help to get through withdrawal.

 CAUSE AND EFFECT What are the causes and effects of withdrawal?

When a young person uses illegal drugs, his or her grades usually fall. He or she also may start to lose friends. ▶

Cocaine and Crack

Cocaine is an illegal drug made from the leaves of the coca plant. It's usually sold as a white powder and sniffed through the nose. Sometimes it's injected into a vein. *Crack* is a rocklike form of cocaine that users smoke. The term *crack* refers to the crackling sound the drug makes when someone smokes it. All forms of cocaine are extremely harmful to the body.

Cocaine affects the user just minutes after it is sniffed. It increases blood pressure and speeds up breathing and heartbeat rates, making the user think he or she is more alert or has more energy. Cocaine is so addictive that it can make the user violent. Cocaine addicts have become violent enough to hurt or even kill people to get money to buy more cocaine.

▲ Coca plants, which grow in South America, are used to make cocaine and crack.

Quick Activity

Analyze Graphs Study the graph showing the number of emergency room visits related to illegal drug use. How many more emergency room visits were caused by using cocaine than by using the other three drugs?

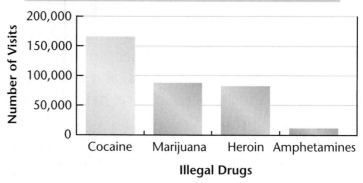

Number of Emergency Room Visits Related to Cocaine and Other Drugs

Number of Visits

200,000
150,000
100,000
50,000
0

Cocaine   Marijuana   Heroin   Amphetamines

Illegal Drugs

1 People who use cocaine sometimes hear and see things that are not there. Long-term cocaine use can lead to brain damage.

2 Sniffing cocaine over a long period can destroy the inside of the nose.

3 Cocaine and crack raise blood pressure, increase heartbeat rate, and can cause a heart attack.

4 When a person takes in cocaine or crack, he or she starts to breathe more rapidly.

The body absorbs crack even faster than powdered cocaine. The user gets a sudden, intense effect in seconds. Some users report feelings of restlessness, anger, and fear. The drug's effects wear off very quickly. The user then becomes very depressed and wants more crack.

Some crack users become addicted after trying it only once. It is considered one of the most addictive illegal drugs. It is also one of the most dangerous. Even a first-time user of crack can die suddenly from a heart attack or a seizure. And it is impossible to predict who might die from a first-time use of crack.

SUMMARIZE List three reasons why using cocaine is dangerous.

Marijuana

Marijuana (mair•uh•WAH•nuh) is an illegal drug that comes from a tall, leafy plant with small white and yellow flowers. Marijuana is made from the crushed, dried leaves and flowering tops of the plant. Marijuana is usually smoked. Some users put it into foods and eat it. Marijuana is sometimes called grass, pot, or weed. The plant's thick, sticky resin, called *hashish* (HASH•eesh), is a powerful drug that is smoked or eaten.

Marijuana contains more than 400 substances that affect the body. Some of the chemicals affects the brain, changing the way a user sees, hears, and feels things.

Marijuana affects different people in different ways. It can even affect one person differently at different times. In general, people who smoke marijuana feel relaxed at first. They may also have a fast heartbeat and a dry mouth and feel hungry. Marijuana affects the mind in strange ways. Time may seem to move more slowly than usual or everything may seem funny for no reason. Marijuana users often do things that embarrass themselves. Sometimes marijuana causes sudden feelings of panic.

Marijuana users often find it hard to concentrate and to remember things. Marijuana disrupts nerve cells in the part of the brain that forms memories. This makes it difficult to learn and do schoolwork. Young people who smoke marijuana tend to lose interest in school and get poor grades.

Heavy marijuana use affects coordination. This makes it hard to do physical things, like playing sports and exercising.

Myth and Fact

Myth: Marijuana is a safe drug.
Fact: Marijuana is addictive and is more harmful to the lungs than tobacco. One marijuana cigarette has more tar than one pack of regular cigarettes.

218

◀ Growing marijuana is illegal in the United States. Each year, law enforcement officers find and destroy tons of marijuana plants. People who grow the plants can be fined or jailed.

A person who has smoked marijuana has slower reflexes, making it dangerous for him or her to drive a car or even ride a bike.

Marijuana use can also damage the lungs. Marijuana smoke contains many of the same harmful chemicals found in tobacco smoke, but in larger amounts. People who use a lot of marijuana face many of the same health problems as people who smoke cigarettes. These problems include asthma, heart disease, and lung cancer. Marijuana use may also lower the body's defenses against other diseases. So, marijuana smokers tend to be ill more often than nonsmokers.

DRAW CONCLUSIONS How can smoking marijuana lead to getting hurt in an accident?

Quick Activity

Research Use the Internet to research the effects of marijuana smoke on the body. Then make a diagram of the body to show all of the effects you learned about.

219

Inhalants

If you look around most homes, you will find chemicals that give off fumes. In many cases, the fumes are poisonous. In fact, some chemical products have warnings that say breathing the fumes can be very harmful. Those products should be used only in places with a lot of fresh air.

As dangerous as these chemical products are, some people breathe the fumes on purpose. Chemicals that people breathe on purpose are called inhalants. **Inhalants** are common products that some people abuse by breathing their fumes. Inhalants are very addictive. Effects of breathing inhalants include nosebleeds, headaches, confusion, memory loss, nausea, and changes in heartbeat and breathing rates. Long-term use of inhalants can damage the brain, kidneys, liver, and lungs and can even cause death.

MAIN IDEA AND DETAILS What are some ways to avoid breathing dangerous fumes?

▲ Many chemicals give off fumes that are dangerous to breathe.

Lesson 3 Summary and Review

❶ Summarize with Vocabulary

Use vocabulary and other terms from this lesson to complete the statements.

_____ are chemicals whose fumes are breathed. They are particularly dangerous when used for a period of time, because people become _____ to them. When someone has a _____ for drugs, it is easier to _____ on the drugs. If drug users suddenly stop taking the drugs they are addicted to, they go through _____.

❷ Critical Thinking Analyze the short-term and long-term effects of two different illegal drugs.

❸ What are the differences between legal and illegal drugs?

❹ (Focus Skill) IDENTIFY CAUSE AND EFFECT

Draw and complete this graphic organizer to show the physical and social effects of taking illegal drugs.

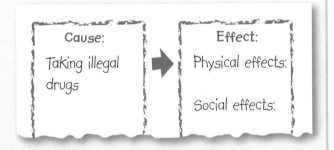

Cause: Taking illegal drugs → Effect: Physical effects: Social effects:

❺ Write to Inform—Explanation

Write an article explaining why people might try illegal drugs, and the consequences of illegal drug use.

Trustworthiness

Be Trustworthy About Not Using Drugs

People who are trustworthy are honest, tell the truth, and keep promises—and other people can trust them. Not using drugs shows your parents that you are trustworthy. Here are some tips on how to be trustworthy about not using drugs:

- **Talk with your parents about illegal drugs.**
- **Don't become friends with people who abuse medicines or who use illegal drugs.**
- **Make friends with people who respect your decision not to use illegal drugs.**
- **Play sports or develop other healthful hobbies.**
- **Avoid events that might involve using illegal drugs.**
- **Practice different ways of refusing to abuse medicines and choosing not to use illegal drugs.**
- **Tell your parents, a teacher, or other trusted adult if someone ever offers you illegal drugs.**

Activity

With a friend, role-play a conversation between a parent and a child about using illegal drugs. Plan a conversation opener. For example, as the "child," you could start by asking your friend—the "parent"—if he or she has ever known somebody who used illegal drugs. After role-playing, try a similar conversation with your mom, dad, or other trusted adult.

Staying Away from Drugs

You Should Refuse Illegal Drugs

To **refuse** something is to say *no* to it. There are many reasons you should refuse to use illegal drugs. If you buy, sell, or use drugs or you simply have an illegal drug in your possession, you are breaking the law.

Using drugs can prevent you from doing well in school and sports. They can stop you from caring about anything except getting more drugs. Drugs can ruin your health, too. They can lead to addiction and overdose. Drugs can even kill you.

Drugs hurt not only the users but also everybody around them. Drug users often stop making positive contributions to their families, friendships, and communities. The use of illegal drugs often leads to

Some kids use drugs to "fit in." What they don't realize is that most kids never use illegal drugs. To really fit in, say *no* to drugs.

Having fun doesn't need to include using drugs.

violence and crimes. Many innocent people become victims of crimes committed by drug users.

People have many good reasons for refusing drugs. They want to stay out of jail. They want to stay in control and healthy. They want to do well in school or in sports. They don't want to disappoint or embarrass their parents or teachers. They have plans for the future, such as sports or college, and they know that drug use can ruin those plans.

Drugs can interfere with your ability to enjoy most activities. How well can you play basketball, ride a bike, read a book, enjoy an amusement park, or take photographs when your mind and body are out of control?

DRAW CONCLUSIONS Describe how family, friends, and school influence a person's choice to refuse illegal drugs.

Consumer Activity

Analyze Media Messages
Many TV ads encourage young people to decide what is more important to them than taking drugs. Research current anti-drug campaigns on TV and other places. How effective do you think the campaigns are in helping people refuse drugs?

You Can Say *No*

Personal Health Plan

Real-Life Situation
There are a lot of
different reasons to
refuse to use
illegal drugs.
Real-Life Plan
Make a list of reasons
you would use to
refuse illegal drugs.

You have the right and a responsibility to refuse drugs. Remember that drug users are the ones who are not cool. Get advice from a parent about how to avoid drugs. Make friends with other drug-free students. Plan ahead for how you will respond if someone asks you to take a drug. You don't have to give excuses, and you don't have to argue with people who want you to use illegal drugs.

Learn from a parent about the harmful effects of drugs. Remember that using drugs is illegal. Think about how drugs can ruin your relationships with your family and friends. Drugs can take over your whole life. They can make you ill and can kill you.

MAIN IDEA AND DETAILS Where can you get good information about the harmful effects of illegal drugs?

224

Quick Activity

Reasons for Saying *No*
Make a poster that shows at least one reason to avoid illegal drugs. Include an alternative to drug use, such as learning to play a musical instrument. After you make your poster, make of list of other ways you can communicate information about drugs.

What reason do you have for not using drugs?

Lesson 4 Summary and Review

❶ Summarize with Vocabulary

Use vocabulary and other terms from this lesson to complete the statements.

"I'm going to _____ drugs because I want to stay _____ and live a long life. If I take _____, I might go to prison. I have too many plans for that. I want to go to college."

❷ Critical Thinking List two social effects and one legal effect that might result from using drugs.

❸ What are three things you can do to avoid using drugs?

❹ (Focus Skill) CAUSE AND EFFECT

Draw and complete this graphic organizer to show some effects of Josh's decision about illegal drugs.

Cause: Josh has decided not to use illegal drugs.		Effect:

❺ Write to Inform—Explanation

Suppose you are a parent. Write a letter to your children, explaining how peer pressure can influence their views about illegal drugs.

225

Refuse

Illegal Drugs

At some time you may be asked if you want to use illegal drugs. You need to have your decision made and your answers ready ahead of that time. Learning several different ways to **Refuse**, such as the ones shown here, will help you stay drug-free.

George is walking home from school when he sees Ned, another student in his class. Ned waves George over and asks if he wants to smoke some marijuana. George has many different options for how to refuse Ned. Which one of the following four options would you choose?

1 **Say *no* and tell why not.**

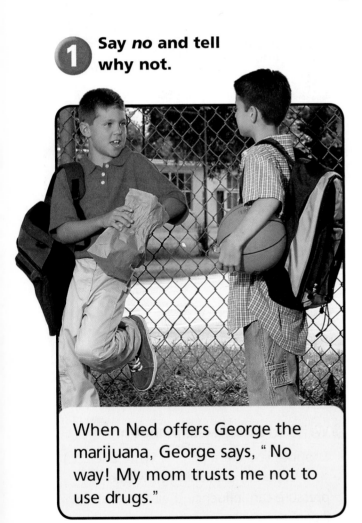

When Ned offers George the marijuana, George says, " No way! My mom trusts me not to use drugs."

2 **Suggest something else to do.**

George says, " No thanks. Why don't we go play basketball instead?"

226

3 **Reverse the peer pressure.**

4 **Just turn and walk away. You can create an opportunity for the other person to join you.**

After Ned suggests they smoke marijuana, George shakes his head and says, "Not on your life! Only losers use drugs."

Hey! Wait up!

George rolls his eyes and starts to walk away. He says over his shoulder as he is leaving, "Ned, I'm going home to shoot some hoops. You can come if you want to, but you've got to get rid of those drugs first."

 Problem Solving

A. Sophia's older brother uses marijuana. One day Sophia walks into the backyard and finds her brother smoking some marijuana. He offers to share it with her. Sophia does not want to use drugs.

• Tell how Sophia can use ways to **Refuse** in this situation.

B. Craig and Bob are cleaning up Craig's father's workshop. Craig tells Bob that he often sniffs fumes from some of the chemicals in the workshop. He offers to show Bob how to do it. Bob knows that his parents trust him not to sniff chemicals.

• Explain the most trustworthy decision for Bob to make to show that he won't disappoint his parents.

227

How Drug Users Can Get Help

Lesson Focus

Drug users and their families can get help from sources at home, at school, and in the community.

Why Learn This?

If you or someone you know needs help to refuse drugs or to stop using drugs, it is important to know where to get help.

When Someone Needs Help

You might know someone who needs help in refusing drugs. Or you might know someone who actually may be abusing medicines or using illegal drugs. How can you help the person? To help someone who is abusing drugs, you must first know what the signs of drug abuse are. One of the signs is changes in behavior. If you know anyone who shows some of the signs listed below, he or she might have a drug problem.

COMPARE AND CONTRAST Compare and contrast normal behaviors with the signs that a person might be using drugs.

Some of the warning signs of medicine abuse or illegal drug use are listed on the notepad. If you know someone who shows some of these warning signs, you can help by telling a parent or other trusted adult. ▶

Drug Abuse Warnings

A person who displays some of the following signs may be abusing drugs.

1. Neglects personal health.
2. Becomes secretive.
3. Suddenly loses weight without trying.
4. Frequently misses school or work.
5. Is anxious and nervous.
6. Has trouble being responsible.
7. Explodes in anger without reason.
8. Often asks to borrow money.

Getting Help

There are many people who can help someone who has a problem with drugs. The drug user can talk to a parent, teacher, school nurse, or school counselor. If you are worried about a family member who may have a drug problem, talk to another adult in your family. Don't worry about getting someone in trouble. You could actually be helping a person with a drug problem.

Many communities have programs to help people who are abusing medicines or using illegal drugs. Drug users can call local drug prevention and treatment centers or community drug hotlines. The people who work there can provide information or counseling to help drug users stop abusing drugs.

Many county and state governments also have drug treatment programs. You could check with the media specialist at your school or the librarian at your local library for the names, phone numbers, and addresses of these programs.

Talk to a parent, grandparent, older brother or sister, teacher, counselor, or other trusted adult if you or someone you know has a drug problem. ▼

There are several national groups that can provide information to help drug users stop abusing drugs. They include the National Clearinghouse for Alcohol and Drug Information, the National Council on Alcoholism and Drug Dependence, and Narcotics Anonymous. Your parents or another trusted adult can help you contact one of these groups for information.

DRAW CONCLUSIONS How can you help a friend or family member who is using illegal drugs to take responsibility for his or her health?

Help Line

If you or someone you know has a problem with drugs, help can be just a phone call away.

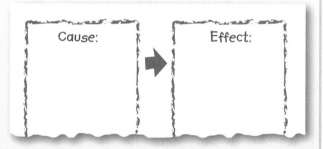

Lesson 5 Summary and Review

① Summarize with Vocabulary

Use terms from this lesson to complete the statements.

If you are worried that a friend is using drugs, watch for _____, such as weight loss and often asking to borrow _____. You can help your friend handle the problem if you talk to a _____.

② List three warning signs of drug use.

③ Critical Thinking Suppose you tell a parent about a family member who shows some signs of drug use. Explain how you are really helping the family member.

④ (Focus Skill) CAUSE AND EFFECT Draw and complete this graphic organizer to show the effects of choosing to get help for a drug problem or choosing not to get help.

Cause:		Effect:

⑤ Write to Express—Business Letter

Write a letter to an organization that deals with drug problems. Request information for a friend who might be abusing drugs.

ACTIVITIES

Language Arts

To Tell or Not to Tell Work in a team of five to eight students. Write a skit about a situation in which someone you know has a drug problem. Perform the skit for your classmates.

Science

Reaction Time With a partner, explore how reaction time might be affected by drug use. Have your partner hold the top of a yardstick so that the zero mark is hanging between your open thumb and forefinger. Your partner should drop the yardstick without warning. You should try to catch it. Record the number of inches that dropped before you caught the stick. Repeat this exercise several times. What do you think might happen to a person's reactions if he or she were using drugs?

Technology Project

Use a computer to make a database containing drug information, such as the effects of drugs on the body. Present your information to your family or classmates.

For more activities, visit The Learning Site. www. harcourtschool.com/health

Home & Community

Promote Health Ask a parent for permission to survey your family's medicine cabinet. List the names of the medicines, their uses, whether they are prescription or OTC medicines, and their side effects.

Career Link

School Resource Officer Imagine you are a school resource officer. A school resource officer is a police officer who provides information to people at schools. Make a pamphlet that can teach the students at your school about illegal drug use. Include information about how and where people can get help if they have drug problems or if they know others who do.

Reading Skill

IDENTIFY CAUSE AND EFFECT

Draw and then use this graphic organizer to answer questions 1 and 2.

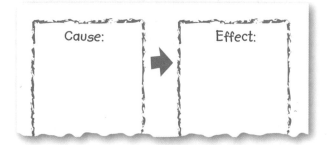

Cause: → Effect:

1 Write three effects of drug use.
2 Write three causes of addiction.

Use Vocabulary

Match each term in Column B with its meaning in Column A.

Column A	Column B
3 Chemical that changes the way the body or mind works	A drug
	B medicine abuse
	C medicine misuse
4 Taking a medicine without following the directions	D overdose
	E side effect
	F withdrawal
5 Unwanted reaction to a medicine	
6 Taking a medicine for a reason other than an illness	
7 Dangerously large dose of a drug	
8 Reaction that occurs when someone suddenly stops using a drug	

Check Understanding

Choose the letter of the correct answer.

9 Medicines you can buy without a doctor's prescription are called _____.
  A illegal drugs   C anabolic steroids
  B drugs   D OTC medicines

10 Illegal drugs include _____.
  F crack
  G marijuana
  H cocaine
  J all of these

11 Which of the following gives off dangerous fumes?
  A paper paste   C soda
  B gasoline   D watercolor paints

12 Which information should be on a prescription medicine label?
  F how much of the medicine to take
  G the name of the patient
  H the number of refills left
  J all of these

13 Deciding what medicine to take without asking a doctor is _____.
  A self-medication
  B medicine misuse
  C medicine abuse
  D overdosing

14 Which of the following is **NOT** a warning sign of drug abuse?
  F missing a lot of school
  G borrowing money often
  H getting angry for no reason
  J doing well in school

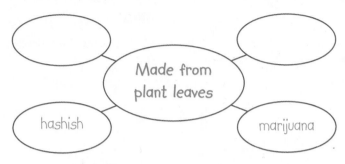

Made from plant leaves

hashish

marijuana

15 Which illegal drugs are missing in the graphic organizer?

   A cocaine   **C** neither A nor B

   B crack   **D** both A and B

16 Which drug is related to hashish?

   F marijuana

   G crack

   H anabolic steroids

   J cocaine

17 Which warning on a label relates to a side effect of a medicine?

   A Take with food.

   B May cause drowsiness.

   C Shake well.

   D No refills.

18 When do drug users begin suffering from withdrawal?

   F when they take too much of a drug

   G when they stop using drugs they are addicted to

   H when they have a high tolerance to a drug

   J when they start using drugs

19 Most medicines should be stored in a _____.

   A warm, bright place

   B place that children can get to easily

   C cool, dark place

   D bottle without a label

 Think Critically

20 Why is it important to know the warning signs of drug use?

21 Why is it difficult for drug users to quit using drugs?

22 Look at this prescription label. Tell what each piece of information means and why it is on the label.

TOWN DRUG

49 HARDING RD. PHONE 555-8531 SPRINGFIELD, OH 46203

Federal law prohibits transfer of this drug to any person
other than patient for whom prescribed.

57146   Dr. Greg Hardy

ADA SPRINGER 21-OCT-03   Q: 20 ORG: 21-OCY-30

ERYTHROMYCIN 500mg   **MAY CAUSE DROWSINESS**

EXPIRES: 21-NOV-03

DIRECTIONS: Take 1 tablet orally four
times daily. Finish all medication

REFILL: NONE

 Apply Skills

23   **BUILDING GOOD CHARACTER**

Trustworthiness Suppose you have a stomachache. Your parents are not at home, but you know where they keep the medicine that they take for stomach problems. Should you take the medicine? Explain what you should do to show that you are trustworthy.

24   **LIFE SKILLS**

Refuse A friend has started to use drugs. She wants you to try them, too. She says that if you're a good friend, you'll join her. Describe two ways you could say *no* to her.

Write About Health

25 Write to Inform—Explanation Why do people use drugs, and what are some reasons not to do so?

233

CHAPTER 7

About Tobacco and Alcohol

Reading Skill

Focus Skill

DRAW CONCLUSIONS Sometimes authors don't directly tell you all the information in what you read. You have to use information from a passage plus what you already know to draw a conclusion. Use the Reading in Science Handbook on pages R19–R27 and this graphic organizer to help you read the health facts in this chapter.

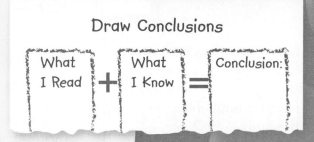

Draw Conclusions

What I Read + What I Know = Conclusion:

Health Graph

INTERPRET DATA The costs of smoking go far beyond the price of cigarettes. Look at the graph below. How much per year are the combined medical and social costs of smoking?

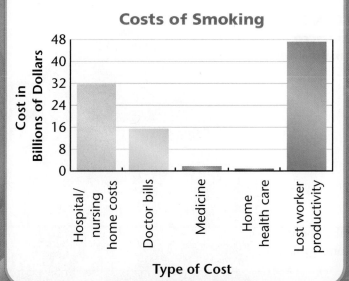

Costs of Smoking

Cost in Billions of Dollars

Type of Cost
- Hospital/nursing home costs
- Doctor bills
- Medicine
- Home health care
- Lost worker productivity

Daily Physical Activity

You should keep alcohol and tobacco out of your life. They can harm your growing body. However, physical activity should be part of your life every day.

Be Active!
Use the selection, Track 9, **Hop To It**, to practice some healthful activity choices.

Tobacco Affects Body Systems

Short-Term Effects of Using Tobacco

In the last fifty years, people have learned more and more about the harm tobacco does to the human body. Many people believe that tobacco will harm them only if they use it for a long time. This just isn't true. There are also many short-term effects of tobacco use.

One of the first effects of smoking tobacco is a bad smell. A smoker's hair and clothes often smell of stale cigarette smoke. A smoker's breath usually smells bad, too. Tobacco smoke makes the eyes and nose burn. People who chew tobacco have bad breath, also, and chewing tobacco turns teeth yellow or brown.

Smoking makes it hard to breathe. People who have trouble breathing have a hard time playing sports and doing other activities. There is another danger that can result from smoking. Ashes from a smoker's cigarette can fall on clothing, carpets, and furniture. Sometimes these ashes burn little holes or even start fires.

Focus Skill DRAW CONCLUSIONS **How can using tobacco affect a person's relationships with others?**

Smoking makes people smell bad—and look bad, too. ▶

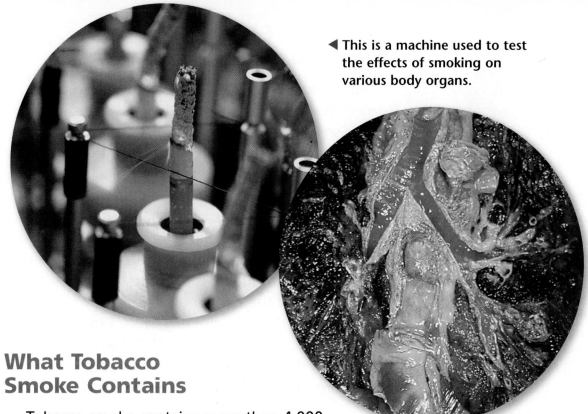

◀ This is a machine used to test the effects of smoking on various body organs.

▲ These lungs are black because of the tar in cigarettes. Tar causes cancer.

What Tobacco Smoke Contains

Tobacco smoke contains more than 4,000 substances. More than 50 of these are linked to cancer. Substances that cause cancer are called **carcinogens** (kar·SIN·uh·juhnz).

One substance tobacco contains is nicotine. **Nicotine** (NIK·uh·teen) is a poison. In fact, in the past it was used to kill insects. Nicotine speeds up the nervous system. It also makes the blood vessels smaller. As a result, the heart must work harder to move blood through the body.

Tobacco smoke contains a poisonous gas called **carbon monoxide** (KAR·buhn muh·NAHK·syd). This gas takes the place of oxygen in the blood. A little carbon monoxide makes you tired. Too much can kill you.

Tobacco smoke also contains tar, a dark, sticky paste. When people smoke, tar coats the air passages in their lungs. The tar builds up and makes breathing difficult. In time, some smokers are not able to get enough oxygen to keep their bodies working. They may even get lung cancer, because tar is a carcinogen.

SUMMARIZE Identify three harmful substances in tobacco smoke, and describe their effects on the body.

Information Alert!

Chemicals in Tobacco Researchers keep finding new chemicals in tobacco smoke that harm the body.

GO ONLINE For the most up-to-date information, visit The Learning Site. www.harcourtschool.com/ health

Long-Term Effects of Using Tobacco

The respiratory system is the body system that is harmed the most by smoking tobacco. Breathing in tobacco smoke over and over again irritates the nose, throat, trachea, and lungs. Eventually, these irritations cause smokers to cough a lot.

Smokers are much more likely to die of *chronic bronchitis* and *emphysema* than nonsmokers. Chronic bronchitis starts with a buildup of tar in the respiratory system. The buildup causes the breathing tubes leading to the lungs to produce excess mucus and to swell. This makes it hard for the person to breathe.

Emphysema destroys the tiny air sacs in the lungs. When these air sacs are destroyed, it takes longer for the lungs to do their job. People with emphysema have a hard time breathing. Often they can't

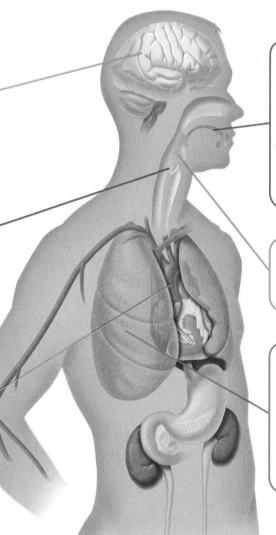

1 **Brain** Nicotine reaches the brain 10 seconds after being inhaled. Taking in nicotine leads to addiction.

3 **Esophagus** Smokers get about 80 percent of all cases of cancer of the esophagus.

5 **Circulatory System** Chemicals in tobacco smoke decrease the amount of oxygen in the blood and narrow the blood vessels. This makes the heart work harder, leading to heart diseases.

2 **Mouth** Tobacco juice damages gums, exposing the roots of the teeth. It also affects the sense of taste. Smokeless, or "spit," tobacco causes mouth, tongue, and lip cancer.

4 **Throat** Tobacco smoke irritates the throat and may cause throat cancer.

6 **Lungs** Tar collects inside the lungs, causing coughing and shortness of breath. Long-term smoking is the leading cause of cancer and other lung diseases.

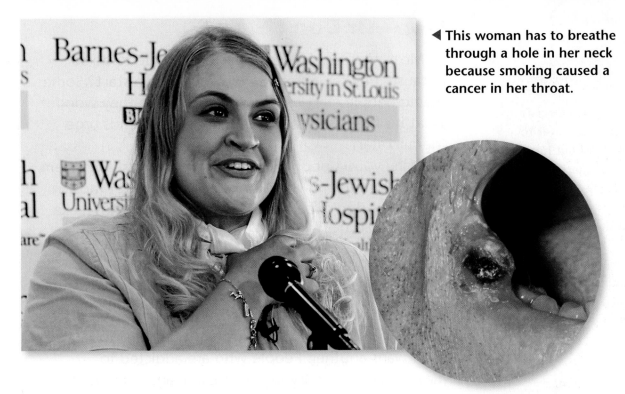

◀ This woman has to breathe through a hole in her neck because smoking caused a cancer in her throat.

▲ Using smokeless tobacco causes sores to form in the mouth. These sores often turn into cancer.

get enough oxygen to exercise or even walk short distances.

Lung cancer is the disease most people relate to smoking. Cancer destroys healthy tissues and organs. The longer a person smokes cigarettes, the more likely he or she is to get lung cancer. Smokers are also at risk of getting cancer of the mouth, esophagus, larynx, throat, and digestive system.

Heart diseases caused by smoking kill people every year. Chemicals in cigarette smoke make the heart work faster and harder. Smokers are four times more likely to die of heart disease than are nonsmokers.

Tobacco smoke also harms nonsmokers. People who are around smokers breathe environmental tobacco smoke (ETS)—tobacco smoke in the air. ETS has the same harmful poisons that smokers inhale. People who breathe ETS all the time can end up with lung diseases, cancer, and heart disease. They also have more allergies, asthma, and respiratory infections than people who stay in smoke-free places.

CAUSE AND EFFECT **List four possible long-term effects of using tobacco.**

Myth and Fact

Myth: Smokeless tobacco is harmless.

Fact: People who use smokeless tobacco are fifty times more likely to get oral cancer than people who don't. Oral cancer is cancer of the mouth, lips, gums, tongue, or inside of the cheeks.

Stop—Or Don't Start

Most people who use tobacco continue to do so because they can't stop. So why do people start? Some young people start using tobacco because they wonder what it's like. Others start because their friends urge them to start.

Many young people think using tobacco makes them look grown-up and cool. But the facts are that most grown-ups don't use tobacco and that cigarettes make people sick! Also, in most states a person under the age of eighteen who is caught buying tobacco can be arrested or fined.

Don't think you can smoke a cigarette once in a while or quit whenever you want. Nicotine is an addictive drug. When you smoke a cigarette, you will soon want another. People who are addicted to nicotine become nervous, depressed, and irritable if they don't use tobacco often. The best way to avoid this is to never use tobacco in the first place!

Most adults who smoke want to quit. As soon as a smoker quits, his or her body begins to heal. The chances of developing cancer, lung diseases, and heart diseases go down.

Nicotine Withdrawal and Recovery

After 12 Hours	After a Few Days	After a Few Weeks
Carbon monoxide and nicotine levels decline	Senses of smell and taste return	Heart and lungs begin to repair themselves
Person feels hungry, tired, edgy, short-tempered	Person often eats more and experiences temporary weight gain	Risk of death from disease, stroke, cancer, emphysema is reduced
Coughing increases	Mouth and tongue are dry	More healthy, productive days
	Most nicotine is gone from the body	Chances for a longer life improve

Many people need help to quit smoking. Hospitals, support groups, and health organizations are sources that offer help. Also, doctors can suggest special medicines to help smokers get over their addiction.

 DRAW CONCLUSIONS Why does taking responsibility for your own health mean not smoking?

◀ **You can be cool and have fun with friends without smoking!**

Lesson 1 Summary and Review

1 Summarize with Vocabulary

Use vocabulary from this lesson to complete the statements.

Tobacco smoke contains cancer-causing substances, or _____, such as the sticky substance known as _____. Tobacco smoke also contains the addictive drug _____ and the poisonous gas _____. Even nonsmokers can be hurt by tobacco by way of _____.

2 Describe two ways in which nicotine affects the body.

3 Critical Thinking Once a person has started using tobacco, why should he or she stop?

4 **DRAW CONCLUSIONS** Draw and complete this graphic organizer to show how you might arrive at the following conclusion.

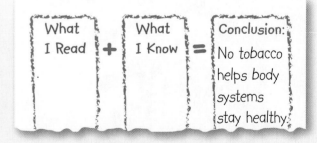

| What I Read | + | What I Know | = | Conclusion: No tobacco helps body systems stay healthy. |

5 Write to Inform—Description

Write a paragraph describing how to avoid tobacco products and ETS. Also describe how avoiding tobacco helps reduce health problems.

Alcohol Affects Body Systems

Lesson Focus

Alcohol is a drug that can cause immediate and long-term effects.

Why Learn This?

Knowing the effects of alcohol will help you make good decisions about its use.

Vocabulary

blood alcohol level (BAL)
intoxicated
alcoholism

Short-Term Effects of Using Alcohol

You may see alcohol being served at family gatherings, in restaurants, or even in church. When used by adults in small amounts, alcohol can even have positive effects on the circulatory system. However, drinking too much alcohol can be dangerous or even deadly. Even small amounts of alcohol can harm a young person.

Alcohol is a drug. It is found in beer, wine, and liquor. Alcohol changes the way a person feels, acts, and thinks. It also changes the way the body works. How much a person is affected by alcohol depends on the person's blood alcohol level. **Blood alcohol level (BAL)** is a measure of the amount of alcohol in a person's blood. The more alcohol a person drinks, the higher the person's BAL. The higher the BAL, the more the person is affected by alcohol.

Each of these drinks contains about $\frac{1}{2}$ ounce of alcohol.

242

◄ It is dangerous for someone who has been drinking a lot to drive a car! It is also illegal. An intoxicated person who drives could have his or her license taken away or even be put in jail.

Alcohol affects the parts of the brain that control speech, balance, and coordination. People who drink a lot of alcohol sometimes have trouble speaking and even standing.

Alcohol also affects the parts of the brain that control judgment, attention, and memory. Drinking a lot of alcohol causes people to make bad decisions. They may do things they would otherwise never do. They may also forget what they have done.

As alcohol builds up in a person's body, the person becomes drunk, or intoxicated. Being **intoxicated** (in•TAHK•sih•kay•tuhd) means being strongly affected by a drug. This happens to different people at different rates. A small or young person will become intoxicated faster than a large adult. Some people become loud, angry, or violent when intoxicated. Some become sleepy, sad, or silly. Others may vomit.

Alcohol slows down a person's breathing. If a person's BAL is high enough, he or she may fall asleep or become unconscious. Alcohol is a poison. Too much alcohol can kill a person.

SEQUENCE **What are some of the short-term effects a person experiences as his or her BAL increases?**

Did You Know?

Every year in the United States, more than 17,000 people die in car crashes linked to drinking alcohol. That's about two people killed every hour.

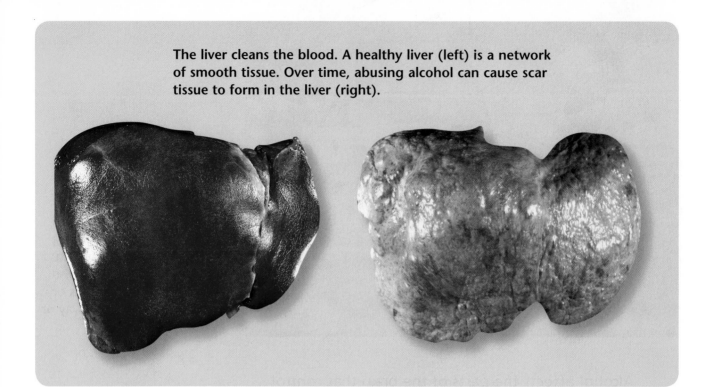

The liver cleans the blood. A healthy liver (left) is a network of smooth tissue. Over time, abusing alcohol can cause scar tissue to form in the liver (right).

Long-Term Effects of Using Alcohol

Drinking alcohol causes changes in a person's brain and body. These changes can cause the person to become addicted to alcohol.

People who start drinking alcohol at a young age become addicted more quickly than people who begin as adults. In fact, a young person can become addicted after drinking alcohol for only a few months. That's one reason why it's against the law for people under the age of twenty-one to buy alcohol.

Drinking a lot of alcohol over a long time can cause many health problems. Alcohol can damage nerve cells in the brain and other parts of the nervous system. This can make it hard for people to remember things or to think clearly.

Drinking alcohol for a long time can also cause damage to the liver, an important organ that cleans the blood of certain wastes. Liver damage due to alcohol or other drugs is called *cirrhosis*.

Myth and Fact

Myth: Alcohol hurts only the people who drink it.
Fact: Each year thousands of nondrinkers are killed in alcohol-related violence or car crashes.

244

Alcohol keeps some people from feeling hungry. So a person who drinks a lot of alcohol may not eat enough. As a result, the body may not get the nutrients it needs. This makes the body less fit and less able to protect itself from disease.

MAIN IDEA AND DETAILS **Describe how alcohol affects the body.**

1 **Brain** Alcohol slows nerve activity that controls speech, motor skills, judgment, thinking, and memory. Alcohol makes the blood vessels in the brain expand, causing headaches. Long-term alcohol use can cause permanent brain damage.

2 **Mouth** Alcohol numbs and irritates a drinker's mouth and esophagus. Long-term use of alcohol can cause cancer of the mouth.

3 **Heart** Alcohol makes the heart beat faster. It also causes blood pressure to rise. Heavy drinking can cause lasting high blood pressure.

4 **Stomach** Alcohol causes the stomach to secrete juices for digestion. If there is no food in the stomach, these juices irritate the stomach, causing small sores, called *ulcers,* to form.

5 **Liver** The poisons in alcohol collect in the liver and form blisters. Over time these blisters form scar tissue that keeps the liver from cleaning the blood. Eventually the liver stops working.

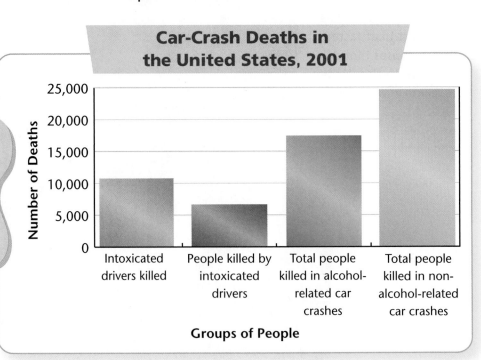

▲ Alcohol use causes more car-crash deaths than any other factor.

Other Problems Caused by Alcohol

Health effects are not the only risks connected to alcohol use. Remember that alcohol affects the brain in many ways. Intoxicated people may say hurtful things, take foolish risks, and damage property. They may also injure or kill themselves and others. Thousands are killed in car crashes each year because of people who think they can drive safely after drinking.

People who can't stop drinking have a disease called alcoholism. **Alcoholism** (AL·kuh·hawl·iz·uhm) is an addiction to alcohol. People who suffer from alcoholism are *alcoholics*

Quick Activity

Analyze Data Look at the bar graph at the right. What percent of car-crash deaths are related to alcohol use?

Car-Crash Deaths in the United States, 2001

Number of Deaths

25,000
20,000
15,000
10,000
5,000
0

Intoxicated drivers killed | People killed by intoxicated drivers | Total people killed in alcohol-related car crashes | Total people killed in non-alcohol-related car crashes

Groups of People

(al•kuh•HAWL•iks). Alcoholism can affect people of any age, any race, and either gender.

Many alcoholics want to stop drinking. When they try to stop, though, they go through withdrawal. Recall that withdrawal is the physical and emotional changes addicts go through when they stop using an addictive drug.

Withdrawal is different for different people. Some sweat a lot or become very confused. Some see or hear things that aren't there. Some get severe headaches or feel sick to the stomach. Others get nervous and are unable to sleep. Nearly all alcoholics in withdrawal want to drink to feel better.

Trained health-care workers at hospitals and treatment centers can help alcoholics going through withdrawal. The workers can offer counseling and medicine to lessen the effects of withdrawal.

Going through withdrawal is not the end for an alcoholic. He or she may still need help for months or years to keep away from alcohol. Most alcoholics can't stop drinking by themselves. They need help from doctors or from organizations that understand alcoholism and know how to treat it.

COMPARE AND CONTRAST **Compare and contrast the health risks of an alcohol user with the health risks of a non-user.**

ACTIVITY

Building Good Character

Trustworthiness You trust people not to use alcohol or other drugs while they are working. For example, a school-bus driver should never drink alcohol before going to work. Name other jobs that require workers to be trustworthy about not using alcohol while they are working.

You may think that all alcoholics look dirty and wear ragged clothes. The truth is that most alcoholics are ordinary people with a problem.

Alcohol Affects Others, Too

Alcoholism doesn't affect just the alcoholic. It causes problems for the alcoholic's family and friends, too. Alcoholics may not always notice others. Their moods may go up and down a great deal, depending on how much they have been drinking. They buy alcohol with money that should be used for family needs. Family members get used to being treated badly. They adjust their lives around the alcoholic's behavior. They lose their sense of worth. Al-Anon is an organization that sponsors support groups for people close to an alcoholic. Alateen support groups are for teens and younger children who have an alcoholic friend or relative.

SUMMARIZE List two programs of support groups for family members of alcoholics.

◀ Alateen offers support groups in most communities. Find out where Alateen groups meet in your community.

Lesson 2 Summary and Review

❶ Summarize with Vocabulary

Use vocabulary and other terms from this lesson to complete the statements.

When a person drinks a lot of _____, he or she can become _____ and have a high _____. A person who continues to drink too much alcohol can become a(n) _____.

❷ Critical Thinking
How is a person's blood alcohol level (BAL) affected by the number of drinks he or she has had?

❸
Make a table showing times or places in which you might be offered alcohol. For each situation, list a reason not to drink.

❹ (Focus Skill) DRAW CONCLUSIONS
Draw and complete this graphic organizer to show how you might arrive at the following conclusion.

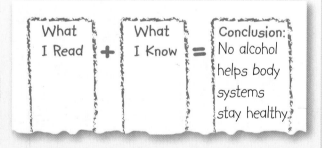

| What I Read | | What I Know | | Conclusion: No alcohol helps body systems stay healthy. |

❺ Write to Inform—How-To
Write a short how-to guide that teaches young people how to reduce health risks related to alcohol use.

Citizenship

Showing Respect for Authority

Being a good citizen means helping to keep your community safe, clean, and a good place to live. There are many ways that you can be a good citizen. One way is to show respect for people who have authority, including parents, teachers, police officers, firefighters, bus drivers, store security guards, and crossing guards. Here are some ways to show respect:

- **Always follow instructions given to you by people in authority.**

- **If you see others not following instructions given by a person in authority, tell the person about it.**

- **When you're outside and you see a person in authority, pay attention in case he or she needs to signal you to stop or come over.**

- **If you see people breaking the law, such as a young person using alcohol or tobacco, tell a parent or report it to someone in authority.**

Activity

Working with a partner, make a list of people in authority, who need respect in order to do their jobs. Then role-play some of these people as they try to enforce rules. Decide how both the authorities and the people they direct should act. Make sure everyone involved shows respect.

Refusing Alcohol and Tobacco

Lesson Focus

Refusing alcohol and tobacco is easier if you know the facts and plan ahead.

Why Learn This?

Many young people face peer pressure to use alcohol and tobacco. But it is illegal, dangerous, and unhealthful for young people to use these drugs.

Some People Choose Not to Use Alcohol and Tobacco

Sometimes it might seem as if you have to use alcohol and tobacco to have fun. You see adults smoking and drinking in movies, videos, magazines, and TV shows. The media make the people using these drugs look glamorous, healthy, and full of energy. However, this image is *not true*. Adults who use tobacco and too much alcohol are harming their bodies. That is why most adults have chosen to avoid tobacco and large amounts of alcohol.

There are many reasons not to use alcohol. Some people find that alcohol makes them feel tense, sad, or worried. Other people are allergic to chemicals in some alcoholic drinks. People may also avoid alcohol because they regret how they act when they drink.

Young people may choose not to use alcohol because it's illegal or because of family rules. They may

Follow your family rules! This will keep you healthy and show your parents that you are trustworthy. ▶

also want to do well in school. They know that alcohol affects their ability to think and remember. They know about the health risks linked to alcohol use, too.

Most people also choose not to use tobacco. For them it's more important to avoid the health risks, like cancer, heart disease, and respiratory diseases. They also know that using tobacco would make it harder for them to enjoy sports and other activities.

The cost of tobacco is also a concern to many people. Smokers may buy a pack or two of cigarettes a day. Users of smokeless tobacco may buy a pouch or tin every day or two. That's a lot of money to spend on things that make people ill!

Many young people don't want to get hooked on a behavior that not only costs a lot of money but also is dangerous. Young people may decide not to use tobacco because it's against the law for them. Bad breath, smelly clothes, and stained teeth may also keep them from smoking or chewing tobacco. Even friends don't want to be around people who smoke or chew.

Focus Skill **DRAW CONCLUSIONS How do family, school, and peers influence your choice not to use alcohol and tobacco?**

PersonaL HeaLth PLan ▶

Real-Life Situation
You're hanging out with your best friends, and all of you are bored. One of your friends suggests you go to her house to drink a few beers.
Real-Life Plan
Make a list of fun activities you and your friend could do that don't involve alcohol.

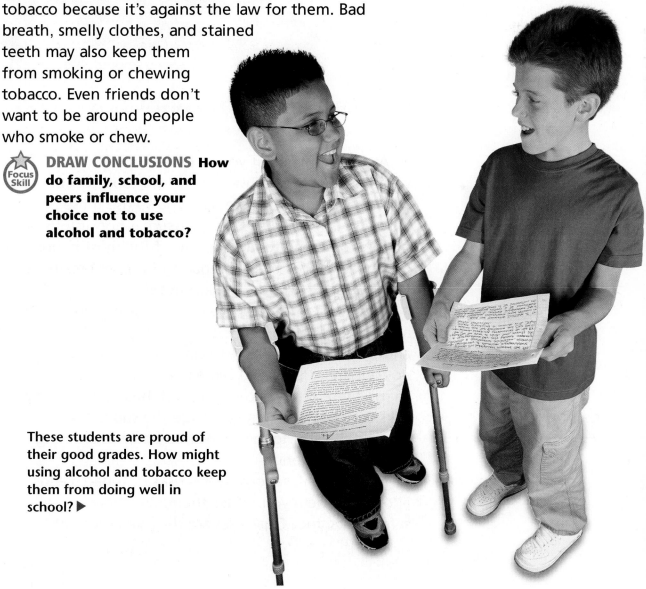

These students are proud of their good grades. How might using alcohol and tobacco keep them from doing well in school? ▶

Ways to Say *No*

1 Politely say *no,* and walk away.

2 Explain that you would rather do something else.

3 Explain that you choose not to use alcohol or tobacco because of the risks.

4 Change the subject.

5 Make a joke.

6 Express surprise that your friend would be so foolish.

7 Express disappointment that your friend would want to do something so unpleasant.

You Can Refuse Alcohol and Tobacco

At some time most young people must decide whether to use or refuse alcohol and tobacco. People your age might try to pressure you to use these products. This is called *peer pressure.* Choosing to say *no* to alcohol and tobacco is one of the most important decisions you can make. Preparing for peer pressure can help you stick to your decision to refuse.

It's important to practice ways of saying *no.* There are many ways to do it. You can simply say " No thanks" and walk away. You can explain that you would rather do something else. You can explain that you don't want to use these drugs because of their health and safety risks. You can also simply change the subject. Any way you can think of to say *no* will be better than using tobacco and alcohol!

Knowing the serious health risks of tobacco and alcohol can help you refuse them. But there are serious safety risks, too. Cigarettes are the main cause of fires

◀ Young people who want to stay healthy say *no* to cigarettes. How can friends help each other say *no*?

in homes, hospitals, and hotels. Alcohol is a leading cause of car crashes.

One of the most important reasons to refuse alcohol and tobacco is to feel good about yourself. When you feel good about yourself, you won't want to follow the bad habits of others. You won't need alcohol or tobacco to feel grown-up.

You can also avoid places where you know there will be drinking or smoking. Parties where there are no responsible adults are often places where young people feel they can get away with drinking or smoking. You can also protect yourself by making friends with young people who don't drink or smoke.

MAIN IDEA AND DETAILS **Identify ways to resist peer pressure to use alcohol and tobacco.**

ACTIVITY

Life Skills

Communicate

Colette is watching television with her older brother Jim when a beer commercial comes on. Jim says, "Hey, we have some of that in the refrigerator! Want one?" What are some ways Colette can say *no*?

Analyze Advertising Messages

Companies that make and sell tobacco and alcohol products spend a lot of money on advertising. Their ads suggest that people who use their products are rich, cool, and always have fun. They want you to think that using alcohol or tobacco products will make you popular and fun to be with.

People who see these ads should remember the harmful effects of alcohol and tobacco. These ads never show how hard it is to quit using the products. They never tell how much money the products cost. You would never know by looking at the ads that people become ill and die from using alcohol and tobacco.

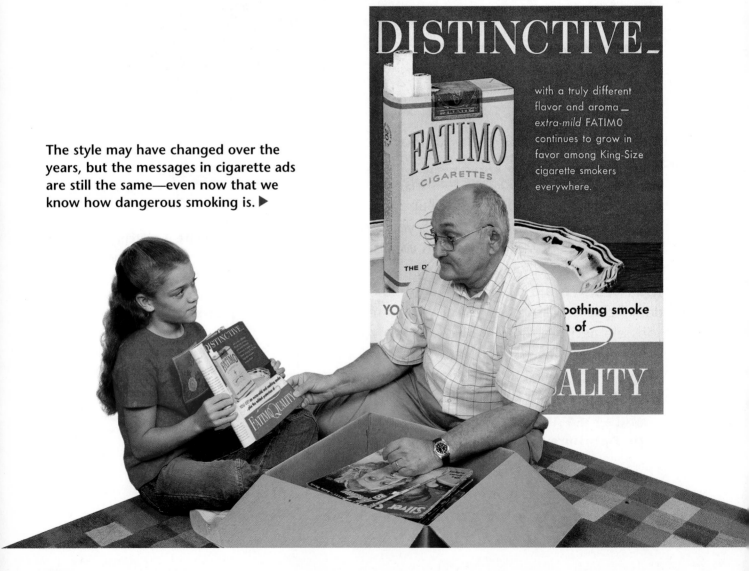

The style may have changed over the years, but the messages in cigarette ads are still the same—even now that we know how dangerous smoking is. ▶

254

Ads for alcohol and tobacco often show young adults using these products. Alcohol and tobacco companies know that young people want to be like adults. These companies also know that people who start drinking and smoking have a hard time stopping.

Beer companies often show their commercials during sporting events. The commercials are designed to make people think that drinking beer is as exciting as playing sports. Cigarette companies are no longer allowed to advertise on TV. But they still get the names of their products on TV by sponsoring sporting and cultural events. When you see the names of alcohol and tobacco products or ads for them, be sure to think about what's not being shown.

SUMMARIZE List ways the media influence a person's view of alcohol and tobacco.

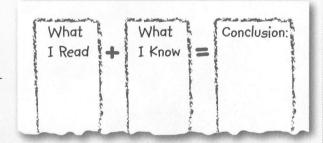

Lesson 3 Summary and Review

1 Summarize with Vocabulary

Use terms from this lesson to complete the statements.

TV, magazines, and other _____ often encourage young people to use alcohol and _____. They don't show how _____ these products are. An honest media message would encourage people to _____ rather than use alcohol and tobacco.

2 Why do you think it's illegal for young people to buy or use tobacco and alcohol?

3 Critical Thinking Why is it a good idea to think of reasons for refusing alcohol and tobacco before you are offered these drugs?

4 (Focus Skill) DRAW CONCLUSIONS Draw and complete this graphic organizer to show a conclusion you might make about using alcohol and tobacco.

What I Read	+	What I Know	=	Conclusion:

5 Write to Inform—How-To

Write a how-to manual that teaches young people the attitudes and skills for making responsible decisions about tobacco and alcohol.

Refuse
Alcohol

There will be times when you need to make decisions for yourself about alcohol and tobacco use. Learning ways to **Refuse** will help you stay healthy.

Cory and Nicki had been playing tennis together. When the game was over, they headed to Nicki's house. Nicki's parents weren't home at the time. Nicki said, "Hey, my dad bought a six-pack of beer last night. Do you want to try one?" Cory may want to drink alcohol but knows she shouldn't. Here are some ways she can say *no*.

1 **Say *no*, and tell why not.**

No way! It's illegal for us to drink!

Cory can say *no* and explain why they shouldn't be drinking alcohol.

2 **Use humor to make your point.**

Girl, I don't want to get a beer belly!

Cory can make a joke, hoping Nicki will forget about drinking.

3 Suggest something else to do.

4 Just ignore what the person has said.

Nah, let's go see that new spy movie.

Cory can suggest something else for them to do instead of drinking alcohol.

Did you see that TV show last night?

Cory can just not respond to Nicki's suggestion and can change the subject.

 # Problem Solving

A. Anna and Kay are looking at a magazine. They see a picture of a beautiful woman advertising cigarettes. Kay suggests that they smoke some cigarettes so they can look like the model. Anna does not want to smoke.
  • Choose and explain one way to **Refuse** in Anna's situation.

B. Dave and his older friend Chuck are camping out. As Chuck is unpacking the food, Dave notices a six-pack of beer. Dave doesn't want to drink alcohol, and he doesn't want to be around if Chuck is going to drink.
  • What are some ways Dave can get out of this situation? How can Dave show respect for his family's rules about not using alcohol?

Where Users Can Find Help

When Someone Needs Help

"I want to do it myself!" You've probably heard small children say this. Maybe you've said it, too. It expresses a natural feeling. You feel proud when you do something without any help. But everyone needs help sometimes. Asking for help when it's needed is a sign of being responsible.

Overcoming a problem with alcohol or tobacco is difficult. Most people need help with it. Fortunately, there are many kinds of help for overcoming alcohol or tobacco addiction.

How much alcohol use is too much? You may be worried about the drinking habits of someone you know. Maybe you've noticed someone drinking more alcohol now than he or she used to. Maybe you've seen someone drinking alone. In both cases, the person might need help.

Did You Know?
Most people who decide to quit using alcohol or tobacco have to try several times before they succeed. Just because a person tries and fails doesn't mean he or she will never be able to quit.

Warning Signs of Problem Drinking
1. Drinking more now than in the past
2. Hiding alcohol or sneaking drinks
3. Forgetting things as a result of drinking
4. Missing school or work as a result of drinking
5. Lying about drinking
6. Needing a drink to have fun or to relax
7. Drinking alone
8. Thinking and talking about alcohol a lot

Drinking more and more alcohol can mean that the person has become an alcoholic. A person who drinks alone may be using alcohol to deal with feelings such as anger, sadness, or grief. To the person who is drinking, alcohol seems to make these feelings go away. In fact, however, alcohol will only make the feelings worse. With the right help, a person can learn to deal with his or her feelings in healthful ways.

If someone's drinking worries you, chances are that the person needs help. To know for sure, check the warning signs listed on page 258. These signs can help you know whether someone needs help.

Anyone who uses tobacco should also get help. Most people who use tobacco want to quit. They know how dangerous and expensive the habit is. But quitting is hard, especially for someone who tries to do it alone. Medicine is available now to help people quit smoking. Encouragement from family and friends helps, too.

CAUSE AND EFFECT Describe a situation that might lead a person to drink too much alcohol.

Quick **Activity**

Be a Friend The attitudes of friends can make a big difference to people who are trying to quit using tobacco. Make a list of ways you could help a person close to you who wants to stop smoking.

If somebody is trying to quit using tobacco or alcohol, you should support that person by encouraging his or her efforts. ▶

If you know somebody who has a problem with alcohol or tobacco, one of the best people to go to is a parent. ▼

Getting Help

If someone close to you has a problem with alcohol or tobacco, talk about the problem with a parent or another adult you trust. You might worry that telling someone will get the person who needs help in trouble. The truth is that people who have an alcohol or tobacco problem need help before they do more harm to themselves. Telling someone about a person's problem will let the person know that you care about him or her. It will also give you the chance to share your concerns with someone else.

Talking with someone can also help the person with the problem find other kinds of support. For example, your community may have clinics, hospitals, or community organizations that help people deal with alcohol and tobacco problems.

SUMMARIZE Describe a plan for getting help for a person who has an alcohol or tobacco problem.

Lesson 4 Summary and Review

1 Summarize with Vocabulary

Use terms from this lesson to complete the statements.

To recognize when a person has a problem with drinking, know the _____. Some people drink because they think it will get rid of unwanted _____. They need _____ to stop drinking. If you know a problem drinker, you should talk with a (an) _____.

2 Suppose you are looking for help for a person with an alcohol or tobacco problem. Name some people and groups in your community that you might call.

3 Critical Thinking Why do you think some people drink when they are feeling stress?

4 **DRAW CONCLUSIONS** Draw and complete this graphic organizer to show what you can conclude from the following facts.

What I Read
Warning signs of problem drinking

+

What I Know
Jim misses school. He talks about drinking.

=

Conclusion:

5 Write to Inform—Description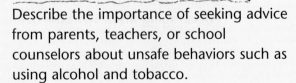

Describe the importance of seeking advice from parents, teachers, or school counselors about unsafe behaviors such as using alcohol and tobacco.

ACTIVITIES

Language Arts

Smoking Skit Write a humorous skit about why some people don't smoke cigarettes. Include several scenes so you can show the many different reasons people have for not smoking. Perform the skit for your class.

Science

Effects of Alcohol Take two leaves from a living plant. Cover one leaf with water. Have your teacher or a parent cover the other leaf with clear alcohol. Keep a log of your observations of what happens to the two leaves over the next three days. At the end of the three days, try to explain some of the changes you observed.

Technology Project

Identify at least ten local athletes who do not use tobacco. Ask them to give their top two reasons for not using tobacco. Use a spreadsheet on a computer to record your results. If you don't have a computer, use a paper spreadsheet.

 For more activities, visit The Learning Site. www. harcourtschool.com/health

Home & Community

Analyze Ads Find three or more magazine ads that feature alcohol or tobacco products. Analyze them by listing the negative results of smoking or drinking that the ads don't show and by describing why the ads are misleading. Then discuss your findings with a parent.

Career Link

Magazine Editor Imagine you are the chief editor for a top-rated teen magazine. You'd like your next issue to include a two-page feature article that gives readers positive and effective tools for refusing tobacco and alcohol. The article should offer readers things they can do and things they can say. As the editor of the magazine, what other guidelines will you give the writer of this article?

Reading Skill

DRAW CONCLUSIONS

Draw and then use this graphic organizer to answer questions 1 and 2.

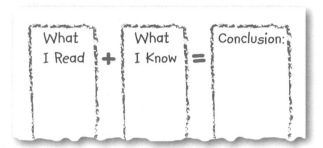

1 Write three facts that lead to the conclusion that tobacco can be dangerous.

2 Write three facts that lead to the conclusion that alcohol can be dangerous.

Use Vocabulary

Match each term in Column B with its meaning Column A.

Column A	Column B
3 Poison that speeds up the nervous system	**A** tar
4 Sticky, dark paste in tobacco smoke	**B** environmental tobacco smoke (ETS)
5 Poisonous gas from burning tobacco	**C** intoxicated
6 Affected by alcohol	**D** carcinogens
7 Causes of cancer	**E** carbon monoxide
8 A person who is addicted to alcohol	**F** blood alcohol level (BAL)
9 Amount of alcohol in the bloodstream	**G** nicotine
10 Tobacco smoke in air	**H** alcoholic

 Check Understanding

Choose the letter of the correct answer.

11 All forms of tobacco contain a poison called _____.
   A tar
   B a tumor
   C carbon dioxide
   D nicotine

12 The only disease below that is **NOT** a serious risk for smokers is _____.
   F cirrhosis   **H** emphysema
   G cancer   **J** heart disease

13 Alcohol is found in all of the following products **EXCEPT** _____.

14 Who probably does **NOT** have a problem with alcohol?
   F a person who hides his or her drinking
   G a person who drinks only at religious celebrations
   H a person who thinks about alcohol often
   J a person who drinks alone

15 People who don't smoke can suffer from respiratory problems and other diseases if they breathe a lot of _____.
   A smokeless tobacco
   B environmental tobacco smoke (ETS)
   C carbon dioxide
   D unfiltered air

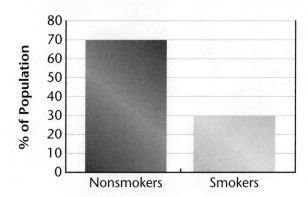

16 Look at the graph above. Which of the
following statements is **TRUE** according to
the data in the graph?

  F Most adults smoke.

  G Almost half of all adults are smokers.

  H Most adults do not smoke.

  J Most adults who smoke are able to quit.

17 Cigarette smoke contains many _____, or
substances that cause cancer.

  A poisons

  B carcinogens

  C depressants

  D fibers

18 Carbon monoxide makes the heart work
harder because it takes the place of _____
in the blood.

  F tars   **H** nicotine

  G air sacs   **J** oxygen

19 The _____ system is the body system
MOST damaged by smoking tobacco.

  A digestive   **C** respiratory

  B circulatory   **D** nervous

20 Alcohol affects a person's _____.

  F judgment

  G personality

  H memory

  J all of these

Think Critically

21 You overhear two adults talking. One of
them says, "Alcohol is not a problem for
me. I drink only a few beers each night."
Review the warning signs of problem
drinking. Then tell whether you agree with
this person or not. Explain your answer.

22 Someone you know quit smoking two days
ago. "Wow," he says, "I thought my cough
was caused by smoking. But I'm coughing
worse than ever now that I've quit." What
would you tell him?

Apply Skills

23 **BUILDING GOOD CHARACTER**
Citizenship You arrive at a party
where an adult was supposed to be in
charge. However, only young people are
there, and many of them have been
drinking. Some of them are intoxicated
and talking about going swimming. What
should you do to be a good citizen?

24 **LIFE SKILLS**
Refuse You've been working hard
all season because you want your team to
make it to the state finals. One day a
teammate takes out a pouch of chewing
tobacco and offers you some. What would
you do or say?

Write About Health

25 **Write to Explain—How-To** Explain what
you should do if you know someone who
has a problem with drinking.

263

UNIT 4

Exploring Ecosystems

LIFE SCIENCE

Carlsbad Caverns National Park

TO: william@hspscience.com

FROM: kaitlyn@hspscience.com

RE: bats, bats, and more bats

William,

On a recent trip to Carlsbad Caverns, in New Mexico, you would think I would have been most fascinated with the amazing cave system. Surprisingly enough, I was more interested by what lived inside those caves—300,000 Mexican free-tail bats. The coolest part was the mass exodus of the bats from the cave. It looked like a plume of smoke. In fact, it was the bats that have made Carlsbad their home for more than 5,000 years.

Now that's incredible!

Kaitlyn

Everett Children's Adventure Garden

TO: teresa@hspscience.com

FROM: dave@hspscience.com

RE: flowers aren't so bad

Dear Teresa,

I went to the New York Botanical Garden with my parents. I was really not looking forward to it, as I knew it would just be a lot of boring flowers. However, I was blown away by the Everett Children's Adventure Garden. Not only did we get to do lab experiments, but we also got to look at plants under high-powered microscopes. Climbing the boulder maze was a real test of my climbing abilities. Were there lots of flowers? You bet, but as it turns out, they weren't so boring after all!

Dave

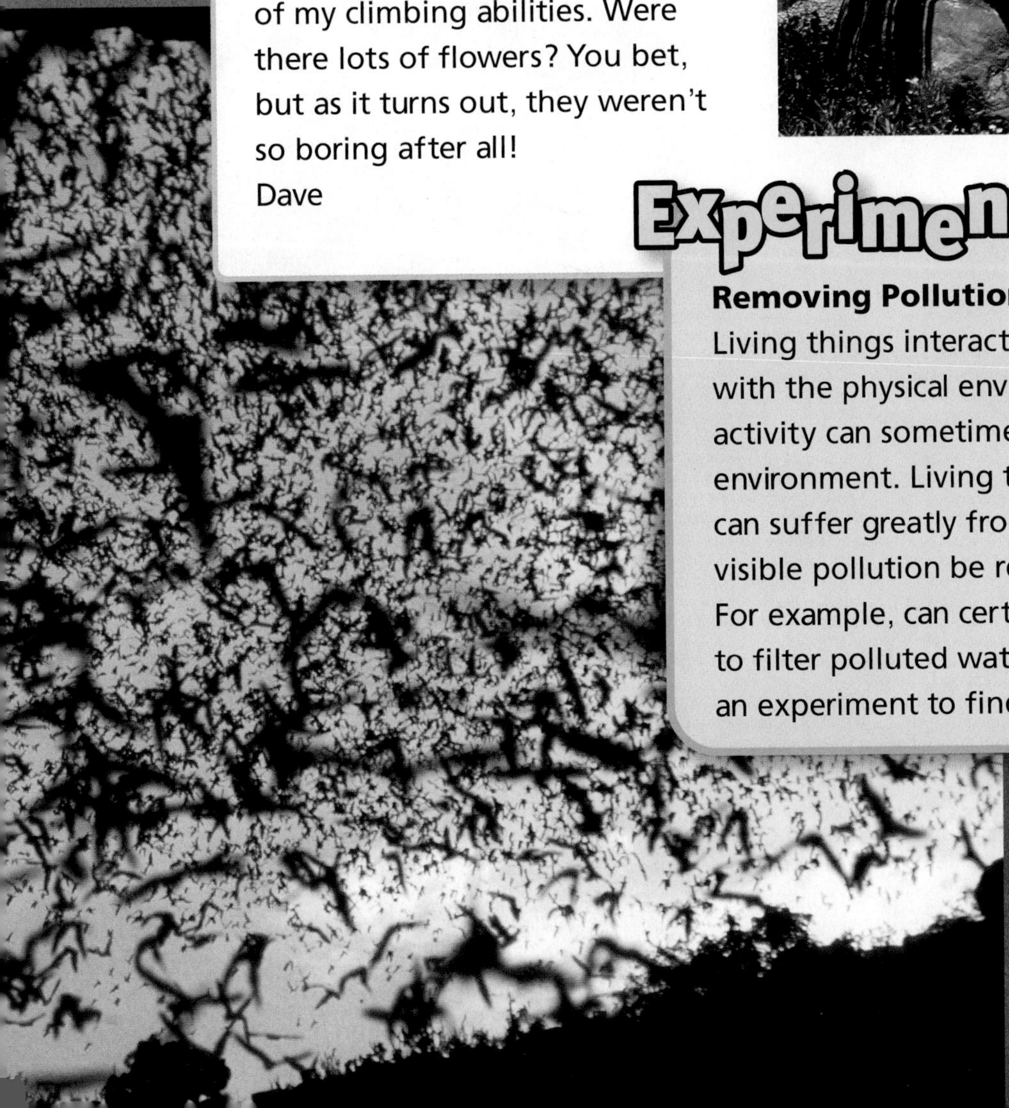

Experiment!

Removing Pollution from Water

Living things interact with each other and with the physical environment. Human activity can sometimes pollute the physical environment. Living things in the ocean can suffer greatly from pollution. How can visible pollution be removed from water? For example, can certain materials be used to filter polluted water? Plan and conduct an experiment to find out.

Energy and Ecosystems

Lesson 1 How Do Plants Produce Food?

Lesson 2 How Is Energy Passed Through an Ecosystem?

Vocabulary

transpiration
photosynthesis
chlorophyll
producer
consumer
ecosystem
herbivore
carnivore
food chain
decomposer
food web
energy pyramid

What do YOU wonder?

Whale sharks are the largest of all sharks, growing up to 15 m (50 ft) long. They also have the largest mouths, as you can see. What do you think a huge shark like this eats? Where does it get the energy it needs?

How Do Plants Produce Food?

Fast Fact

Working Plants These flowers and trees produce some of the oxygen you breathe. They also take carbon dioxide out of the air. In the Investigate, you will observe that a plant takes in carbon dioxide.

Using Carbon Dioxide

Materials
- safety goggles
- 2 plastic cups
- water
- dropper
- bromothymol blue (BTB)
- 2 test tubes with caps
- *Elodea*
- funnel
- plastic straw

Procedure

1. **CAUTION: Wear safety goggles.** Fill one cup about two-thirds full of water. Use the dropper to add BTB until the water is blue.

2. Put the straw into the cup, and blow into it. **CAUTION: DO NOT suck on the straw. If the solution gets in your mouth, spit it out and rinse your mouth with water.**

3. Observe and record changes in the water.

4. Put the *Elodea* in one test tube. Use the funnel to fill both test tubes with the BTB solution. Cap both tubes.

5. Turn the tubes upside down, and put them in the empty cup. Place the cup on a sunny windowsill. Predict what changes will occur in the test tubes.

6. After 1 hour, observe both tubes and record your observations.

Draw Conclusions

1. What changes did you observe in the BTB solution during the activity?

2. **Inquiry Skill** Scientists use what they know to predict what will happen. After you blew into the water, how did your observations help you predict what would happen next?

Step 2

Step 5

Investigate Further

Plan and conduct an experiment to test the effect of sunlight on the changes in the BTB solution. Predict what will happen. Then carry out your experiment.

Reading in Science

VOCABULARY

transpiration p. 271
photosynthesis p. 272
chlorophyll p. 272
producer p. 274
consumer p. 274

SCIENCE CONCEPTS

▶ how leaves use carbon dioxide and give off oxygen

▶ how the parts of plants make food by means of photosynthesis

READING FOCUS SKILL

MAIN IDEA AND DETAILS Look for details about how plants make and store food.

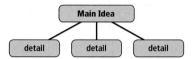

Plant Structures

You are probably familiar with the basic parts of plants. These parts include roots, stems, and leaves. Some of those parts produce food for the plant.

Roots Roots have two main jobs. They anchor plants, and they take in water and nutrients. Tubes in the roots carry water to the stems. The roots of some plants, such as carrots, also store food.

Different plants have different types of roots. For example, the roots of desert plants spread out just below the surface to catch any rain that falls. Some plants, like the dandelion, have one main root to reach water deep underground.

Stems Stems support a plant and enable its leaves to reach the sunlight. Stems also contain tubes that carry water and nutrients to the leaves. Other tubes carry food to all parts of the plant. The stems of some plants, such as sugar cane, store food.

Just as plants have different roots, they also have different stems. Small plants tend to have flexible, green stems. Most of these plants live for just one year. Larger plants and

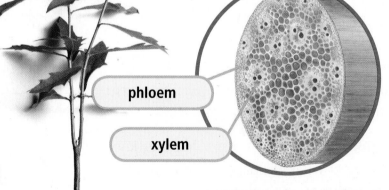

phloem

xylem

xylem

phloem

◀ Both roots and stems have tubes running through them. *Xylem* (ZY•luhm) carries water and nutrients from the soil to the leaves. *Phloem* (FLOH•em) carries food from the leaves to other parts of the plant.

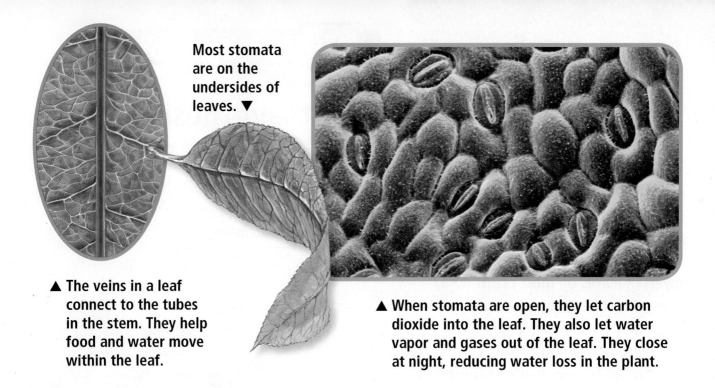

Most stomata are on the undersides of leaves. ▼

▲ The veins in a leaf connect to the tubes in the stem. They help food and water move within the leaf.

▲ When stomata are open, they let carbon dioxide into the leaf. They also let water vapor and gases out of the leaf. They close at night, reducing water loss in the plant.

trees need more support. They usually have stiff, woody stems, and live for many years.

Leaves Leaves have one main job—to make food for the plant. A leaf can be as small as the head of a pin, or it can be wide enough to support a frog on the surface of a pond. Some leaves are very specialized. The leaves of the Venus' flytrap are able to catch food for the plant. They snap shut when an insect lands on them. Then the leaves help digest the insect.

Most leaves are thin and have several layers of cells. The outer layer, called the *epidermis* (ep•uh•DER•mis), keeps the leaf from drying out. The upper epidermis is often covered with a layer of wax. This helps keep water in. The lower epidermis has many small openings called *stomata*.

Stomata usually open during the day so the leaf can take in carbon dioxide to make food. Stomata close at night to keep the plant from drying out. The loss of water through leaves is called **transpiration**.

Just below the upper epidermis is a closely packed layer of cells in which most of the food is made. Just above the lower epidermis is a spongy layer of cells. Air spaces among these cells contain carbon dioxide, oxygen, and water vapor.

Veins, which connect to the tubes in the stems, are found in the center of most leaves. In broad leaves, the veins have many branches. They bring the water needed to make food to cells throughout the leaf.

MAIN IDEA AND DETAILS What is the main job of each plant part?

Insta-Lab

Moving Out

Partially break five toothpicks, leaving the halves connected. Arrange them in a grouping, as shown. Wet the center of the grouping with several drops of water. How does this activity show the way water moves through plants?

Photosynthesis

Plants make food in a process that uses water from the soil, carbon dioxide from the air, and energy from sunlight. This process, called **photosynthesis**, produces food for the plant and releases oxygen into the air.

Recall that plant cells contain organelles called chloroplasts. Cells with chloroplasts are found in the inner layers of leaves on most plants. Only cells with chloroplasts can make food.

Chloroplasts contain a green pigment, or coloring matter, called chlorophyll (KLAWR•uh•fil). **Chlorophyll** enables a plant to absorb light energy so that it can produce food. It also makes plants green. Plants contain small amounts of other pigments as well. In autumn, many plants stop producing chlorophyll, so you can see the other pigments. This is what makes some leaves change color in autumn.

Photosynthesis begins when sunlight hits the chloroplasts. The energy absorbed by the chlorophyll causes water and carbon dioxide to combine to form sugar—the food that plants need to live and grow.

Oxygen is produced as a byproduct of photosynthesis. It is released into the air through the stomata. About 90 percent of the oxygen you breathe is produced during photosynthesis by plants and plantlike protists. Plants also help you by taking carbon dioxide, which your body does not need, out of the air.

 MAIN IDEA AND DETAILS What does a plant need for photosynthesis?

Science Up Close

Photosynthesis

Sunlight provides energy for plants to make food.

Plants take in carbon dioxide from the air.

After making food, the leaves release oxygen through their stomata.

Chlorophyll absorbs energy from sunlight. The plant needs this energy, along with carbon dioxide and water, to make food.

The food made by the plant is stored in the plant's leaves, stems, seeds, and—in some plants—roots.

Plant roots take in water, which is necessary for photosynthesis.

For more links and activities, go to www.hspscience.com

It All Starts with Plants

All organisms need energy to live and grow. That energy comes from food. Plants are called **producers** because they produce, or make, their own food. Animals can't make their own food, but they need energy from food to survive. When animals eat plants, the animals receive the energy that's stored in those plants. The word *consume* means "to eat," so we call animals that eat plants or other animals **consumers**.

You are a consumer. For example, when you eat a salad, you take in the energy stored in the lettuce leaves and carrot roots. When you eat strawberries, you get the energy that was stored in the fruit and seeds of the strawberry plants.

In fact, you and every animal on Earth depend on plants. Even animals that eat only other animals depend on plants. Without plants, animals such as deer and rabbits, which eat only plants, would starve. Then animals such as wolves, which eat deer and rabbits, would have nothing to eat. They, too, would starve.

The energy from sunlight moves from plants, to animals that eat plants, to animals that eat other animals. Without sunlight, every living thing on Earth would die.

 MAIN IDEA AND DETAILS Define the terms *producer* and *consumer*.

These bison get the energy they need by eating grasses. Without plants, the bison couldn't survive.

Focus Skill

1. MAIN IDEA AND DETAILS Draw and complete the graphic organizer.

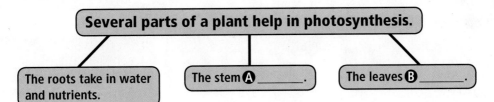

Several parts of a plant help in photosynthesis.

The roots take in water and nutrients.

The stem **A** _____.

The leaves **B** _____.

2. SUMMARIZE Write two sentences that explain what this lesson is about.

3. DRAW CONCLUSIONS What would happen if all plants had the same kind of roots?

4. VOCABULARY Make a crossword puzzle, including clues, using this lesson's vocabulary terms. Then exchange puzzles with a partner, and solve his or her puzzle.

Test Prep

5. Critical Thinking How would Earth's atmosphere change if plants stopped carrying out photosynthesis?

6. Which gas do plants need for photosynthesis?

A. carbon dioxide
B. carbon monoxide
C. nitrogen
D. oxygen

Links

Writing

Narrative Writing

Write a **myth** that "explains" a concept in this lesson, such as why plants have roots, why some leaves change color in the fall, or why animals depend on plants. Illustrate your story.

Math

Make a Table

Suppose you want to conduct a two-week experiment to see how different amounts of sunlight affect five sunflower seedlings. Make a table that you could use to record your results.

Language Arts

Word Meanings

Identify the parts of the word *photosynthesis*. Explain how the parts' meanings relate to the fact that plants make their own food. Then list at least three other words that have one of the word parts found in *photosynthesis*.

 For more links and activities, go to **www.hspscience.com**

How Is Energy Passed Through an Ecosystem?

Fast Fact

Bear Chow Bears eat just about anything. A bear weighing 91 kg (200 lb) can eat more than 13 kg (29 lb) of salmon in one day. Or it might eat nearly 32 kg (70 lb) of berries or apples. In the Investigate, you will classify and order organisms that eat one another.

Ordering What Eats What

Materials
- index cards
- markers
- pushpins
- bulletin board
- yarn

Procedure

1. You will be assigned an organism. On an index card, draw it, write its name, or both.

2. Do some research to classify your organism. Is it a producer, a plant-eating consumer, or a meat-eating consumer? Is it a consumer that eats both plants and meat? Or is it an organism that gets its energy from the remains of dead organisms?

3. Work with members of your group to put your cards in an order that shows what eats what.

4. Pin your team's cards in order on the bulletin board. Connect your cards with yarn to show what eats what. Then use yarn to show which of your team's organisms eat organisms from other teams.

Draw Conclusions

1. Classify each organism on your group's cards. In which group does each belong?

2. **Inquiry Skill** When scientists order things, they better understand relationships between them. Could you put your team's cards in another order? Why or why not? Which card must always be first? Which card must always be last?

Step 1

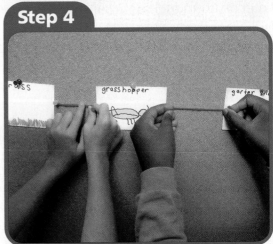

Step 4

Investigate Further

Draw the order of organisms that eat one another in the ocean. Share your drawing with the class.

Reading in Science

VOCABULARY

ecosystem p. 278
herbivore p. 278
carnivore p. 278
food chain p. 279
decomposer p. 279
food web p. 280
energy pyramid p. 283

SCIENCE CONCEPTS

▶ how food energy is passed from plant to animal to animal in an ecosystem
▶ how food chains make up food webs

 READING FOCUS SKILL

SEQUENCE Look for the order of events in the transfer of energy.

Energy Transfer

You read that plants make their own food through the process of photosynthesis. So do a few other organisms, such as algae and lichens (LY•kuhnz). Plants are the main producers in most land ecosystems.

An **ecosystem** (EE•koh•sis•tuhm) includes all the organisms in an area and the environment in which they live. This is a tundra ecosystem. All the organisms shown here are part of a tundra ecosystem. An ecosystem includes many kinds of organisms.

Some tundra animals, like caribou, eat plants and other producers. The food energy stored in the reindeer moss is transferred to the caribou. An animal that eats plants or other producers is an **herbivore**. Herbivores are also called first-level consumers.

Other tundra animals, such as wolves, don't eat plants. They get their energy by eating other animals, like caribou. Food energy stored in the caribou is transferred to the wolf. An animal that eats mainly other animals is a **carnivore**. Carnivores are also called second-level consumers.

Reindeer moss, a lichen, makes food by photosynthesis. The food energy is stored in the organism.

The caribou gets its energy by eating reindeer moss.

Some animals, called *omnivores,* eat both plants and other animals. Omnivores can be first-level or second-level consumers. The bear shown on the first page of the lesson is an omnivore. So are most people.

In another ecosystem, a large carnivore, such as a hawk, might eat a smaller carnivore, such as a snake. That makes the hawk a third-level consumer. Each time something eats something else, food energy is transferred from one organism to the next. The transfer of food energy between organisms is called a **food chain**.

When plants and animals die, what happens to the food energy stored in their remains? The remains are broken down and the food energy is used by decomposers. A **decomposer** is a consumer that gets its food energy by breaking down the remains of dead organisms. Decomposers can be animals, such as earthworms. Many decomposers are fungi. Others are single-celled organisms—protists or bacteria.

Decomposers use some of the nutrients as food. The rest become mixed into the soil. Then plant roots can take up these nutrients. In this way, decomposers connect both ends of a food chain.

You know that all the organisms in an ecosystem depend on producers to make food. Then food energy is transferred through the ecosystem from one consumer level to another. All along the way, decomposers get energy from the remains of dead organisms. Any nutrients not used are returned to the soil.

Focus Skill **SEQUENCE** What can happen next to food energy taken in by a second-level consumer?

The wolf gets the energy it needs by eating caribou.

When the moss, caribou, and wolf die, decomposers break down their remains. Then the reindeer moss and other producers can take up any remaining nutrients.

Food Webs

You know that most animals eat more than one kind of food. For example, a hawk might eat a mouse that ate seeds. The same hawk might also eat a small snake that ate grasshoppers and other insects. The insects, in turn, might have eaten grass. An organism, such as the hawk, can be a part of several food chains. In this way, food chains overlap. A **food web** shows the relationships among different food chains.

Carnivores eat herbivores, omnivores, and sometimes other carnivores. Carnivores also

Prairie Food Web

The producers in this prairie ecosystem include grasses, clover, and purple coneflowers. First-level consumers, or herbivores, include insects, mice, ground squirrels, and bison. Second-level and third-level consumers—carnivores— include spiders, snakes, and hawks. The decomposers that you can see are mushrooms. What you can't see are the millions of single-celled decomposers. They are in the soil, helping recycle nutrients.

Pond Food Web

In this pond ecosystem, the producers include water plants and algae. Here the first-level consumers, or herbivores, include insects and tadpoles. Second-level and third-level consumers include fish. Some of the birds, such as ducks, are herbivores, while others are carnivores. The turtle is an omnivore, eating insects, tiny fish, and plants. The water is full of decomposers, such as snails, worms, and single-celled protists.

limit the number of animals below them in a food web. For example, without snakes, the number of mice in the prairie ecosystem would keep increasing. In time, the mice would eat all the available food. Then the mice would starve, and so would hawks, which eat mice.

Organisms in an ecosystem depend on one another for survival. A change in the number of one kind of organism can affect the entire ecosystem!

SEQUENCE If all the mosquitoes in a pond died, what might happen next?

Energy Pyramid

Not all the food energy of plants is passed on to the herbivores that eat them. Producers use about 90 percent of the food energy they produce for their own life processes. They store the other 10 percent in their leaves, stems, roots, fruits, and seeds.

Animals that eat the producers get only 10 percent of the energy the producers made. These herbivores then use for their life processes 90 percent of the energy they got from the producers. They store the other 10 percent in their bodies.

Math in Science
Interpret Data

Suppose the grasses at the base of this energy pyramid produce 100,000 kilocalories of energy. How many kilocalories would be passed to each of the other levels?

The owl is a third-level consumer. It takes a lot of grass, locusts, and snakes to provide the owl with the energy it needs.

Owl

The snakes are second-level consumers. They pass on to the owl only 10 percent of the energy they receive from the locusts.

Snakes

The locusts are first-level consumers. They pass on to the snakes only 10 percent of the energy they receive from the grasses.

Locusts

The grasses are producers. They pass on to the locusts only 10 percent of the energy they produce.

Grasses

An **energy pyramid** shows that each level of a food chain passes on less food energy than the level before it. Most of the energy in each level is used at that level. Only a little energy is passed on to the next level.

Because each level passes so little energy to the next, the first-level consumers need many producers to support them. In the same way, the second-level consumers need many first-level consumers to support them. This pattern continues up to the top of the food chain.

That's why the base of an energy pyramid is so wide. That's also why only one or two animals are at the top of the pyramid.

Most food chains have only three or four levels. If there were more, a huge number of producers would be needed at the base of the pyramid! Sometimes, things in the environment may cause the number of organisms at one level of the pyramid to change. Then the whole food chain is affected. Suppose a drought kills most of the grasses in an area. Then some of the first-level consumers will starve. Many second-level and third-level consumers will go hungry, too.

Suppose people cut down a forest to provide space for houses. The second-level and third-level consumers may not be able to find enough small animals to eat, so they may leave that ecosystem. With fewer carnivores to eat them, the number of small animals will increase over time. If there isn't enough food for their larger numbers, many will starve.

When a change in numbers occurs at any level of a food chain, the entire chain will be affected.

 SEQUENCE What can happen to a food chain if the number of second-level consumers increases?

Insta-Lab

A Tale of Two Pyramids

Compare the energy pyramid with this pyramid that was once used to classify foods. How are they alike? How are they different? Who are the consumers at each level of the food pyramid?

Natural Cycles

Most ecosystems depend on the water cycle to provide plants with the water they need for photosynthesis. Other cycles affect ecosystems, too.

For example, nitrogen also has a cycle. Nitrogen compounds are important for all living organisms. Nitrogen is a gas that makes up most of Earth's atmosphere. Before nitrogen gas can be used as a nutrient, it must be changed to a form that plants can take up through their roots.

Some nitrogen is changed, or fixed, by lightning. Lightning burns air, producing nitrogen-rich compounds that dissolve in rain. Plant roots can absorb these compounds. Bacteria found in some plant roots also change nitrogen gas into compounds that plants can use.

When a plant or animal dies and decays, nitrogen returns to the soil. Animal wastes also contain nitrogen. Decomposers change these wastes and remains of organisms into the nitrogen compounds plants need.

Carbon and oxygen also have a cycle. You learned that plants use carbon dioxide to make food and that they release oxygen as a byproduct. Plants and animals use this oxygen and release more carbon dioxide.

Carbon is stored in organisms, too. Burning wood, coal, and natural gas releases carbon dioxide into the air.

SEQUENCE What part do decomposers play in the nitrogen cycle?

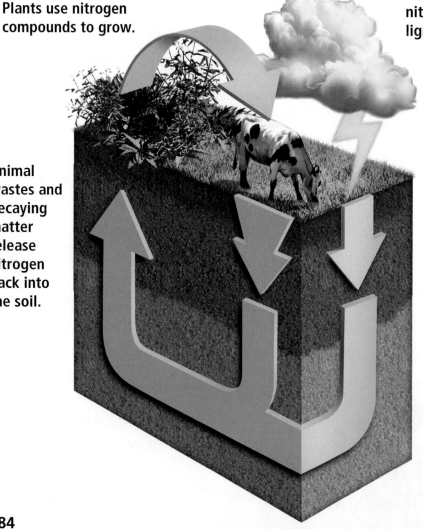

Plants use nitrogen compounds to grow.

A small amount of nitrogen is "fixed" by lightning.

Animals eat plants that contain nitrogen compounds.

Animal wastes and decaying matter release nitrogen back into the soil.

Bacteria in nodules (NAH•joolz), or lumps, on some plant roots change nitrogen into a form plants can use.

1. **SEQUENCE** Draw and complete this graphic organizer. Put the organisms in an order that forms a food chain, ending with a decomposer.

bear   grass   grasshopper   mushroom   salmon

A _____ → B _____ → C _____ → D _____ → E _____

2. **SUMMARIZE** Write a summary of this lesson, beginning with this sentence: *Energy moves through an ecosystem.*

3. **DRAW CONCLUSIONS** What is your role in a food chain or a food web? Explain your answer.

4. **VOCABULARY** Write a sentence for each of this lesson's vocabulary terms. Leave a blank space in each sentence for the term. Have a partner fill in the correct terms.

Test Prep

5. **Critical Thinking** What is your favorite food? What level of consumer are you for that food?

6. Which of these is **not** essential in a food chain?
   A. decomposer
   B. first-level consumer
   C. producer
   D. second-level consumer

Links

Writing

Expository Writing
Imagine that you have discovered an animal that was thought to be extinct. Write a **paragraph** that describes the animal and explains how it fits into a food web in its ecosystem.

Math

Solve a Problem
An eagle ate 2 fish and received 20 kilocalories of energy. The fish had eaten many insects. How many kilocalories were produced by the plants that the insects ate?

Social Studies

Food Choices
In some parts of the world, meat protein is scarce. Find out what kinds of insects some people eat to add protein to their diets. Present a report to share what you learn.

 For more links and activities, go to **www.hspscience.com**

Trash Man

Chad Pregracke grew up on the banks of the Mississippi River. He spent summers fishing, sailing, water-skiing, and canoeing. When Pregracke was 15, he started working with his brother, a commercial shell diver.

Like a modern-day Tom Sawyer and Huck Finn, the brothers spent their nights camping on river islands and their days combing the pitch-black river bottom for clamshells.

During their travels, Pregracke noticed that the riverbanks were lined with trash. "We're talking refrigerators, barrels, tires. There was this one pile of 50 or 60 barrels that had been there for [more than] 20 years. ... I saw there was a problem, basically in my backyard. And I wanted to do something about it," explained Pregracke.

Taking Action

In addition to collecting clamshells, Pregracke started picking up garbage. He

also wrote letters to local companies requesting donations to launch a river cleanup. When he started in 1997, Pregracke single-handedly cleaned 160 kilometers (100 miles) of the Mississippi River shoreline with community donations and a grant from a local corporation.

Since then, Pregracke's project has grown. He now has a ten-person crew, a fleet of barges and boats, and thousands of volunteers to help keep the Mississippi and other rivers in the United States clean. "There's been a lot of accomplishments, and I've had a lot of help," said Pregracke. "But I feel like I'm just getting started."

Phantom Garbage

Although Pregracke has hauled tons of garbage from the Mississippi, the river is still polluted by a type of waste that can't be picked up with a forklift: runoff.

Rainwater either soaks into the ground or flows over Earth's surface as runoff. Runoff transports ground pollution to rivers, oceans, lakes, and wetlands. Many of the pollutants in runoff come from oil, antifreeze, and gasoline leaked by automobiles; pesticides sprayed on lawns; and fertilizers spread on fields. Other water pollutants include heavy metals, such as iron, copper, zinc, tin, and lead; oil from spills; and sewage.

Water pollution can cause human health problems and harm aquatic ecosystems. An ecosystem is a community of living things and its environment.

Think About It

1. How might runoff pollution affect your drinking water?
2. What can you do to help keep rivers clean?

Did You Know?

- The majority of Americans live within 10 miles of a polluted body of water.

- Water pollution has caused fishing and swimming to be prohibited in 40 percent of the nation's rivers, lakes, and coastal waters.

- Your own daily habits can help reduce water pollution. For more information, visit the U.S. Environmental Protection Agency's water Web site for kids.

 Find out more! Log on to **www.hspscience.com**

Looking for Trouble

Most people think of marine biologists as swimming in the open ocean, studying whales or sharks. Fu Lin Chu is a marine biologist, but the animals she studies are usually a lot smaller than a whale and can be found in the creeks and shallow areas of the Chesapeake Bay, on the east coast of the United States.

Chu works at the Virginia Institute of Marine Science. She spends most of her time studying shellfish and how they are affected by their environment. This is especially important research in the Chesapeake Bay region, where oysters, a type of shellfish, are in trouble because of pollution and overfishing.

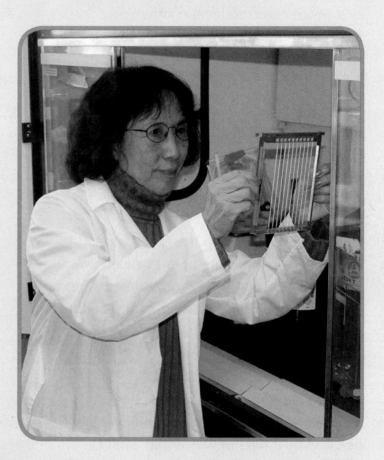

Career Lab Technician

When water samples from field research are sent to the laboratory, they are not just thrown under a microscope and analyzed. Samples have to be catalogued, prepared, and tested. Lab technicians usually are given specific instructions by scientists about how to test or analyze a sample.

Quick and Easy Project

Clover's Secret

Materials
- clover plant
- trowel
- outside faucet or hose

Procedure

1. Find in a field a clover plant at least 15 cm (6 in.) tall. Get permission to dig it up.
2. Use the trowel to dig up the soil around the plant. Then carefully lift the roots out of the soil.
3. Gently shake the loose soil off the roots. Then use water to rinse off the rest of the soil.
4. Look for light-colored lumps on the roots. These lumps are nodules. They contain bacteria that change nitrogen gas from the air into nitrogen compounds that plants can use.

Draw Conclusions

How does nitrogen gas reach the nodules? Are the bacteria in the nodules helpful or harmful? Explain. How do the nodules affect any plants growing around the clover plant?

Design Your Own Investigation

Sweaty Leaves

You read in Lesson 1 that plant leaves can lose water vapor through their stomata. How could you use a green plant and a plastic bag to show that this happens? Design an experiment. Write down the steps you will use to carry it out. Then do your experiment. Be sure to get permission before using someone else's plant. After observing what happens and recording your findings, draw some conclusions about your results.

Review and Test Preparation

Vocabulary Review

Use the terms below to complete the sentences. The page numbers tell you where to look in the chapter if you need help.

producers p. 274   **decomposers** p. 279
herbivores p. 278   **food web** p. 280
food chain p. 279   **energy pyramid** p. 283

1. To survive, all consumers rely on
   _____.

2. Nutrients are returned to the soil by
   _____.

3. Animals that eat producers are _____.

4. Grass-insect-bird-hawk is an example of
   a _____.

5. The fact that each level of a food chain
   passes on less food energy than the
   level before it is shown in an _____.

6. The relationship among different food
   chains in an ecosystem is a _____.

Check Understanding

Write the letter of the best choice.

7. Which of the following is the process
   in which stomata release water from a
   leaf?
   A. chlorophyll
   B. photosynthesis
   C. respiration
   D. transpiration

8. Which of the following is the substance
   that enables a leaf to use sunlight to
   produce food?
   F. chlorophyll
   G. photosynthesis
   H. respiration
   J. transpiration

9. How much energy is passed from each
   level of an energy pyramid to the next?
   A. 10 percent
   B. 20 percent
   C. 80 percent
   D. 90 percent

10. **SEQUENCE** To which group do
    herbivores pass their energy?
    F. first-level consumers
    G. plants
    H. producers
    J. second-level consumers

11. **MAIN IDEA AND DETAILS** What is the
    source of all food energy on Earth?
    A. decomposers
    B. herbivores
    C. producers
    D. carnivores

12. Which process produces most of the
    oxygen in Earth's atmosphere?
    F. burning
    G. photosynthesis
    H. respiration
    J. transpiration

13. Which of these is **not** a consumer?

   A. caribou   **C.** owl

   B. mouse   **D.** reindeer moss

14. The relationships between organisms in an ecosystem can be shown in many ways. Which way is shown here?

   F. energy pyramid

   G. food chain

   H. food pyramid

   J. food web

15. Which gas does photosynthesis produce?

   A. ammonia

   B. carbon dioxide

   C. nitrogen

   D. oxygen

16. Which of the following must plants have for photosynthesis?

   F. soil   **H.** warmth

   G. stems   **J.** water

Inquiry Skills

17. Which three of the organisms below should be **classified** in the same group? Explain your answer.

18. Kendra will perform an experiment in which she cuts the stem of a sunflower and then puts the stem into the soil. **Predict** what will happen, and explain why.

Critical Thinking

19. Not all producers are plants. Some protists are also producers. How can you tell by looking at a protist whether it is a producer?

20. The diagram shows a sequence of four organisms.

grass ➡ grasshopper ➡ snake ➡ hawk

   Part A What does the direction of the arrows tell you?

   Part B If this were part of a food web, would more arrows point toward the second-level consumer or away from the second-level consumer? Explain.

Chapter 9

Ecosystems and Change

Lesson 1 How Do Organisms Compete and Survive in an Ecosystem?

Lesson 2 How Do Ecosystems Change over Time?

Lesson 3 How Do People Affect Ecosystems?

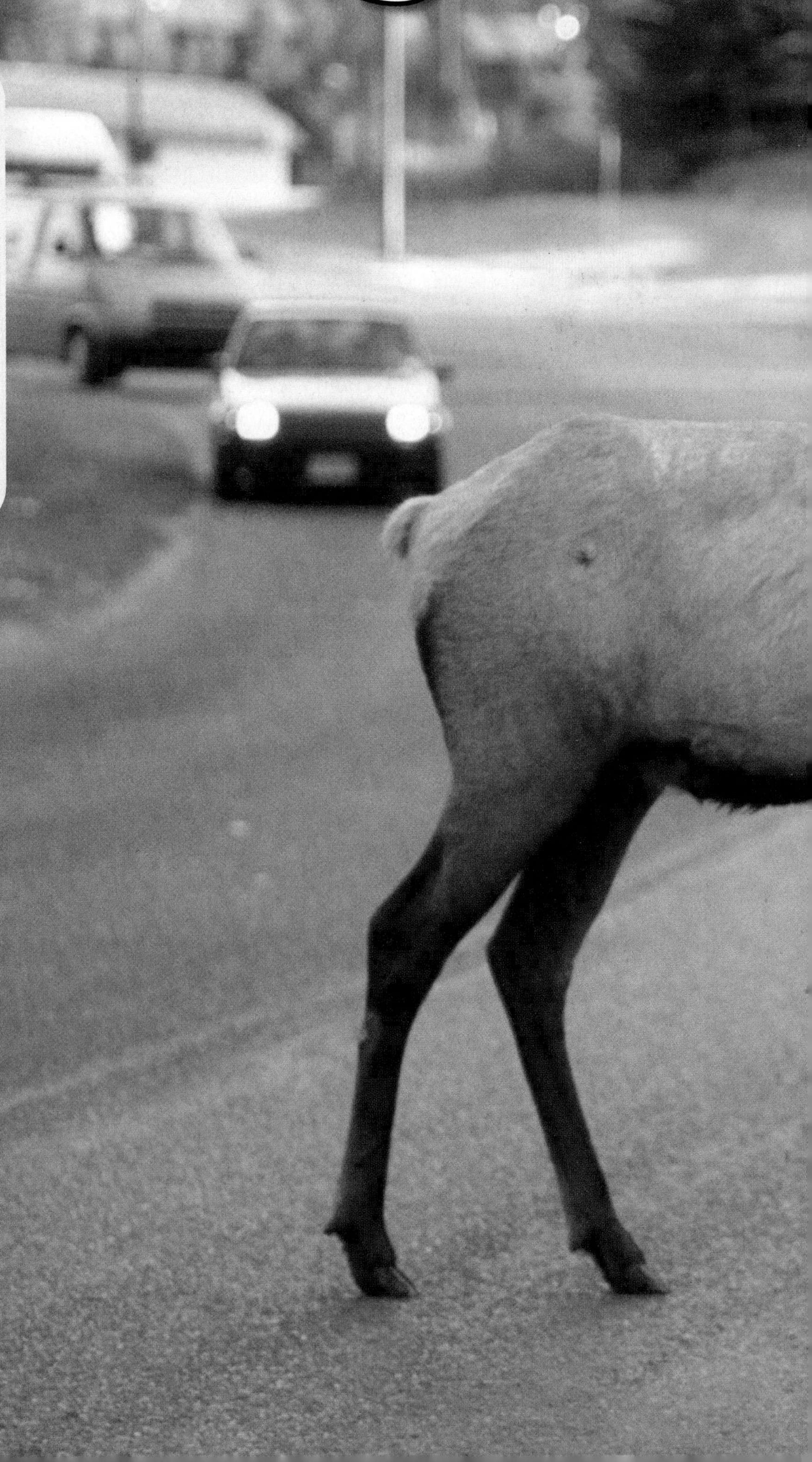

Vocabulary

population
community
competition
adaptation
symbiosis
predator
prey
succession
extinction
pollution
acid rain
habitat
conservation
reclamation

What do YOU wonder?

Many animals share their ecosystems with people. Here an elk is searching for food and water in a neighborhood. How might the neighborhood—a dramatic change in the natural ecosystem of elk—affect the survival of these animals?

How Do Organisms Compete and Survive in an Ecosystem?

Fast Fact

That's Fast! This chameleon's tongue shoots out at about 21.6 km/hr (13.4 mi/hr)! This enables the chameleon to catch fast-moving insects. It can even zap insects more than one and a half body lengths away. In the Investigate, you'll find out how some insects avoid being captured, even by chameleons.

Using Color to Hide

Materials
- hole punch
- red, blue, green, and yellow sheets of acetate
- large green cloth
- clock or watch with a second hand

Procedure

1. Make a table like the one shown.

2. Using the hole punch, make 50 small "insects" from each color of acetate.

3. Predict which color would be the easiest and which would be the hardest for a bird to find in grass. Record your predictions.

4. Spread the green cloth on the floor, and randomly scatter the insects over it.

5. At the edge of the cloth, kneel with your group. In 15 seconds, each of you should pick up as many insects as you can, one at a time.

6. Count the number of each color your group collected. Record the data in the table.

7. Repeat Steps 5 and 6 three more times. Then total each column.

Draw Conclusions

1. Which color did you predict would be easiest to find? Which color was collected most often? Least often? Why?

2. **Inquiry Skill** Scientists predict what they expect to happen and then observe what happens. Predict what might happen to green insects if the grass turns brown.

Step 2

Number of Insects Found			
	Red	Blue	Green	Yellow
Hunt 1				
Hunt 2				
Hunt 3				
Hunt 4				
Total				

Investigate Further

Predict how different body shapes might help insects hide in grass. Then plan an investigation to test your prediction.

Reading in Science

VOCABULARY
population p. 296
community p. 296
competition p. 297
adaptation p. 297
symbiosis p. 298
predator p. 300
prey p. 300

SCIENCE CONCEPTS
▶ how populations depend on and compete with one another
▶ how adaptations help plants and animals compete

 READING FOCUS SKILL

MAIN IDEA AND DETAILS Look for details about how organisms interact.

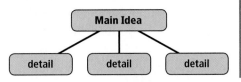

Interactions in Nature

In the last chapter, you learned about different kinds of ecosystems. You also learned that ecosystems include many kinds of plants and animals. All the organisms of one kind in an ecosystem are called a **population**. For example, a pond ecosystem might have populations of frogs, waterlilies, insects, duckweed, and protists.

Populations living and interacting with each other form a **community**. For example, in a pond community, some insects eat plants. Then frogs eat insects.

Another part of an ecosystem is the physical environment, which includes the sun, air, and water. The soil and climate are also part of the environment. Populations interact with the environment. Plants grow in sunlight and take water and nutrients from soil. Fish and frogs live in water that birds and other animals drink.

To survive, each population needs a certain amount of food, water, shelter, and space. The challenge of meeting these

As this water hole dries up, many organisms compete for water.

Competition can take many forms. These moray eels compete for shelter in a coral reef.

Counting the Survivors

This graph shows the average number of young produced and the number that survive the first year. What can you say about survival rates compared to the numbers of young produced?

Survivors

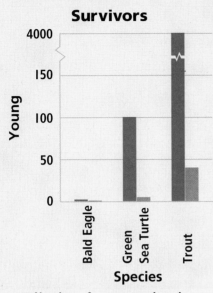

Young (y-axis: 0, 50, 100, 150, 4000)

Species (x-axis: Bald Eagle, Green Sea Turtle, Trout)

- ■ Number of young produced
- ■ Number of young that survive the first year

After sea horses hatch, they are on their own. Many starve or are eaten by other fish. Sea horses have as many as 1000 young, which helps increase their chances of survival.

Some animals have few young, but take care of them after birth. This care helps the young survive.

needs leads to **competition**, a kind of contest among populations.

Populations often compete for the same sources of food. For example, alligators and snapping turtles both eat fish. When there isn't much food, individuals of the same population compete with each other.

In winter, deer compete with each other for food.

Too little food leads to increased competition. Increased competition limits the number of organisms that can share an ecosystem. For this reason, food is a *limiting factor*. It limits the size of a population.

To survive and compete in an ecosystem, animals have developed many kinds of adaptations. An **adaptation** is a characteristic that helps an organism compete in an ecosystem. A turtle survives the winter by burrowing into the mud. A tiger's coloring enables it to sneak up on prey. Some plants smell so bad that animals won't eat them. All of these characteristics are adaptations.

 MAIN IDEA AND DETAILS What do organisms compete for in an ecosystem?

Mistletoe sends its roots into the tree on which it grows. It takes nutrients from the tree. The mistletoe benefits, but the tree is harmed.

▲ The barnacles on this humpback whale eat scraps the whale misses. The barnacles benefit, but the whale is not affected.

Symbiosis

Populations don't always compete with each other. Sometimes a relationship between organisms helps each of them meet basic needs. A relationship between different kinds of organisms is called **symbiosis** (sim•by•OH•SIS).

There are three kinds of symbiosis. In the first kind, both organisms benefit. For example, some ants take care of tiny insects called aphids. The ants guide the aphids to leaves. Then the ants protect the aphids while the aphids eat. When an ant rubs an aphid, the aphid gives off a sweet liquid. The ant drinks this liquid. This relationship, called *mutualism*, helps both the ant and the aphid.

In the second kind of symbiosis, only one organism benefits and the other isn't affected. An example is the relationship between sharks and small fish called remora.

A remora attaches itself to the shark by using a sucker on its head. Being near a shark protects the remora. The remora also eats scraps from the shark's meals. The remora benefits, and the shark isn't affected much. This relationship is called *commensalism*.

Some bacteria in your large intestine have this kind of relationship with you. They feed on the food in your intestine without harming you. Other bacteria help supply you with vitamin K. This relationship is an example of mutualism. You provide food, and the bacteria help keep you well. You both benefit.

In the third kind of symbiosis, called *parasitism*, one organism benefits but the other is harmed. The organism that benefits is called a *parasite*. The organism that is harmed is called a *host*. Parasites steal food

▲ The birds on this rhino are eating insects that bother the rhino. The birds get dinner, and the rhino gets relief from the insects. Both benefit.

from hosts or harm them in some other way. Some parasites release chemicals into the host. In time, these chemicals may kill the host.

Viruses and many one-celled organisms—such as bacteria, some protists, and some fungi—are parasites. They cause diseases such as polio, measles, and influenza. During the Middle Ages, a parasite caused an illness called the Black Plague, which killed about one-third of the population of Europe.

Bacteria and viruses spread as long as they can find hosts. Vaccinations can stop the spread of some of these parasites. When the parasites can't find new hosts, they die.

Roundworms and tapeworms are parasites that live in their hosts' intestines. They absorb food from their hosts, harming or killing them.

The sea lamprey is also a parasite. This eel attaches itself to a fish. Unlike the remora, the lamprey drills a hole into the fish and sucks its blood. The wound often becomes infected.

 MAIN IDEA AND DETAILS Give examples of the three kinds of symbiosis.

Human Symbiosis

With a partner, think of human activities that are examples of symbiosis. Then act out your examples. Have classmates classify the types of symbiosis being acted out.

299

Predator-Prey Relationships

To survive, animals must eat. They must also avoid being eaten. An animal that eats other animals is called a **predator**. For example, hawks and wolves are predators. Animals that are eaten, such as mice and rabbits, are called **prey**.

It's easy to see why predators need prey. However, prey need predators, too. Otherwise, prey populations would grow very large. Then the prey would have to compete with each other to meet their basic needs. Many would end up starving.

The number of prey and the number of predators are closely related. Any change in one leads to a change in the other. For example, if a prey animal's food supply increases, it will be easier for more prey to survive long enough to reproduce. More prey means more food for predators, so the number of predators goes up, too.

On the other hand, a drought might kill much of the grass and other plants in an ecosystem. Then the number of prey that eat the plants is likely to drop. Soon the ecosystem will have fewer predators, too.

Predators help keep the number of prey in balance. For example, wolves keep the deer in some ecosystems to a manageable number. If there were too many deer, they might eat all of the available food. Then more deer would die of starvation than from the attacks of wolves.

 MAIN IDEA AND DETAILS What symbiotic relationship is most like a predator-prey relationship?

The cheetah's markings keep it hidden until it gets close to its prey—an antelope. Then the predator's speed enables it to chase down its prey. ▼

1. MAIN IDEA AND DETAILS Draw this graphic organizer, and add the missing details.

> Organisms depend on and compete with one another.

A Two examples of mutualism:

_____

_____

B Four things that organisms compete for to meet their needs:

_____
_____
_____
_____

2. SUMMARIZE Write a summary of this lesson by using the vocabulary terms in a paragraph.

3. DRAW CONCLUSIONS A certain forest is home to a large number of hawks. What does this tell you about the number of mice and other small animals that live there?

4. VOCABULARY Use the lesson vocabulary terms to create a quiz that uses matching.

Test Prep

5. Critical Thinking What are three of the populations in an ecosystem near you?

6. Which of these is an adaptation that helps a skunk defend itself against predators?

A. its stripe   **C.** its odor

B. its tail   **D.** its size

Links

Writing

Expository Writing
You have discovered a new kind of organism in a rain forest. Write a brief **description** explaining how this organism meets its needs. Include any symbiotic relationships it has.

Math

Solve a Problem
For a certain fish, only 5 of every 100 eggs hatch and survive to adulthood. If this fish lays 5,000 eggs, how many will become adults?

Health

Parasites
Learn more about the parasites that affect people, such as tapeworms or the viruses that cause smallpox or influenza. Then, in an oral or written report, share what you learned.

 For more links and activities, go to www.hspscience.com

How Do Ecosystems Change over Time?

Fast Fact

Missing Marshes Many of the world's ecosystems are changing. Salt marshes like this one are quickly disappearing. By 2025, two-thirds of Africa's farmable land will be too dry for growing crops. In the Investigate, you'll model how an ecosystem can change from a pond into dry land.

Observing Changes

Materials
- ruler
- potting soil
- plastic dishpan
- water
- duckweed
- birdseed

Procedure

1. Make a model of a pond by spreading 5 cm of potting soil in the dishpan. Dig out a low space in the center, leaving 1 cm of soil. Pile up soil around the low space to make sides about 10 cm high.

2. Slowly pour water into the low spot until the water is 4 cm deep. Put duckweed in the "pond."

3. Sprinkle birdseed over the soil. Do not water it. Make a drawing or take a photograph to record how your pond looks.

4. After three or four days, measure and record the depth of the water in the pond. Record how the pond looks now.

5. Sprinkle more birdseed over the soil, and water it lightly.

6. Wait three or four more days, and observe how your pond has changed. Measure and record the depth of the water. Compare your three observations.

Draw Conclusions

1. What caused the changes you observed?

2. **Inquiry Skill** Scientists often make models and observe changes, just as you did. Which of the changes you observed might occur in a real pond? What other changes do you think might occur in a real pond?

Step 1

Step 3

Investigate Further

Make a model of another ecosystem, such as a forest floor. If possible, include some insects. Observe and record the changes that take place over time.

Reading in Science

VOCABULARY
succession p. 304
extinction p. 308

SCIENCE CONCEPTS
▶ how changes in ecosystems affect the organisms there
▶ how these changes can cause the extinction of some organisms

 READING FOCUS SKILL

CAUSE AND EFFECT Look for the causes of changes in ecosystems.

Primary Succession

Ecosystems change every day, but the changes are usually too slow to notice. Some organisms die out, while others start to thrive. A gradual change in the kinds of organisms living in an ecosystem is called **succession**. Unlike the changes you observed in the Investigate, succession in nature can take thousands of years.

What causes succession? One cause is a change in climate. When a region becomes drier, for example, some of the organisms that live there will no longer be able to meet their needs. If fewer plants survive in the dry climate, herbivores will have to move to find food or they'll die. A loss of herbivores leads to a loss of predators. Meanwhile, plants and animals that can live with less water begin to thrive. They will slowly replace the organisms that cannot live in the drier climate.

Succession can also be caused by the organisms living in an ecosystem. For example, a large herd of deer can kill many trees by eating too many leaves. Then the deer and other animals in the ecosystem

Primary Succession

①

At the edge of a pond, plants trap soil in their roots. As the plants die and decay, the soil gains nutrients.

②

More plants begin to grow in the rich new soil at the edge of the pond. The pond is starting to get smaller.

can no longer find enough food or shelter. To survive, they must move to a new area. With fewer small animals to eat, the predators also leave or die. Because fewer trees shade the forest floor, plants that thrive in the sun begin to grow. Much of the ecosystem has changed.

Adding new plants or animals to an ecosystem is another cause of succession. For example, a vine called *kudzu* has taken over many ecosystems of the southern United States. Kudzu was brought to the United States from Japan in 1876. Farmers were paid to plant it because, they were told, kudzu could control erosion and feed animals.

The climate of the South was perfect for kudzu. It could grow 30 cm (1 ft) a day! Soon this vine was everywhere. It killed whole forests by climbing on trees and preventing sunlight from reaching the trees' leaves. In 1972, kudzu was declared to be a weed. By then, it had affected many ecosystems in the South by changing both the plants and the animals that lived there.

Succession can be primary or secondary. *Primary succession* begins with bare rock. The first plants to grow, such as lichens, are called *pioneer plants*. Lichens can grow without soil, and they can survive harsh conditions. As they grow, lichens produce chemicals that help weather the rock they grow on. In time, a thin layer of soil forms, allowing mosses to grow.

As mosses grow and die, they add nutrients to the thin soil. Soon grass seeds begin to sprout. Then birds and other animals come to eat the grasses and their seeds. The animals' droppings add more nutrients to the soil. When the soil is deep enough and rich enough, larger plants, including trees, begin to grow. In time, the ecosystem becomes stable, and changes stop. The result is known as a *climax community*.

Focus Skill **CAUSE AND EFFECT** **What are three causes of succession?**

The pond ecosystem continues to grow smaller, while the land ecosystem grows larger.

Small shrubs now grow where the pond was. In time, they will be replaced by larger trees.

Secondary Succession

Rebirth of a Forest

1. Fire destroys all the organisms living above ground.

2. Roots that survive underground and seeds blown in by the wind begin to sprout, forming new plants.

Secondary Succession

Secondary succession helps rebuild damaged ecosystems. This kind of succession occurs in places that already have soil. It often happens after a forest fire or a volcanic eruption has destroyed the original ecosystem.

Primary succession is a very slow process. Secondary succession is not. It happens quickly because soil is already there and the soil usually contains many seeds. Animals and wind bring in more seeds. Some roots of original plants survive underground, and they start sending up new shoots. In secondary succession, as with primary succession, the first plants are hardy. But they don't have to be as hardy as those growing on bare rock. The soil is deep enough for strong roots, and ashes from burned trees add nutrients to the soil.

You might have heard about eruptions of Mount St. Helens in Washington State. This volcano exploded on May 18, 1980, covering the mountain with a thick layer of ash and mud. Yet by the summer of 1981, the mountainside bloomed with pink fireweed flowers. A few years later, shrubs began to grow there. Many insects, birds, and other animals have already returned. Now you can find young fir trees on the mountain's slopes. Even with more eruptions, a mature forest will one day cover Mount St. Helens again.

3. New growth appears among the blackened tree trunks. Many insects and other small animals return to the forest.

 For more links and activities, go to **www.hspscience.com**

Where secondary succession occurs, there is also some primary succession. Secondary succession cannot occur without primary succession. You can find bare rock after a volcanic eruption. Fire, followed by erosion of the soil, also uncovers bare rock. Lichens would begin growing on the rock. Mosses would grow next, and so on, until the ecosystem of the bare rock would be the same as that restored by secondary succession. But this may take hundreds of years. Remember, primary succession happens very slowly.

CAUSE AND EFFECT What is the main result of primary succession and of secondary succession?

Insta-Lab

Regrowth
Make a drawing showing regrowth of a climax community in an area that has had a fire, a flood, a volcano, or other natural disaster. Be sure to include several stages of secondary succession in your drawing.

Extinction

Sometimes changes in an ecosystem cause the extinction of an entire species. **Extinction** is the death of all the organisms of a species.

Many organisms can adapt to slow changes in an ecosystem. But some cannot. When an environment changes, some organisms living in it will die. Plants and some animals can't move to other ecosystems to meet their needs.

A species with just a few small populations in different places is more likely to become extinct than a species with many large populations. A population that lives in a small area, such as on a remote island, is in more danger than a population spread out over a large area. Any change in the island environment could wipe out an entire population.

An environmental change can be so great that it affects many populations of different species. You might know that most dinosaurs became extinct about 65 million years ago. But did you know that more than 70 percent of all the other organisms on Earth were also wiped out? This mass extinction was probably due to a drastic change in the worldwide climate.

Some scientists hypothesize that the cause may have been a huge meteor. It may have thrown up a dust cloud so big that it blocked out the sun. Some plants died, followed by many herbivores and most carnivores. Of course, most changes in ecosystems are more gradual.

Many human actions, too, can lead to extinctions. You'll learn more about that in the next lesson.

 CAUSE AND EFFECT How can a change in climate cause extinctions?

Beginning 40,000 years ago, thousands of plants and animals became trapped in tar that rose to Earth's surface. Fossils of nearly 200 kinds of organisms, including saber-toothed cats, have been identified in the La Brea tar pits in California. ▼

Saber-toothed cats became extinct about 11,000 years ago. The cause was probably climate change or hunting.

1. CAUSE AND EFFECT Draw and complete these graphic organizers. For B–D, describe three causes of the same effect.

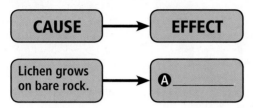

CAUSE	→	EFFECT

Lichen grows on bare rock. → Ⓐ _____

CAUSE	→	EFFECT

Ⓑ _____

Ⓒ _____

Ⓓ _____

Succession occurs.

2. SUMMARIZE Write two sentences to summarize this lesson.

3. DRAW CONCLUSIONS How are pioneer plants different from plants in a climax community?

4. VOCABULARY Write a paragraph using each vocabulary term twice.

Test Prep

5. Critical Thinking Describe ways that people affect succession.

6. Which of these is the final result of secondary succession?

A. adaptation

B. rebuilt ecosystem

C. competition

D. final extinction

Links

Writing

Narrative Writing

Choose a wild area or park near you. Write a **description** of its present stage of succession. Describe how human activities have influenced its natural succession.

Math

Make an Estimate

Florida is 65,700 sq mi in area. Texas covers 268,600 sq mi. Florida has 111 species in danger of extinction. Texas has 91. Which state has more endangered species per square mile?

Art

Succession

Use any kind of media to illustrate the stages of primary or secondary succession. Set the succession in a certain climate, and research the plants that should be shown.

 For more links and activities, go to **www.hspscience.com**

How Do People Affect Ecosystems?

Fast Fact

Too Much Paper! More than 40 percent of the trash in this landfill is paper! Despite widespread recycling programs, paper is still the most common item tossed in the trash. Unfortunately, paper buried in a landfill is very slow to decay. Newspapers can still be read 40 years after they were buried. In the Investigate, you'll explore how human actions can affect other parts of our ecosystems.

Observing Effects of Fertilizer

Materials
- marker
- 4 jars with lids
- pond water
- dropper
- liquid fertilizer

Procedure

1. Use the marker to number the jars 1–4.

2. Fill each jar with the same amount of pond water.

3. Use the dropper to put 10 drops of liquid fertilizer in Jar 1, 20 drops in Jar 2, and 40 drops in Jar 3. Do not put any fertilizer in Jar 4.

4. Put the lids on the jars, and place them in a sunny window.

5. Observe the jars every day for two weeks, and record your observations.

Draw Conclusions

1. Which jar had the most plant growth? Which had the least? What conclusion can you draw about fertilizer and plant growth?

2. As organisms die and decay in water, they use up the oxygen in the water. Which jar do you infer will eventually contain the least amount of oxygen? Explain your answer.

3. **Inquiry Skill** Scientists identify and control variables in their experiments so they can observe the effect of one variable at a time. Which variables did you control in setting up the four jars? Which variable did you change?

Step 1

Step 3

Investigate Further

Suppose you want to study the effect of sunlight on fertilizer in pond water. Plan an experiment that will identify and control the variables. Then carry out your experiment.

311

Reading in Science

VOCABULARY
pollution p. 312
acid rain p. 312
habitat p. 313
conservation p. 314
reclamation p. 316

SCIENCE CONCEPTS
▶ how people's actions can change the environment
▶ how the environment can be protected and restored

READING FOCUS SKILL

MAIN IDEA AND DETAILS Look for details about how people damage ecosystems.

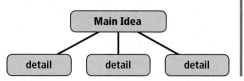

Damaging Ecosystems

In the Investigate, you observed how fertilizer affects pond water. You observed that it speeds up plant growth. But isn't plant growth a good thing?

In time, plants in water will die. As they decay, they will use up oxygen in the water. Without oxygen, any fish living there will also die. The decaying fish will use up still more oxygen.

Decaying organic matter can pollute water. **Pollution** is any waste product that damages an ecosystem. Chemicals used on crops and lawns also pollute water. Heavy rain carries them from the fields to streams, rivers, and lakes.

Air can be polluted, too. Burning fossil fuels, such as coal, oil, and gas, is a major cause of air pollution. Certain chemicals in fossil fuels mix with water vapor in the air. The combination produces acids. When these acids fall to Earth with rain, we call it **acid rain**.

Acid rain can damage trees, crops, and other plants. It has made many bodies of clean-looking water acidic. Acidic water affects organisms differently. For example, it might kill all the small fish in a pond but not harm the larger fish. Then that pond's food chain would be affected.

A strip mine can pollute the groundwater as well as the land.▼

This bear now has to share its ecosystem with people.

Trash threatens wildlife in many ways. Animals can get cut by broken glass or snared by plastic drink-can holders. Small animals can even get trapped inside containers.

▲ Every year, snowmobiles add tons of pollutants to the air in places such as Yellowstone National Park.

Ecosystems can also be damaged by changing them. For example, most of our prairie ecosystems have been turned into farms. Prairies once had many communities. Now most of them are used to grow only one crop.

People fence off many ecosystems. This reduces the size of habitats or forces animals to share habitats with people. A **habitat** is an area where an organism can find everything it needs to survive. Fences make it hard for animals to migrate, or move, to different habitats. Fences also cut through hunting grounds of predators such as mountain lions and wolves.

When people cut down forests for timber, they destroy habitats. Habitats are also destroyed when people fill wetlands to make space for houses and shopping malls.

Sometimes people introduce organisms from other regions, such as the kudzu vine you read about. These organisms crowd out native plants and animals, changing and often damaging the ecosystem.

 MAIN IDEA AND DETAILS What are three ways that people damage ecosystems?

Melting a Sculpture

Make a "sculpture" from a piece of chalk. Use a paper clip to carve the chalk. Then stand the chalk upright in a clay base. Drip vinegar or lemon juice onto your sculpture. How does the vinegar, an acid, affect your sculpture? How is this like acid rain affecting a statue?

313

▲ Beach walkovers help protect the fragile ecosystem of the dunes.

Protecting Ecosystems

Many laws have been passed to protect ecosystems. For example, most wetlands can no longer be filled in. Regulations control how industries can get rid of possible pollutants. New cars must have devices that reduce air pollution. And before developers can build, they must describe how a project might affect the environment.

But laws alone are not enough. Each person can have a role in protecting ecosystems. One way is through the **conservation**, or saving, of resources.

Conservation of resources includes three actions: reduce, reuse, and recycle.

Reduce means "use fewer resources." For example, if you walk or ride your bike instead of riding in a car, you save gasoline. Opening windows instead of turning on an air conditioner helps reduce the amount of coal burned to produce electricity. Burning gasoline and coal also causes acid rain.

Reuse means "use resources again, instead of throwing them away." For example, you can give outgrown clothes and toys to a charity. That way, someone else can use them. You can also use glasses and dishes that can be washed and used again and again. That saves plastic and paper that would be thrown away.

Some items can be reused for a new purpose. For example, a plastic drink bottle can be reused as a planter, a bird feeder, or a funnel. Reusing items saves resources and space in landfills, too.

Recycle means "collect used items so their raw materials can be used again." For example, glass, paper, aluminum, and some plastics can be ground up or melted and made into new products. And recycling often uses less energy than producing the same items from new resources.

Most glass can be recycled. Recycled glass melts at a lower temperature than the resources used to make new glass. Recycling glass requires 30 percent less energy than making new glass.

Nearly all kinds of paper can be recycled. Making new paper from old paper uses 20 percent less energy than making paper from trees. However, paper coated with wax, foil, or plastic is too costly to recycle.

Recycling aluminum helps a lot. Recycling just two cans saves the energy equal to a cup of gasoline. Making a can from recycled aluminum uses only 4 percent of the energy needed to make a can from new resources.

Plastics make up about 10 percent of our waste. Some kinds of plastic are hard to recycle. However, soft-drink bottles are easy. The recycled bottles can be used to make carpeting, boards, new bottles, and many other products.

Reducing, reusing, and recycling save resources and energy. These actions reduce pollution and help protect ecosystems.

 MAIN IDEA AND DETAILS List six ways you can help protect ecosystems.

Juice boxes are hard to recycle because most contain paper, plastic, and aluminum. Pouring juice from a large container into a glass means fewer juice boxes end up in landfills.

Discarded batteries can leak pollutants into the soil. In some states, it is illegal to put batteries in the trash. Instead, use rechargeable batteries.

Old newspapers take up about 13 percent of all the space in landfills. Yet they are easy to recycle into new paper.

Restoring Ecosystems

Damaged ecosystems are not always lost. Some can be cleaned and restored. The process is called **reclamation**. But reclamation is costly and takes time.

Removing pollutants is often part of reclamation. We now know that wetlands can help filter pollutants out of water. Yet the United States has lost most of its wetlands. In the 1970s, builders were filling in 500,000 acres of wetlands a year.

Now the rate of wetland loss has slowed. Many programs are helping to protect remaining wetlands or even to restore them.

For example, many wetlands have been restored along Florida's Gulf Coast. The bays of Fort DeSoto Park, near St. Petersburg, Florida, had become clogged with soil. The water quality was poor. The plants and animals were struggling to survive. Now the water moves freely. This change has also improved water quality in wetlands nearby.

Fragile ecosystems are being restored across the nation. Perhaps there is a reclamation project near you.

 MAIN IDEA AND DETAILS Why are wetlands important in reclamation?

This area used to be a strip mine. The first step in reclaiming a strip mine is removing mining wastes. Then soil must be added to provide a base for trees and plants. Reclamation of a large strip mine can take many years and cost millions of dollars. ▼

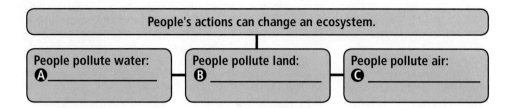

1. MAIN IDEA AND DETAILS Draw and complete this graphic organizer by adding two details to support the main idea.

People's actions can change an ecosystem.

People pollute water:	People pollute land:	People pollute air:
A_____	**B**_____	**C**_____

2. SUMMARIZE Write one sentence that describes three ways people affect ecosystems.

3. DRAW CONCLUSIONS How is conservation different from reclamation?

4. VOCABULARY Make up quiz-show answers for the vocabulary terms. See if a partner knows the correct questions for the answers, such as "What is pollution?"

Test Prep

5. Critical Thinking What specific things can people do to avoid the cost of restoring an ecosystem?

6. Which of these is a cause of acid rain?

   A. burning forests

   B. burning fuels

   C. runoff from farmers' fields

   D. decaying organisms in the water

Links

Writing

Persuasive Writing
Some people think recycling is not worth the effort. Write a **letter** for your school or community newspaper, urging readers to recycle. Try to motivate them to help protect ecosystems.

Math

Make a Pictograph
Make a pictograph showing U.S. recycling rates: cardboard, 70%; newspaper, 60%; aluminum cans, 49%; soft-drink bottles, 36%; glass, 22%.

Literature

Life Preservers
Read about the life of a well-known naturalist, such as Rachel Carson, Henry David Thoreau, John Burroughs, or John Muir. In a written or oral report, share what you learned.

 For more links and activities, go to www.hspscience.com

317

Saving the EVERGLADES

What blood is to the human body, water is to Florida's Everglades. And over the past half-century, the Everglades have been slowly and steadily bleeding to death. In 2001, the federal government passed the Everglades Restoration Act to stop the bleeding and save the Everglades. The restoration will cost more than $8 billion and continue for 30 years.

River of Grass

The Everglades is a slow-moving river that is less than 30 centimeters (1 foot) deep and 80 kilometers (50 miles) wide and covers millions of acres from Lake Okeechobee to Florida Bay. In 1947, the federal government established Everglades National Park. In 1948, Congress ordered the U.S. Army Corps of Engineers to drain large parts of the Everglades outside the park.

The corps began construction on a series of dams and canals that drained hundreds of thousands of acres. That changed the natural flow of water and eventually funneled 6.4 billion liters (1.7 billion gallons) of fresh water into the ocean every day. Builders put up new housing developments, and even whole cities, on drained Everglades.

The canals and other artificial barriers prevented some animal species from migrating. Drainage caused the populations of some wading birds, for instance, to plummet by 90 percent. Chemical and sewage runoff from Florida's growing towns and factories also spilled into natural areas, killing both animals and plants.

Undoing the Damage

The Everglades Restoration Act is aimed at restoring the Everglades to its natural state. One important part of the plan calls for the removal of dams, dikes, and flood-control gates that stop or slow the flow of water. The act also aims to improve water treatment plants. Those plants clean wastewater coming from farms and towns near the Everglades. The improved plants will allow less-polluted water to flow into the Everglades.

Many people, from environmental groups to private citizens, applaud the

The Whole World Is Watching

This is the first time the restoration of an entire ecosystem has been tried.

plan, saying it is a major step in stopping the destruction of a great natural resource.

Think About It

1. Why would the government want to drain wetlands such as the Everglades?
2. Why might it be harmful to change the flow of water in the Everglades?

Find out more! Log on to
www.hspscience.com

319

Working on the River

Most field trips allow students to see cool sights or visit historical places. However, Portia Johnson recently had a chance to spend a day up to her knees in mud helping to protect an important river in Virginia. Portia and her classmates were part of a project organized by the Friends of the Rappahannock.

During the project, students planted seedlings from the school's nursery along eroded sections of the river. The trees will help to keep the riverbank's soil in place and slow down erosion.

The Rappahannock River runs about 184 miles through Virginia until it empties into the Chesapeake Bay. This river is an important source of water and habitat for many plants and animals.

You Can Do It!

Quick and Easy Project

Plant Power

Materials
- 2 pots filled with soil
- 6 beans
- water
- flour

Procedure

1. Plant 3 beans in each pot, and water both pots in the same way.
2. Mix some flour and water until it forms a thick batter.
3. Pour the batter into one pot, covering the soil with a thick layer.
4. Put both pots at a sunny window.
5. Observe the pots for 10 to 14 days. Water the uncovered pot when it feels dry.

Draw Conclusions

What conclusion can you draw from your observations? What variable did you test? What does this experiment tell you about plants' role in restoring damaged ecosystems?

Design Your Own Investigation

Taking Out the Trash

Which kinds of trash decay quickly in a landfill, and which kinds take up space forever? Form a hypothesis. Then check your hypothesis by designing an investigation and carrying it out. For example, you might make a model of a landfill and bury different kinds of trash in it. Be sure to ask for permission before you start your investigation. Also, wear plastic gloves when you check your results.

Review and Test Preparation

Vocabulary Review

Use the terms below to complete the sentences. The page numbers tell you where to look in the chapter if you need help.

competition p. 297   **succession** p. 304
adaptation p. 297   **extinction** p. 308
predators p. 300   **conservation** p. 314
prey p. 300   **reclamation** p. 316

1. Grasses replace mosses in a process called _____.

2. Recycling is one kind of _____.

3. The number of organisms in a population is limited by _____.

4. A hummingbird's long beak is an _____.

5. Cleaning up polluted water is an example of _____.

6. Earthworms can be _____.

7. The death of all earthworms would be an _____.

8. Big cats are usually _____.

Check Understanding

Write the letter of the best choice.

9. How can we reduce the amount of acid rain that falls?
   A. by driving less
   B. by restoring wetlands
   C. by planting more trees
   D. by cleaning up polluted water

10. What forms a community?
    F. symbiotic relationships
    G. several populations
    H. an ecosystem
    J. succession

11. Which of these is usually in the last stage of succession?
    A. bushes   **C.** mosses
    B. lichen   **D.** trees

12. **CAUSE AND EFFECT** Which of these could possibly lead to an extinction?
    F. adaptation   **H.** reclamation
    G. pollution   **J.** symbiosis

13. **MAIN IDEA** Which statement is most accurate?
    A. All ecosystems change in a way that is often gradual.
    B. People cause all the changes in ecosystems.
    C. Succession is a cause of change in ecosystems.
    D. Competition is the main cause of change in ecosystems.

14. Which of these is **not** a predator or prey?

    F. corn

    G. alligator

    H. ant

    J. antelope

15. Which of these is **not** a result of human actions?

    A. acid rain

    B. conservation

    C. extinction

    D. symbiosis

16. What is shown in the photo below?

    F. competition

    G. extinction

    H. succession

    J. symbiosis

Inquiry Skills

17. In an experiment, you water one plant with a certain amount of plain water. You water an identical plant with the same amount of a mixture of vinegar and water. You put both plants in a sunny window. Which **variables are you controlling** in this experiment?

18. Suppose the number of organisms in one population in a community suddenly increases. **Predict** what might happen, and explain why.

Critical Thinking

19. Explain how recycling is like mutualism.

20. Study the photograph below, and answer both questions.

Part A What concept from this chapter does the photograph illustrate?

Part B What organisms probably grew here before this photograph was taken? What kinds of organisms will grow here next?

References

Contents

Health Handbook

Reading in Science Handbook

Math in Science Handbook   R28

Your Skin

Your skin is your body's largest organ. It provides your body with a tough protective covering. It produces sweat to help control your body temperature. It protects you from disease. Your skin also provides your sense of touch that allows you to feel pressure, textures, temperature, and pain.

When you play hard or exercise, your body produces sweat, which cools you as it evaporates. The sweat from your skin also helps your body eliminate excess salts and other wastes.

The skin is the body's largest organ. ▼

Epidermis
Many layers of dead skin cells form the top of the epidermis. Cells in the lower part of the epidermis are always making new cells.

Dermis
The dermis is much thicker than the epidermis. It is made up of tough, flexible fibers.

Hair Follicle
Each hair follicle has a muscle that can contract and make the hair " stand on end."

Pore
These tiny holes on the surface of your skin lead to your dermis.

Oil Gland
Oil glands produce oil that keeps your skin soft and smooth.

Sweat Gland
Sweat glands produce sweat, which contains water, salt, and various wastes.

Fatty Tissue
This tissue layer beneath the dermis stores food, provides warmth, and attaches your skin to underlying bone and muscle.

Caring for Your Skin

- To protect your skin and to keep it healthy, you should wash your body, including your hair and your nails, every day. This helps remove germs, excess oils and sweat, and dead cells from the epidermis, the outer layer of your skin. Because you touch many things during the day, you should wash your hands with soap and water frequently.

- If you get a cut or scratch, you should wash it right away and cover it with a sterile bandage to prevent infection and promote healing.

- Protect your skin from cuts and scrapes by wearing proper safety equipment when you play sports or skate, or when you're riding your bike or scooter.

- Always protect your skin from sunburn by wearing protective clothing and sunscreen when you are outdoors in bright sun.

Your Senses

Eyes

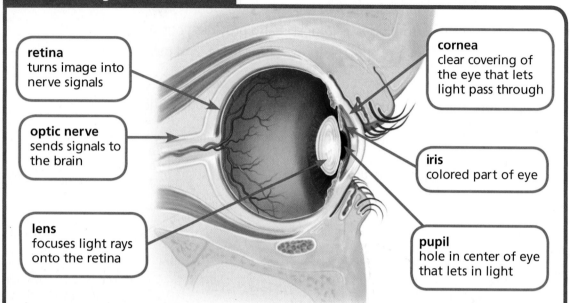

retina
turns image into nerve signals

optic nerve
sends signals to the brain

lens
focuses light rays onto the retina

cornea
clear covering of the eye that lets light pass through

iris
colored part of eye

pupil
hole in center of eye that lets in light

Light rays bounce off objects and enter the eye through the pupil. A lens inside the eye focuses the light rays, and the image of the object is projected onto the retina at the back of the eye. In the retina the image is turned into nerve signals. Your brain analyzes these signals to "tell" you what you're seeing.

Ears

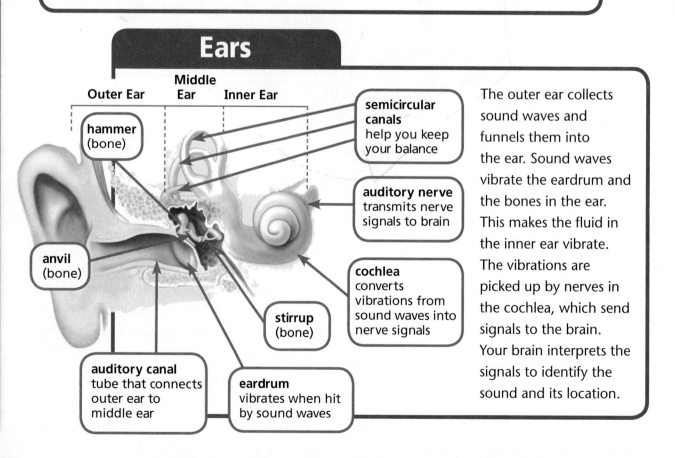

Outer Ear   Middle Ear   Inner Ear

hammer
(bone)

semicircular canals
help you keep your balance

auditory nerve
transmits nerve signals to brain

anvil
(bone)

cochlea
converts vibrations from sound waves into nerve signals

stirrup
(bone)

auditory canal
tube that connects outer ear to middle ear

eardrum
vibrates when hit by sound waves

The outer ear collects sound waves and funnels them into the ear. Sound waves vibrate the eardrum and the bones in the ear. This makes the fluid in the inner ear vibrate. The vibrations are picked up by nerves in the cochlea, which send signals to the brain. Your brain interprets the signals to identify the sound and its location.

Nose

When you breathe in, air is swept upward to nerve cells in the nasal cavity. The nasal cavity is the upper part of the nose, inside the skull. Different nerve cells respond to different chemicals in the air and send signals to your brain.

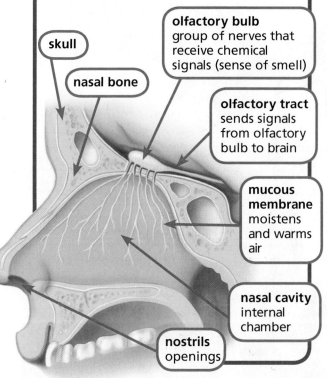

skull

nasal bone

olfactory bulb group of nerves that receive chemical signals (sense of smell)

olfactory tract sends signals from olfactory bulb to brain

mucous membrane moistens and warms air

nasal cavity internal chamber

nostrils openings

Skin

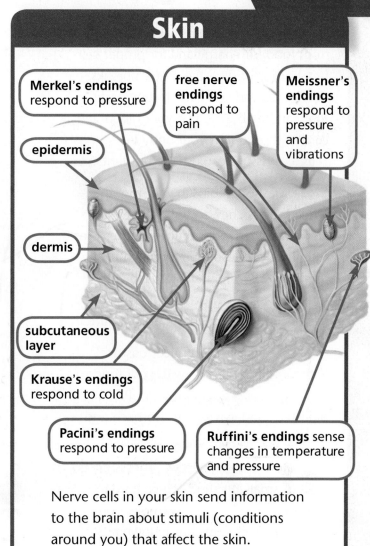

Merkel's endings respond to pressure

free nerve endings respond to pain

Meissner's endings respond to pressure and vibrations

epidermis

dermis

subcutaneous layer

Krause's endings respond to cold

Pacini's endings respond to pressure

Ruffini's endings sense changes in temperature and pressure

Nerve cells in your skin send information to the brain about stimuli (conditions around you) that affect the skin.

Caring for Your Senses

- Injuries to these organs can affect your senses.

- Protect your skin and eyes by wearing sunscreen and sunglasses. Protect your ears from loud sounds. Protect your nose from harsh chemicals and your tongue from hot foods and drinks.

Tongue

The tongue is covered with about 10,000 tiny nerve cells, or taste buds, that detect basic tastes in things you eat and drink. Different taste buds respond to different chemicals and send signals to your brain.

taste buds

Your Digestive System

Your body systems need nutrients from food for energy and for proper cell function. Your digestive system breaks down the food you eat into tiny particles that can be absorbed by your blood and carried throughout your body, so various cells and tissues can use the nutrients.

Digestion begins in your mouth when food is chewed, mixed with saliva, and swallowed. Your tongue pushes the food into your esophagus, which pushes the food down to your stomach with a muscular action, much like the one you use to squeeze toothpaste from a tube.

Your stomach produces gastric juices and mixes them with your food to begin breaking down proteins. Partially digested food leaves your stomach and moves to your small intestine.

Most of the digestive process occurs in your small intestine, where partially digested food is mixed with bile from your liver. This helps break down fats. Your pancreas also produces digestive juices that continue the process of digesting fats and proteins in the small intestine. Your pancreas also produces a special substance called insulin, which helps your body move sugar from your blood into your cells.

As food moves through your small intestine, nutrients are absorbed by the villi and pass into your blood.

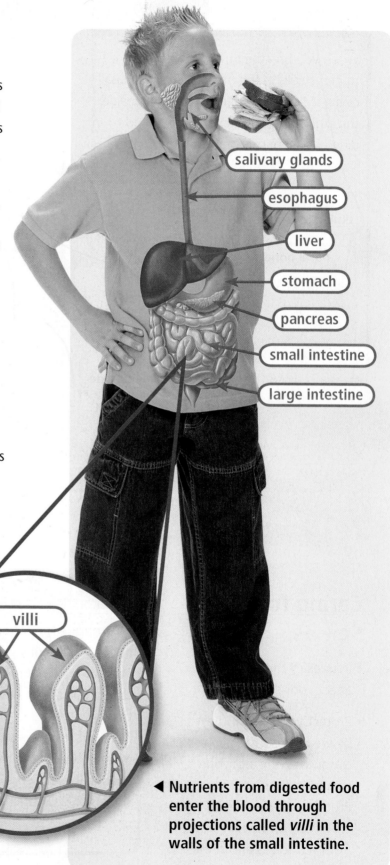

salivary glands

esophagus

liver

stomach

pancreas

small intestine

large intestine

villi

◀ **Nutrients from digested food enter the blood through projections called *villi* in the walls of the small intestine.**

Specialized Digestive Organs

Your liver produces a fluid called bile that helps break down fats. Bile is stored in your gallbladder. During digestion, the stored bile flows through the bile duct into your small intestine, to help with the digestive process.

Material that is not absorbed by your small intestine passes into your large intestine. This organ absorbs water and vitamins from the undigested materials. The remaining solid wastes are stored by your large intestine until it leaves your body.

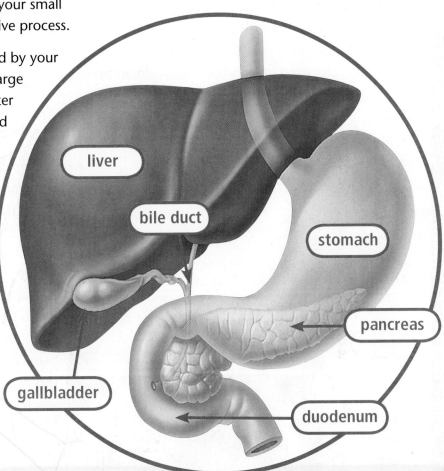

liver

bile duct

stomach

pancreas

gallbladder

duodenum

Caring for Your Digestive System

- Drink plenty of water every day. Water helps move food through your digestive system and helps your body replenish saliva, gastric juices, and bile consumed during digestion.

- Eat a variety of foods, choose a well-balanced diet, and maintain a healthy weight.

- Eat plenty of fruits and vegetables. These foods contain essential nutrients and help your digestive system function effectively.

- Chew your food thoroughly before swallowing.

Your Circulatory System

Your body relies on your circulatory system to deliver essential nutrients and oxygen to your organs, tissues, and cells. These materials are carried by your blood. As it circulates, your blood also removes wastes from your tissues. Your circulatory system includes your heart, arteries that carry oxygen and nutrient-rich blood away from your heart, tiny capillaries that exchange gases and nutrients between your blood and your body's tissues, and veins that carry blood and wastes back to your heart. Your veins have a system of one-way valves that maintains the direction of blood flow within your circulatory system and helps maintain an even distribution of oxygen and nutrients to all parts of your body.

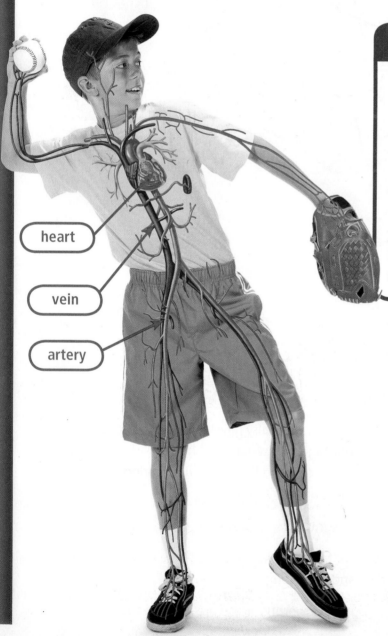

heart

vein

artery

Your Heart

Your heart is a strong, muscular organ that contracts rhythmically to pump blood throughout your circulatory system. When you exercise or work your muscles hard, your heart beats faster to deliver more oxygen and nutrient-rich blood to your muscles. When you rest, your heartbeat slows. Regular exercise helps keep your heart muscle and the rest of your circulatory system strong.

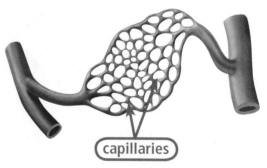

capillaries

▲ Oxygen and nutrients pass from the blood, through capillary walls, and into the cells. Cell wastes pass through capillary walls and into the blood.

Blood Flow and Your Excretory System

Your veins carry blood from your tissues back to your lungs, where carbon dioxide and other waste gases are removed from your red blood cells and expelled when you exhale. Your blood also travels through your kidneys, where small structures called nephrons remove salts and liquid wastes. Urine formed in your kidneys is held in your bladder until it is eliminated. Your liver removes other wastes from your blood, including blood cells. Red blood cells live for only 120 days. Specialized cells in your spleen and liver destroy damaged or dead red blood cells.

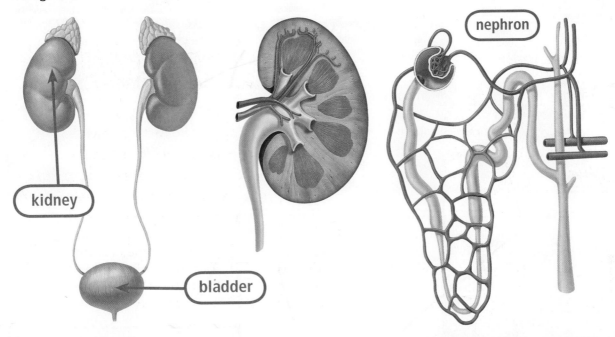

kidney

bladder

nephron

Caring for Your Circulatory System

- Eat foods that are low in fat and high in fiber. Fiber helps take away substances that can lead to fatty buildup in your blood vessels. Eat foods high in iron to help your red blood cells carry oxygen.

- Drink plenty of water to help your body replenish your blood fluid.

- Avoid contact with another person's blood.

- Exercise regularly to keep your heart and blood vessels strong.

- Never smoke or use tobacco. It can strain your heart and damage your blood vessels.

- Don't use illegal drugs or alcohol. They can damage your liver and your heart.

- Follow directions for all medicines carefully. Misuse of medicine can damage your blood's ability to clot after a cut, and can damage your liver and heart.

Your Immune System

A pathogen is an organism or virus that causes illness. An infection is the growth of pathogens in the body. Some pathogens weaken or kill body cells. A disease is an illness that damages or weakens the body, so you are not able to do the things you normally do. You may have a sore throat, or you may feel achy or tired, or you may have an unusually high body temperature, or fever. These are signs that your body is fighting an infection.

Infectious diseases have different symptoms because they are caused by different pathogens. There are four main types of pathogens: viruses, bacteria, fungi, and protozoa.

Diseases Caused by Pathogens

Pathogen	Characteristics	Diseases
Viruses	The smallest pathogens; the ones that cause most infectious diseases	Colds, chicken pox, HIV, infectious hepatitis, influenza (flu), measles, mumps, polio, rabies, rubella (German measles)
Bacteria	One-celled organisms that can—but do not always—cause disease; they make people ill by producing harmful wastes	Strep throat, pertussis (whooping cough), some kinds of pneumonia, Salmonella food poisoning, tetanus, tuberculosis (TB), Lyme disease
Fungi	Small, simple organisms like yeasts and molds; they most often invade the skin or respiratory system	Ringworm, athlete's foot, allergies
Protozoa	One-celled organisms somewhat larger than bacteria; they can cause serious diseases	Ameobic dysentery, giardiasis, malaria

There are pathogens all around you. You don't become ill often because your body has a complex system of defenses that prevents most pathogens from entering your body and destroys the ones that get through.

Sometimes pathogens do manage to overcome your body's defenses. When they do, your body's next line of defense is in your blood. Your blood contains white blood cells that have their own role to play in fighting infection.

Some white blood cells manufacture substances called antibodies. Each antibody is designed to fight a specific kind of pathogen. The antibodies attach themselves to the pathogen and either kill it or mark it to be killed by another kind of white blood cell. When a pathogen enters your body, your immune system produces antibodies to fight it. This process may take several days, during which you may have a fever and feel some other symptoms of the disease. When you have recovered from an illness, your white blood cells "remember" how to make the antibody needed to fight the pathogen that made you ill. The ability to recognize pathogens and "remember" how to make antibodies to fight disease is called *immunity*.

You can also develop immunity to certain diseases by getting vaccinations from your doctor that prevent the disease. A vaccine is usually a killed or weakened form of the pathogen that causes a particular disease.

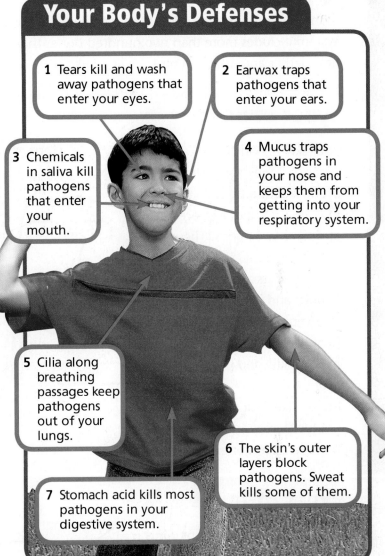

Your Body's Defenses

1 Tears kill and wash away pathogens that enter your eyes.

2 Earwax traps pathogens that enter your ears.

3 Chemicals in saliva kill pathogens that enter your mouth.

4 Mucus traps pathogens in your nose and keeps them from getting into your respiratory system.

5 Cilia along breathing passages keep pathogens out of your lungs.

6 The skin's outer layers block pathogens. Sweat kills some of them.

7 Stomach acid kills most pathogens in your digestive system.

Caring for Your Immune System

- Exercise regularly and get plenty of rest. This helps your body rebuild damaged tissues and cells.

- Eat a healthful, balanced diet. Good nutrition keeps your immune system strong.

- Avoid substances like illegal drugs, tobacco, and alcohol, that can weaken your immune system.

- Wash your hands frequently and avoid touching your eyes, nose, and mouth.

Your Skeletal System

All of the bones in your body form your skeletal system. Your bones protect many vital organs and support the soft tissues of your body. Your skeletal system includes more than two hundred bones that fit together and attach to muscles at joints.

Types of Bones

Your skeleton includes four basic types of bones: long, short, flat, and irregular. Long bones, like the ones in your arms and legs, are narrow and have large ends. These bones support weight. Short bones, found in your wrists and ankles, are chunky and wide. They allow maximum movement around a joint. Flat bones, like the ones in your skull and ribs, protect your body. Irregular bones, like your vertebrae, have unique shapes and fall outside of the other categories.

Types of Joints

Each of the three types of joints is designed to do a certain job.

Ball-and-Socket Joints like your hips and shoulders allow rotation and movement in many directions.

Hinge Joints like your elbow and knees only move back and forth.

Gliding Joints like the vertebrae in your spine or the bones in your wrists and feet allow side-to-side and back-and-forth movement.

Some joints, like the ones in your skull do not allow any movement. These flat bones fit tightly together to protect your brain.

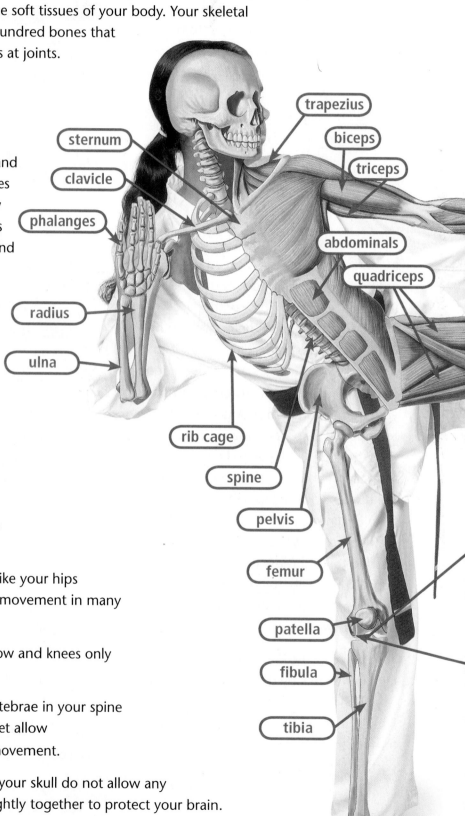

sternum
clavicle
phalanges
radius
ulna
rib cage
spine
pelvis
femur
patella
fibula
tibia
trapezius
biceps
triceps
abdominals
quadriceps

Parts of a Joint

Your bones attach to your muscles and to each other at joints. Your muscles and bones work together to allow your body to move. Joints are made up of ligaments and cartilage. Ligaments are tough, elastic tissues that attach one bone to another. Cartilage is a soft cushioning material at the ends of bones that helps bones move smoothly and absorbs some of the impact when you move. Tendons are dense, cordlike material that joins muscles to bones.

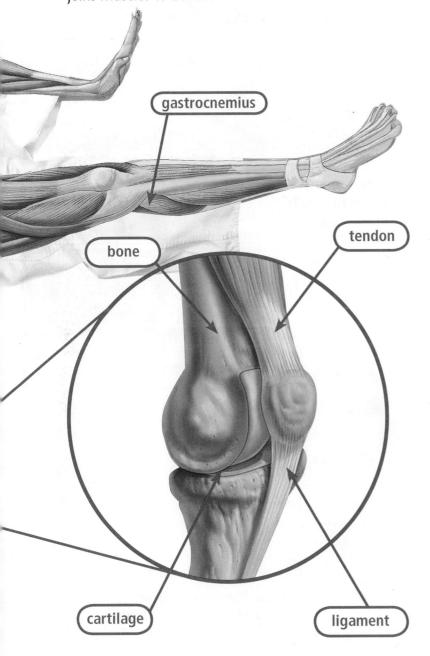

gastrocnemius

bone

tendon

cartilage

ligament

Caring for Your Skeletal System

- Always wear a helmet and proper safety gear when you play sports, skate, or ride a bike or a scooter.
- Your bones are made mostly of calcium and other minerals. To keep your skeletal system strong and to help it grow, you should eat foods that are high in calcium like milk, cheese, and yogurt. Dark green, leafy vegetables like broccoli, spinach, and collard greens are also good sources of calcium.
- Exercise to help your bones stay strong and healthy.
- Always warm up before you exercise.
- Get plenty of rest to help your bones grow.
- Stand and sit with good posture. Sitting slumped over puts strain on your muscles and on your bones.

Your Muscular System

A muscle is a body part that produces movement by contracting and relaxing. All of the muscles in your body make up the muscular system.

Types of Muscle

Your muscular system is made up of three types of muscle. The muscles that make your body move are attached to the bones of your skeletal system. These muscles are called skeletal muscles. A skeletal muscle has a bulging middle and narrow tendons at each end. Tendons are strong flat bands of tissue that attach muscles to bones near your joints. Skeletal muscles are usually under your control, so they are also called voluntary muscles.

Your muscular system includes two other types of muscle. The first of these is called smooth muscle. This specialized muscle lines most of your digestive organs. As these muscles contract and relax, they move food through your digestive system.

Your heart is made of another specialized muscle called cardiac muscle. Your heart's muscle tissue squeezes and relaxes every second of every day to pump blood through your circulatory system. Smooth muscle and cardiac muscle operate automatically. Their contraction is not under your control, so they are also called involuntary muscles.

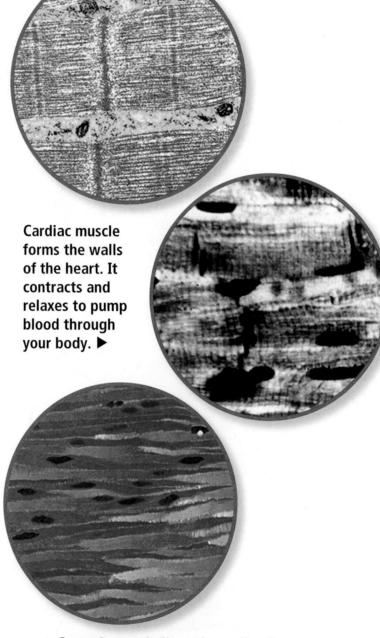

▼ Skeletal muscle appears striped. It is the kind of muscle that moves bones.

Cardiac muscle forms the walls of the heart. It contracts and relaxes to pump blood through your body. ▶

▲ Smooth muscle lines the walls of blood vessels and of organs such as your esophagus and stomach.

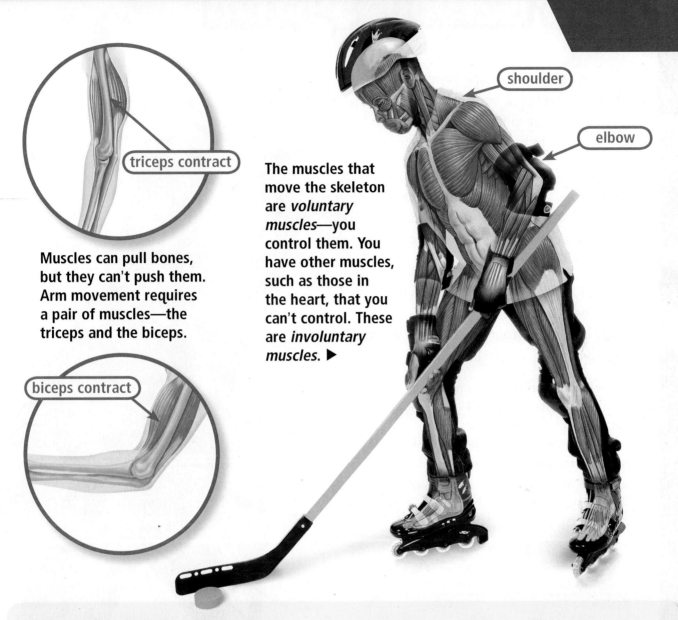

triceps contract

Muscles can pull bones, but they can't push them. Arm movement requires a pair of muscles—the triceps and the biceps.

biceps contract

The muscles that move the skeleton are *voluntary muscles*—you control them. You have other muscles, such as those in the heart, that you can't control. These are *involuntary muscles*. ▶

shoulder

elbow

Caring for Your Muscular System

- Always stretch and warm up your muscles before exercising or playing sports. Do this by jogging slowly or walking for at least ten minutes. This brings fresh blood and oxygen to your muscles, and helps prevent injury or pain.

- Eat a balanced diet of foods to be sure your muscles have the nutrients they need to grow and remain strong.

- Drink plenty of water when you exercise or play sports. This helps your blood remove wastes from your muscles and helps you build endurance.

- Always cool down after you exercise. Walk or jog slowly for five or ten minutes to let your heartbeat slow and your breathing return to normal. This helps you avoid pain and stiffness after your muscles work hard.

- Stop exercising if you feel pain in your muscles.

- Get plenty of rest before and after you work your muscles hard. They need time to repair themselves and to recover from working hard.

Your Nervous System

Your body consists of a number of different systems. Each of your body's systems plays a different role. The different systems of your body work together to keep you alive and healthy.

Just as a leader directs the work of a group, your nervous system controls your body's activities. Some activities, like the beating of your heart and breathing, are controlled automatically by your nervous system.

Your nervous system allows you to move and to see, hear, taste, touch, and smell the world around you. Your brain also allows you to learn, remember, and feel emotions.

Your nervous system is made up of your brain, your spinal cord, and your nerves.

Your spinal cord is a thick bundle of nerves inside the column of bone formed by your vertebrae. Your nerves are bundles of specialized cells branching from your spinal cord. They send messages about your environment to your brain and send signals to your muscles.

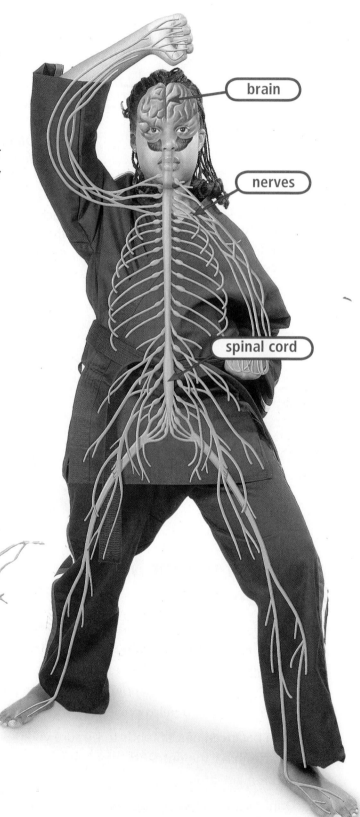

brain

nerves

spinal cord

A nerve cell is called a neuron. Signals travel to and from your brain along branching fibers of one neuron to branching fibers of other neurons.

Your brain contains about 100 billion neurons.
Different areas of your brain control different activities.

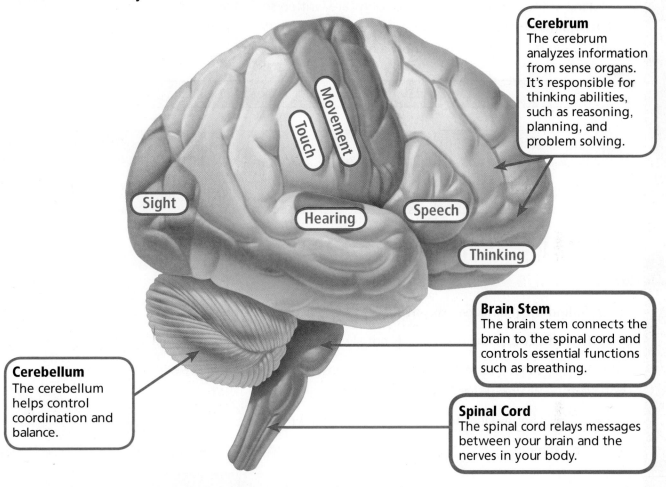

Cerebrum
The cerebrum analyzes information from sense organs. It's responsible for thinking abilities, such as reasoning, planning, and problem solving.

Movement

Touch

Sight

Hearing

Speech

Thinking

Brain Stem
The brain stem connects the brain to the spinal cord and controls essential functions such as breathing.

Cerebellum
The cerebellum helps control coordination and balance.

Spinal Cord
The spinal cord relays messages between your brain and the nerves in your body.

Caring for Your Nervous System

- Don't take illegal drugs, and avoid alcohol. These substances can impair your judgment, which may cause you to react slowly or improperly to danger. They can also damage your nervous system.

- When your doctor prescribes medicines, follow the instructions your doctor gives you. Too much medicine can affect your nervous system. Never take medicine prescribed for someone else.

- Eat a well-balanced diet to be sure your nervous system receives the nutrients it needs.

- Protect your brain and spine from injury by wearing proper safety equipment when you play sports, ride a bike or scooter, or skate.

- Get plenty of rest. Sleep helps keep your mind sharp. Like all of your body's systems, your nervous system requires rest to stay healthy.

Identify the Main Idea and Details

Many of the lessons in this science book are written so that you can understand main ideas and the details that support them. You can use a graphic organizer like this one to show a main idea and details.

> **Main Idea:** The most important idea of a selection

> **Detail:**
> Information that tells more about the main idea

> **Detail:**
> Information that tells more about the main idea

> **Detail:**
> Information that tells more about the main idea

Tips for Identifying the Main Idea and Details

- To find the main idea, ask—*What is this mostly about?*

- Remember that the main idea is not always stated in the first sentence.

- Be sure to look for details that help you answer questions such as *Who?, What?, Where?, When?, Why?* and *How?*

- Use pictures as clues to help you figure out the main idea.

Here is an example.

Main Idea

> All living things are made up of one or more cells. Cells that work together to perform a specific function form tissues. Tissues that work together make up an organ. Each organ in an animal's body is made up of several kinds of tissues. Organs working together form a body system.

Detail

You could record this in the graphic organizer.

> **Main Idea:** All living things are made up of one or more cells.

> **Detail:**
> Cells that work together form tissues.

> **Detail:**
> Tissues that work together make up an organ.

> **Detail:**
> Organs that work together form a body system.

More About Main Idea and Details

Sometimes the main idea of a passage is at the end instead of the beginning. The main idea may not be stated. However, it can be understood from the details. Look at the following graphic organizer. What do you think the main idea is?

Main Idea:

Detail:
Bones make up the skeletal system.

Detail:
The muscular system is made up of voluntary muscles, smooth muscles, and cardiac muscles.

Detail:
Muscles are controlled by the central nervous system.

A passage can contain details of different types. In the following paragraph, identify each detail as a reason, an example, a fact, a step, or a description.

Digestion begins as you chew food. When you swallow, food passes through the esophagus. Gastric juice breaks down proteins. After several hours in the stomach, partly digested food moves into the small intestine. Digestion of food into nutrients is completed in the small intestine. From the small intestine, undigested food passes into the large intestine. In the large intestine, water and minerals pass into the blood and wastes are removed from the body.

Skill Practice

Read the following paragraph. Use the Tips for Identifying Main Idea and Details to answer the questions.

The circulatory, respiratory, digestive, and excretory systems work together to keep the body alive. The circulatory system transports oxygen, nutrients, and wastes through the body. In the respiratory system, oxygen diffuses into the blood and carbon dioxide diffuses out of the blood. The digestive system provides the nutrients your cells need to produce energy. The excretory system removes cell wastes from the blood.

1. What is the main idea of the paragraph?

2. What supporting details give more information?

3. What details answer any of the questions *Who?, What?, Where?, When?, Why?* and *How?*

Compare and Contrast

Some lessons are written to help you see how things are alike or different. You can use a graphic organizer like this one to compare and contrast.

> **Topic:** Name the topic—the two things you are comparing and contrasting.

> **Alike**
> List ways the things are alike.

> **Different**
> List ways the things are different.

Tips for Comparing and Contrasting

- To compare, ask—*How are people, places, objects, ideas, or events alike?*

- To contrast, ask—*How are people, places, objects, ideas, or events different?*

- When you compare, look for signal words and phrases such as *similar, both, too,* and *also.*

- When you contrast, look for signal words and phrases such as *unlike, however, yet,* and *but.*

Here is an example.

Compare

The two basic kinds of energy are kinetic energy and potential energy. Kinetic energy is the energy of motion. Any matter in motion has kinetic energy. However, potential energy is the energy of position or condition. Transformation of energy is the change between kinetic energy and potential energy. The total amount of energy does not change when energy is transformed.

Contrast

Here is what you could record in the graphic organizer.

> **Topic: Kinetic and Potential Energy**

> **Alike**
> Both are basic kinds of energy.
> The total amount of energy stays the same when it changes forms.

> **Different**
> Kinetic energy is the energy of motion.
> Potential energy is the energy of position or condition.

R18

More About Comparing and Contrasting

Identifying how things are alike and how they're different can help you understand new information. Use a graphic organizer to sort the following information about kinetic energy and potential energy.

| kinetic energy | electric energy | thermal energy | mechanical energy | light energy |

| potential energy | elastic potential energy | gravitational potential energy | chemical energy |

Sometimes a paragraph compares and contrasts more than one topic. In the following paragraph, one topic of comparison is underlined. Find a second topic for comparison or contrast.

Material that conducts electrons easily is called a conductor. An insulator is a material that does not carry electrons. An electric circuit is any path along which electrons can flow. Some circuits are series circuits. They have only one path for the electrons. Other circuits are parallel circuits, where each device is on a separate path.

Skill Practice

Read the following paragraph. Use the Tips for Comparing and Contrasting to answer the questions.

Within an atom, electrons have a negative charge and protons have a positive charge. Most objects have equal numbers of protons and electrons. Both protons and electrons attract each other. Sometimes, however, electrons are attracted to the protons of another object and rub off. These objects become negatively charged.

1. What are two ways protons and electrons are alike?

2. Explain a difference between protons and electrons.

3. Name two signal words that helped you identify likenesses or differences in this paragraph.

Cause and Effect

Some of the lessons in this science book are written to help you understand why things happen. You can use a graphic organizer like this one to show cause and effect.

| **Cause:** A cause is an action or event that makes something happen. | → | **Effect:** An effect is what happens as a result of an action or event. |

Tips for Identifying Cause and Effect

- To find an effect, ask—*What happened?*

- To find a cause, ask—*Why did this happen?*

- Remember that events can have more than one cause or effect.

- Look for signal words and phrases, such as *because* and *as a result,* to help you identify causes and effects.

Here is an example.

Earth's surface is made up of many plates. Plates are rigid blocks of crust and upper mantle rock. Earth's plates fit together like the pieces of a puzzle. Plate movement is very slow. As plates move around, they cause great changes in Earth's landforms. Where plates collide, energy is released, and new landforms are produced. On land, mountains rise and volcanoes erupt.

Here is what you could record in the graphic organizer.

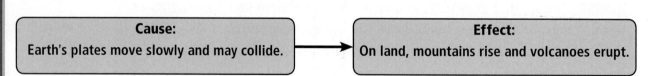

| **Cause:** Earth's plates move slowly and may collide. | → | **Effect:** On land, mountains rise and volcanoes erupt. |

More About Cause and Effect

Events can have more than one cause or effect. For example, suppose a paragraph included a sentence that said "On the ocean floor, deep trenches form." You could then identify two effects of Earth's plates colliding.

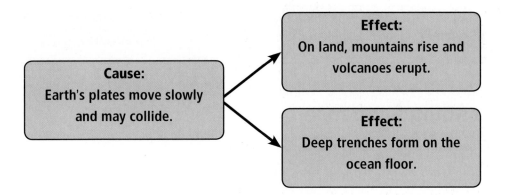

Cause:
Earth's plates move slowly and may collide.

Effect:
On land, mountains rise and volcanoes erupt.

Effect:
Deep trenches form on the ocean floor.

Some paragraphs contain more than one cause and effect. In the paragraph below, one cause and its effect are underlined. Find the second cause and its effect.

As Earth's plates pull apart on land, valleys with volcanoes develop. Africa's Great Rift Valley was formed by the African and Arabian plates pulling apart. When plates pull apart under the sea, ridges and volcanoes form. New sea floor is formed at the ridges.

Skill Practice

Read the following paragraph. Use the Tips for Identifying Cause and Effect to help you answer the questions.

When energy is suddenly released in Earth's crust, the ground shakes and an earthquake occurs. The earthquake is a result of plates crushing together, scraping past each other, or bending along jagged boundaries. Because Earth shakes in an earthquake, great damage can occur, such as streets splitting open and bridges collapsing.

1. What causes an earthquake to occur?

2. What are some effects of an earthquake?

3. What two signal words or phrases helped you identify the causes and effects in this paragraph?

Sequence

Some lessons in this science book are written to help you understand the order in which things happen. You can use a graphic organizer like this one to show sequence.

I. The first thing that happened	→ **2. The next thing that happened**	→ **3. The last thing that happened**

Tips for Understanding Sequence

- Pay attention to the order in which events happen.

- Remember dates and times to help you understand the sequence.

- Look for signal words such as *first, next, then, last,* and *finally*.

- Sometimes it's helpful to add your own time-order words to help you understand the sequence.

Here is an example.

Time-order words

A substance is buoyant, or will float in a liquid, if its density is less than that of the liquid. Here is a procedure that will show you what it takes for an egg to float in water. First, place an egg in a cup of water. Observe whether or not it floats. Next, remove the egg and stir several spoonfuls of salt into the water. Finally, replace the egg in the water and observe whether or not it floats. By changing the density of the water, you allow its density to become greater than the density of the egg.

You could record this in the graphic organizer.

I. First, place an egg in a cup of water and observe.	→ **2. Next, remove the egg and stir salt into the water.**	→ **3. Finally, replace the egg in the water and observe.**

More About Sequence

Sometimes information is sequenced by dates. For example, models of the atom have changed since the late 1800s. Use the graphic organizer to sequence the order of how the model of an atom has changed over time.

I. Near the end of the 1800s, Thomson's model of an atom was the first to include subatomic particles. →	**2.** In the early 1900s, Rutherford's model suggested that the atom was made up mostly of empty space. Bohr's model showed different orbits for electrons. →	**3.** Today, the modern model of an atom includes a cloud of electrons around the central positive nucleus.

When time-order words are not given, add your own words to help you understand the sequence. In the paragraph below, one time-order word has been included and underlined. What other time-order words can you add to help you understand the paragraph's sequence?

> A person riding a bicycle changes the chemical energy in his or her cells to mechanical energy in order to push the pedals. The energy is transferred from the pedals through the chain to the rear wheel. <u>Finally,</u> the kinetic energy of the turning of the wheel is transferred to the whole bicycle.

Skill Practice

Read the following paragraph. Use the Tips for Understanding Sequence to answer the questions.

> First, a flashlight is switched on. Then, the chemical energy stored in the battery is changed into electric energy. Next, the circuit is closed. Finally, the electric energy is changed to light energy in the flashlight bulb.

1. What is the first thing that happened in this sequence?

2. About how long did the process take?

3. What signal words helped you identify the sequence in this paragraph?

Draw Conclusions

At the end of each lesson in this science book, you will be asked to draw conclusions. To draw conclusions, use information from the text you are reading and what you already know. Drawing conclusions can help you understand what you read. You can use a graphic organizer like this.

| **What I Read** List facts from the text. | + | **What I Know** List related ideas from your own experience. | = | **Conclusion:** Combine facts from the text with your own experience. |

Tips for Drawing Conclusions

- Ask—*What text information do I need to think about?*

- Ask—*What do I know from my own experience that could help me draw a conclusion?*

- Pay close attention to the information in the text and to your experience to be sure the conclusion is valid, or makes sense.

Here is an example.

> The shore is the area where the ocean and land meet and interact. Waves grind pebbles and rocks against the shore which can cause erosion. The water pressure from a wave can loosen pebbles and small rocks, which outgoing waves carry into the ocean. Long shore currents move sand, pebbles, and shells along the shore.

Here is what you could record in the graphic organizer.

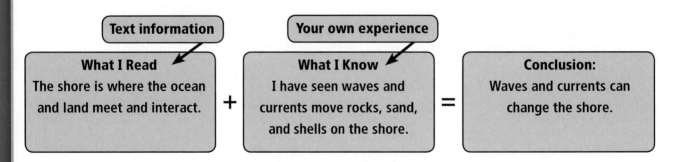

More About Drawing Conclusions

Sensible conclusions based on your experience and the facts you read are valid. For example, suppose a paragraph had ended with the sentence "Human activities can also change the shore." You might have come to a different conclusion about what changes the shore.

What I Read		**What I Know**		**Conclusion:**
The shore is where the ocean and land meet and interact.	**+**	Waves loosen rocks and pebbles. Currents move sand, pebbles, and shells. Structures can be built to prevent erosion.	**=**	Waves, currents, and human activities can change the shore.

Sometimes a paragraph might not contain enough information for drawing a valid conclusion. Read the paragraph below. Think of one valid conclusion you could draw. Then think of one invalid conclusion someone might draw from the given information.

> A jetty is a wall-like structure made of rocks that sticks out into the ocean. Jetties are usually built on either side of an opening to a harbor. Jetties catch sand and pebbles that normally flow down the coast with the current. Jetties can change the shore by building up the beach.

Skill Practice

Read the following paragraph. Use the Tips for Drawing Conclusions to answer the questions.

> Most of the movement of water on the ocean's surface is due to waves. A wave is the up-and-down movement of surface water. On a calm day, ocean waves may only be 1.5 meters high or less. However, during a storm, waves can reach heights of 30 meters.

1. What conclusion did you draw about the height of a wave?

2. What information from your personal experience did you use to draw the conclusion?

3. What text information did you use?

Summarize

At the end of every lesson in this science book, you will be asked to summarize. When you summarize, you use your own words to tell what something is about. In the lesson, you will be given ideas for writing your summary. You can also use a graphic organizer like this one to summarize.

Main Idea:		Details:		Summary:
Tell about the most important information you have read.	**+**	Add details that answer important questions *Who?*, *What?*, *Where?*, *When?*, *Why?*, and *How?*	**=**	Retell what you have just read, including only the most important details.

Tips for Summarizing

- To write a summary, ask—*What is the most important idea of the paragraph?*

- To include details with your summary, ask—*Who?, What?, When?, Where?, Why?* and *How?*

- Remember to use fewer words than the original has.

- Don't forget to use your own words when you summarize.

Here is an example.

Main Idea

Sound waves are carried by vibrating matter. Most sound waves travel through air, but they may also travel through liquids and even some solids. As the sound waves travel, the energy of the wave decreases. The frequency at which the sound wave moves determines the pitch of the sound. The greater the frequency, the higher the pitch. The strength of a sound wave can also be measured. The more energy a sound has, the louder it is.

Details

Here's what you could record in your graphic organizer.

Main Idea:		Details:		Summary:
Sound waves are carried by vibrating matter.	**+**	Pitch is determined by the frequency at which the sound wave moves. The more energy a sound has, the louder it is.	**=**	Sound waves are carried by vibrating matter. Pitch is determined by the frequency at which the sound wave moves. The loudness of a sound is determined by how much energy it has.

More About Summarizing

Sometimes a paragraph includes information that should not be included in a summary. For example, suppose a paragraph included a sentence that said "High musical notes have high pitch and high frequency, and low musical notes have low pitch and low frequency." The graphic organizer would remain the same, because that detail is not important to understanding the paragraph's main idea.

Sometimes the main idea of a paragraph is not in the first sentence. In the following paragraph, two important details are underlined. What is the main idea?

Air, water, clear glass, and clear plastic are substances which objects can clearly be seen through. Substances that light can travel through are transparent. Substances that are transparent are used to make things like windows and eyeglasses. Some substances are transparent only to certain colors of light. They are described as clear since you can see objects through them, but they have a color.

Skill Practice

Read the following paragraph. Use the Tips for Summarizing to answer the questions.

Light can be absorbed, reflected, or refracted. Sometimes light waves are absorbed when they strike an object. Most objects absorb some colors of light. Other colors of light bounce off objects, or are reflected. These are the colors we see. The change in speed of light causes it to bend. This bending of light waves is called refraction.

1. If a friend asked you what this paragraph was about, what information would you include? What would you leave out?

2. What is the main idea of the paragraph?

3. What two details would you include in a summary?

Using Tables, Charts, and Graphs

As you do investigations in science, you collect, organize, display, and interpret data. Tables, charts, and graphs are good ways to organize and display data so that others can understand and interpret your data.

The tables, charts, and graphs in this Handbook will help you read and understand data. You can also use the information to choose the best ways to display data so that you can use it to draw conclusions and make predictions.

Reading a Table

A bird-watching group is studying the wingspans of different birds. They want to find out the birds with the greatest wingspans. The table shows the data the group has collected.

Largest Wingspans	
Type of Bird	**Wingspan (in feet)**
Albatross	12
Trumpeter Swan	11
California Condor	10
Marabou Stork	10

Title

Headings

Data

How to Read a Table

1. **Read the title** to find out what the table is about.

2. **Read the headings** to find out what information is given.

3. **Study the data.** Look for patterns.

4. **Draw conclusions.** If you display the data in a graph, you might be able to see patterns easily.

By studying the table, you can see the birds with the greatest wingspans. However, suppose the group wants to look for patterns in the data. They might choose to display the data in a different way, such as in a bar graph.

Reading a Bar Graph

The data in this bar graph is the same as in the table. A bar graph can be used to compare the data about different events or groups.

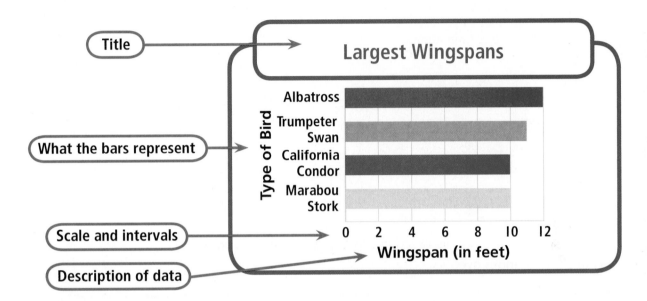

Title

What the bars represent

Scale and intervals

Description of data

Largest Wingspans

Type of Bird: Albatross, Trumpeter Swan, California Condor, Marabou Stork

Wingspan (in feet): 0 2 4 6 8 10 12

How to Read a Bar Graph

1. **Look** at the graph to determine what kind of graph it is.

2. **Read** the graph. Use the labels to guide you.

3. **Analyze** the data. Study the bars to compare the measurements. Look for patterns.

4. **Draw conclusions.** Ask yourself questions, like the ones in the Skills Practice.

Skills Practice

1. Which two birds have the same wingspan?

2. How much greater is the wingspan of an albatross than the wingspan of a California condor?

3. A red-tailed hawk has a wingspan of 4 feet. Which type of bird has a wingspan that is three times that of the hawk?

4. **Predict** A fifth-grade student saw a bird that had a wingspan that was about the same as her height. Could the bird have been an albatross?

5. Was the bar graph a good choice for displaying this data? Explain your answer.

Reading a Line Graph

A scientist collected this data about how the amount of ice in the Nordic Sea area of the Arctic Ocean has changed over the years.

Nordic Sea Area Ice

Year	Number of Square Kilometers (in millions)
1860	2.8
1880	2.7
1900	2.2
1920	2.4
1940	2.0
1960	1.8
1980	1.5
2000	1.6

Here is the same data displayed in a line graph. A line graph is used to show changes over time.

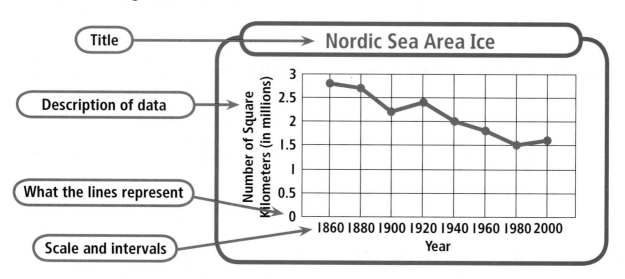

- Title
- Description of data
- What the lines represent
- Scale and intervals

How to Read a Line Graph

1. **Look** at the graph to determine what kind of graph it is.

2. **Read** the graph. Use the labels to guide you.

3. **Analyze** the data. Study the points along the lines. Look for patterns.

4. **Draw conclusions.** Ask yourself questions, like the ones in the Skills Practice to help you draw conclusions.

Skills Practice

1. By how much did the ice in the Nordic Sea area change from 1940 to 1980?

2. **Predict** Will there be more or less than 2.5 million square kilometers of ice in the Nordic Sea area in 2020?

3. Was the line graph a good choice for displaying this data? Explain why.

Reading a Circle Graph

A fifth-grade class is studying U.S. energy sources. They want to know which energy sources are used in the U.S. They classified the different sources by making a table. Here is the data they gathered.

U.S. Energy Sources

Source of Energy	Amount Used
Petroleum	0.38
Natural Gas	0.24
Coal	0.22
Hydroelectric and Nuclear Power	0.12
Other	0.04

The circle graph shows the same data as the table. A circle graph can be used to show data as a whole made up of different parts.

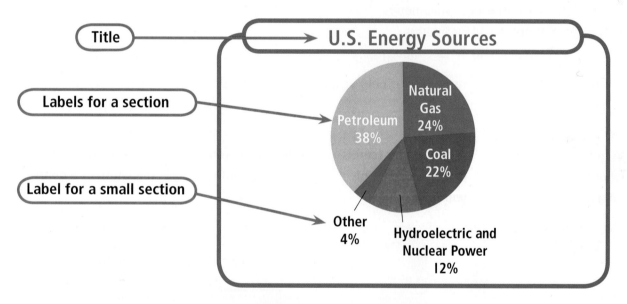

How to Read a Circle Graph

1. **Look** at the title of the graph to learn what kind of information is shown.

2. **Read** the graph. Look at the label of each section to find out what information is shown.

3. **Analyze** the data. Compare the sizes of the sections to determine how they are related.

4. **Draw conclusions.** Ask yourself questions, like the ones in the Skills Practice.

Skills Practice

1. Which source of energy is used most often?

2. **Predict** If wind, geothermal, and solar make up some of the other energy sources, will they be a greater or lesser part of U.S. energy sources in the future?

3. Was the circle graph a good choice for displaying this data? Explain why.

Using Metric Measurements

A measurement is a number that represents a comparison of something being measured to a unit of measurement. Scientists use many different tools to measure objects and substances as they work. Scientists almost always use the metric system for their measurements.

Measuring Length and Capacity

When you measure length, you find the distance between two points. The distance may be in a straight line, along a curved path, or around a circle. The table shows the metric units of **length** and how they are related.

Equivalent Measures
1 centimeter (cm) = 10 millimeters (mm)
1 decimeter (dm) = 10 centimeters (cm)
1 meter (m) = 1,000 millimeters
1 meter = 10 decimeters
1 kilometer (km) = 1,000 meters

You can use these comparisons to help you understand the size of each metric unit of length.

A **millimeter (mm)** is about the thickness of a dime.

A **centimeter (cm)** is about the width of your index finger.

A **decimeter (dm)** is about the width of an adult's hand.

A **meter (m)** is about the width of a door.

Sometimes you may need to change units of length. The following diagram shows how to multiply and divide to change to larger and smaller units.

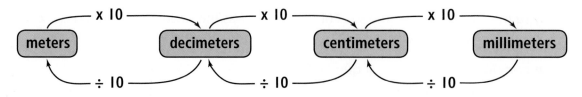

The photos below show the metric units of **capacity** and common comparisons. The metric units of volume are the milliliter (mL) and the liter (L). You can use multiplication to change liters to milliliters. You can use division to change milliliters to liters.

A **milliliter (mL)** is the amount of liquid that can fill part of a medicine dropper.

1 mL

A **liter (L)** is the amount of liquid that can fill a plastic bottle.

1 L

1 L = 1,000 mL

To change *larger* units to *smaller* units, you need more of the *smaller units*. So, **multiply** by 10, 100, or 1,000. To change *smaller* units to *larger* units, you need *fewer of the larger units*. So, **divide** by 10, 100, or 1,000.

500 dm = ___ cm
Think: There are 10 cm in 1 dm.
500 dm = 500 x 10 = 5,000
So, 500 dm = 5,000 cm.

4,000 mL = ____ L
Think: There are 1,000 mL in 1 L.
4,000 ÷ 1,000 = 4
So, 4,000 mL = 4 L.

Skills Practice

Complete. Tell whether you multiply or divide by 10, 100, or 1,000.

1. 7 m = _____ cm

2. 4 m = _____ dm

3. 800 _____ = 8 m

4. 9,000 mm = _____ m

5. 9 L = _____ mL

6. 6,000 mL = _____ L

7. 3,000 mL = _____ L

8. 8 _____ = 8,000 mL

Measuring Mass

Matter is what all objects are made of. Mass is the amount of matter that is in an object. The metric units of mass are the gram (g) and the kilogram (kg).

You can use these comparisons to help you understand the masses of some everyday objects.

A paper clip is about **1 gram (g)**.

A slice of wheat bread is about **20 g**.

A box of 12 crayons is about **100 g**.

A large wedge of cheese is **1 kilogram (kg)**.

You can use multiplication to change kilograms to grams.

You can use division to change grams to kilograms.

2 kg = ___ g	4,000 g = ____ kg
Think: There are 1,000 g in 1 kg.	Think: There are 1,000 g in 1 kg.
2 kg = 2 x 1,000 = 2,000 g	4,000 ÷ 1,000 = 4
So, 2 kg = 2,000 g.	So, 4,000 g = 4 kg.

Skills Practice

Complete. Tell whether you multiply or divide by 1,000.

1. 4,000 g = _____ kg

2. 3,000 g = _____ kg

3. 7 kg = _____ g

4. 8 _____ = 8,000 g

Measurement Systems

SI Measures (Metric)

Temperature

Ice melts at 0 degrees Celsius (°C)

Water freezes at 0°C

Water boils at 100°C

Length and Distance

1000 meters (m) = 1 kilometer (km)

100 centimeters (cm) = 1 m

10 millimeters (mm) = 1 cm

Force

1 newton (N) = 1 kilogram x

    1 meter/second/second (kg-m/s²)

Volume

1 cubic meter (m³) = 1 m x 1 m x 1 m

1 cubic centimeter (cm³) =

    1 cm x 1 cm x 1 cm

1 liter (L) = 1000 millimeters (mL)

1 cm³ = 1 mL

Area

1 square kilometer (km²) =

    1 km x 1 km

1 hectare = 10 000 m²

Mass

1000 grams (g) = 1 kilogram (kg)

1000 milligrams (mg) = 1 g

Rates (Metric and Customary)

km/hr = kilometers per hour

m/s = meters per second

mi/hr = miles per hour

Customary Measures

Volume of Fluids

2 c = 1 pint (pt)

2 pt = 1 quart (qt)

4 qt = 1 gallon (gal)

Temperature

Ice melts at 32 degrees

    Fahrenheit (°F)

Water freezes at 32°F

Water boils at 212°F

Length and Distance

12 inches (in.) = 1 foot (ft)

3 ft = 1 yard (yd)

5,280 ft = 1 mile (mi)

Weight

16 ounces (oz) = 1 pound (lb)

2,000 pounds = 1 ton (T)

Safety in Science

Doing investigations in science can be fun, but you need to be sure you do them safely. Here are some rules to follow.

1. **Think ahead.** Study the steps of the investigation so you know what to expect. If you have any questions, ask your teacher. Be sure you understand any caution statements or safety reminders.

2. **Be neat.** Keep your work area clean. If you have long hair, pull it back so it doesn't get in the way. Roll or push up long sleeves to keep them away from your activity.

3. **Oops!** If you should spill or break something, or get cut, tell your teacher right away.

4. **Watch your eyes.** Wear safety goggles anytime you are directed to do so. If you get anything in your eyes, tell your teacher right away.

5. **Yuck!** Never eat or drink anything during a science activity.

6. **Don't get shocked.** Be especially careful if an electric appliance is used. Be sure that electric cords are in a safe place where you can't trip over them. Don't ever pull a plug out of an outlet by pulling on the cord.

7. **Keep it clean.** Always clean up when you have finished. Put everything away and wipe your work area. Wash your hands.

Glossary

As you read your science book, you will notice that new or unfamiliar terms have been respelled to help you pronounce them while you are reading. Those respellings are called *phonetic respellings*. In this Glossary you will see the same kind of respellings.

In phonetic respellings, syllables are separated by a bullet [•]. Small, uppercase letters show stressed syllables.

The boldfaced letters in the examples in the Pronunciation Key below show how certain letters and combinations of letters are pronounced in the respellings.

The page number (in parentheses) at the end of a definition tells you where to find the term, defined in context, in your book. Depending on the context in which it is used, a term may have more than one definition.

Pronunciation Key

Sound	As in	Phonetic Respelling	Sound	As in	Phonetic Respelling
a	b**a**t	(BAT)	oh	**o**ver	(OH•ver)
ah	l**o**ck	(LAHK)	oo	p**oo**l	(POOL)
air	r**a**re	(RAIR)	ow	**ou**t	(OWT)
ar	**ar**gue	(AR•gyoo)	oy	f**oi**l	(FOYL)
aw	l**aw**	(LAW)	s	**c**ell	(SEL)
ay	f**a**ce	(FAYS)		**s**it	(SIT)
ch	**ch**apel	(CHAP•uhl)	sh	**sh**eep	(SHEEP)
e	t**e**st	(TEST)	th	**th**at	(THAT)
	m**e**tric	(MEH•trik)		**th**in	(THIN)
ee	**ea**t	(EET)	u	p**u**ll	(PUL)
	f**ee**t	(FEET)	uh	med**a**l	(MED•uhl)
	sk**i**	(SKEE)		tal**e**nt	(TAL•uhnt)
er	pap**er**	(PAY•per)		pen**ci**l	(PEN•suhl)
	f**er**n	(FERN)		**o**ni**o**n	(UHN•yuhn)
eye	**i**dea	(eye•DEE•uh)		play**fu**l	(PLAY•fuhl)
i	b**i**t	(BIT)		d**u**ll	(DUHL)
ing	go**ing**	(GOH•ing)	y	**y**es	(YES)
k	**c**ard	(KARD)		r**i**pe	(RYP)
	kite	(KYT)	z	bag**s**	(BAGZ)
ngk	ba**nk**	(BANGK)	zh	trea**s**ure	(TREZH•er)

abyssal plain [uh•BIS•uhl PLAYN] A large, flat area of the ocean floor

acceleration [ak•sel•er•AY•shuhn] The rate at which velocity changes over time

acid rain [AS•id RAYN] A mixture of rain and acids from air pollution that falls to Earth **(312)**

adaptation [ad•uhp•TAY•shuhn] A trait or characteristic that helps an organism survive **(297)**

addiction (uh•DIK•shuhn): A constant need for and use of a substance even though the user knows it is harmful **(212)**

additives [AD•uh•tivz] Things that food manufacturers add to food; some are nutrients, such as vitamins or minerals, and some simply improve taste **(163)**

aerobic exercise [air•OH•bik EK•ser•syz]: Exercise that strengthens the heart and lungs and helps build cardiovascular finess **(187)**

air mass [AIR MAS] A large body of air that has the same temperature and humidity throughout

air pressure [AIR PRESH•er] The weight of the atmosphere pressing down on Earth

alcoholism [AL•kuh•hawl•iz•uhm]: Addiction to alcohol **(246)**

anabolic steroids [a•nuh•BAH•lik STIR•oydz]: Prescription medicines that treat health problems but are abused by people who want to increase the size of their muscles **(213)**

anaerobic exercise [an•er•OH•bik EK•ser•syz]: Brief, intense activity that helps build muscle strength **(187)**

angiosperm [AN•jee•oh•sperm] A flowering plant that has seeds protected by fruits

anorexia [an•uh•REKS•ee•uh]: An eating disorder in which a person diets too much or even starves himself or herself **(151)**

astigmatism [uh•STIG•muh•tiz•uhm]: A condition in which the lens of the eye is curved unevenly and everything looks blurry **(119)**

atmosphere [AT•muhs•feer] The blanket of air surrounding Earth

atom [AT•uhm] The smallest particle that still behaves like the original matter it came from

axis [AK•sis] An imaginary line that passes through Earth's center and its North and South Poles

balance [BAL•uhns] A tool that measures the amount of matter in an object (the object's mass) **(11)**

balanced forces [BAL•uhnst FAWRS•iz] Forces that act on an object but cancel each other

blood alcohol level (or BAL) [BLUHD AL•kuh•hawl LEH•vuhl]: The amount of alcohol in a person's blood **(242)**

buoyant force [BOY•uhnt FAWRS] The upward force exerted on an object by water

calories [KAL•uh•reez]: The units used for measuring the amount of energy in a food **(152)**

carbohydrates [kar•boh•HY•drayts]: The starches and sugars that supply most of the body's energy **(140)**

carbon monoxide [KAR•buhn muh•NAHK•syd]: A poisonous gas in tobacco smoke; takes the place of oxygen in the blood **(237)**

carcinogens [kar•SIN•uh•juhnz]: Substances that cause cancer **(237)**

cardiovascular fitness [kar•dee•of•VAS•kyoo•ler FIT•nuhs]: Good health of the circulatory system, including a strong heart **(186)**

carnivore [KAHR•nuh•vawr] An animal that eats other animals; also called a second-level consumer **(278)**

cast [KAST] A fossil formed when dissolved minerals fill a mold and harden

cell [SEL] The basic unit of structure and function of living things

cell membrane [SEL MEM•brayn] The thin covering that surrounds every cell

chemical energy [KEM•ih•kuhl EN•er•jee] Energy that can be released by a chemical reaction

chlorophyll [KLAWR•uh•fil] A green pigment that allows a plant to absorb the sun's light energy **(272)**

chromosome [KROH•muh•sohm] A threadlike structure in the nucleus, made up of DNA

circulatory system [SER•kyoo•luh•tawr•ee SIS•tuhm] The organ system—made up of the heart, blood vessels, and blood—that transports materials throughout the body

classification [klas•uh•fih•KAY•shuhn] The process of grouping similar things together

climate [KLY•muht] The pattern of weather an area experiences over a long period of time

combustibility [kuhm•buhs•tuh•BIL•uh•tee] A measure of how easily a substance will burn

community [kuh•MYOO•nuh•tee] A group of populations that live together **(296)**

competition [kahm•puh•TISH•uhn] A kind of contest among populations that need to get a certain amound of food, water, and shelter to survive **(297)**

concave lens [kahn•KAYV LENZ] A lens that is thicker at the edges than it is at the center

condensation [kahn•duhn•SAY•shuhn] The process of a gas changing into a liquid

conduction [kuhn•DUK•shuhn] The transfer of heat from one object directly to another

conductor [kuhn•DUK•ter] A material that carries electricity well

conservation [kahn•ser•VAY•shuhn] The use of less of a resource to make the supply last longer **(314)**

constellation [kahn•stuh•LAY•shuhn] A pattern of stars named after a mythological or religious figure, an object, or an animal

consumer [kuhn•SOOM•er] An animal that eats plants, other animals, or both **(274)**

continental shelf [kahnt•uhn•ENT•uhl SHELF] The part of the ocean floor that drops gently near the land

continental slope [kahnt•uhn•ENT•uhl SLOHP] The part of the ocean floor that slopes steeply

convection [kuhn•VEK•shuhn] The transfer of heat through the movement of a gas or a liquid

convex lens [kahn•VEKS LENZ] A lens that is thicker at the center than it is at the edges

crater [KRAYT•er] A low, bowl-shaped area on the surface of a planet or moon

current [KER•uhnt] A stream of water that flows like a river through the ocean

current electricity [KER•uhnt ee•lek•TRIS•uh•tee] A kind of kinetic energy that flows as an electric current

cytoplasm [SYT•oh•plaz•uhm] The jellylike material inside a cell between the cell membrane and the nucleus

decibels [DES•uh•buhlz]: The units used for measuring the loudness of sounds **(123)**

decomposer [dee•kuhm•POHZ•er] A consumer that obtains food energy by breaking down the remains of dead plants and animals **(279)**

delta [DEL•tuh] An area of new land at the mouth of a river, formed from sediments carried by the river **(81)**

density [DEN•suh•tee] The measure of how closely packed an object's atoms are

deposition [dep•uh•ZISH•uhn] The process in which sediment settles out of water or is dropped by wind **(46)**

digestive system [dih•JES•tiv SIS•tuhm] The organ system that turns food into nutrients that body cells need for energy, growth, and repair

dominant trait [DAHM•uh•nuhnt TRAYT] A trait that appears even if an organism has only one factor for the trait

dosage [DOH•sij]: The correct amount of medicine to take **(211)**

drug [DRUHG]: A substance, other than food, that affects the way the body or mind works **(204)**

earthquake [ERTH•kwayk] A movement of the ground, caused by a sudden release of energy in Earth's crust **(90)**

eclipse [ih•KLIPS] An event that occurs when one object in space passes through the shadow of another object in space

ecosystem [EE•koh•sis•tuhm] A community of organisms and the environment in which they live **(278)**

electric circuit [ee•LEK•trik SER•kit] The path an electric current follows

electric current [ee•LEK•trik KER•uhnt] The flow of electrons

electric energy [ee•LEK•trik EN•er•jee] Energy that comes from an electric current

electricity [ee•lek•TRIS•ih•tee] A form of energy produced by moving electrons

electromagnet [ee•lek•troh•MAG•nit] A magnet made by coiling a wire around a piece of iron and running electric current through the wire

element [EL•uh•muhnt] Matter made up of only one kind of atom

energy [EN•er•jee] The ability to cause changes in matter

energy balance: Taking in the same number of calories you use

energy pyramid [EN•er•jee PIR•uh•mid] A diagram that shows how much food energy is passed from each level in a food chain to the next **(283)**

energy transfer [EN•er•jee TRANS•fer] Movement of energy from one place or object to another

environment [en•VY•ruhn•muhnt] All the living and nonliving things that surround and affect an organism

environmental tobacco smoke (or ETS) [en•vy•ruhn•MEN•tuhl tuh•ba•koh SMOHK: Tobacco smoke in the air; can harm nonsmokers **(239)**

enzyme [EN•zym]: A chemical, found in saliva, that helps change food into a form the body can use **(139)**

epicenter [EP•ih•sent•er] The point on Earth's surface directly above the focus of an earthquake **(90)**

equator [ee•KWAYT•er] An imaginary line around Earth equally distant from the North and South Poles

erosion [uh•ROH•zhuhn] The process of moving sediment by wind, moving water, or ice **(55)**

evaporation [ee•vap•uh•RAY•shuhn] The process of a liquid changing into a gas

excretory system [EKS•kruh•tawr•ee SIS•tuhm] The organ system, including the kidneys and bladder, that removes waste materials from the blood

experiment [ek•SPEHR•uh•muhnt] A procedure carried out under controlled conditions to test a hypothesis **(19)**

expiration date [ek•spuh•RAY•shuhn DAYT]: The date at which a medicine should not be used **(211)**

extinction [ek•STINGK•shuhn] The death of all the organisms of a species **(308)**

farsighted [FAR•syt•uhd]: Able to see faraway objects clearly, while nearby objects look blurry **(119)**

fats [FATS]: The nutrients that contain the most energy **(140)**

fault [FAWLT] A break in Earth's crust **(91)**

flexibility [FLEK•suh•BIL•uh•tee]: The ability to bend and twist your body comfortably **(194)**

food allergy [FOOD AL•er•jee]: A bad reaction to a food that most other people can eat without becoming ill **(159)**

food chain [FOOD CHAYN] The transfer of food energy between organisms in an ecosystem **(279)**

food poisoning [FOOD POY•zuhn•ing]: An illness caused by eating or drinking something that contains harmful germs **(168)**

food web [FOOD WEB] A diagram that shows the relationships between different food chains in an ecosystem **(280)**

force [FAWRS] A push or pull that causes an object to move, stop, or change direction

fossil [FAHS•uhl] The remains or traces of past life, found in sedimentary rock

frequency [FREE•kwuhn•see] The number of vibrations per second

friction [FRIK•shuhn] A force that opposes motion

front [FRUHNT] The border where two air masses meet

fulcrum [FUHL•kruhm] The balance point on a lever that supports the arm but does not move

galaxy [GAL•uhk•see] A grouping of gas, dust, and many stars, plus any objects that orbit those stars

gene [JEEN] The part of a chromosome that contains the DNA code for an inherited trait

germinate [JER•muh•nayt] To sprout

gingivitis [jin•juh•VYT•is]: a gum disease that occurs when plaque hardens on the teeth and irritates the gums **(116)**

glacier [GLAY•sher] A large, thick sheet of ice **(72)**

gravitational force [grav•ih•TAY•shuhn•uhl FAWRS] The pull of all objects in the universe on one another

gravity [GRAV•ih•tee] The attraction between objects and Earth

gymnosperm [JIM•noh•sperm] A plant that produces naked seeds

habitat [HAB•i•tat] An area where an organism can find everything it needs to survive **(313)**

hair follicle [HAIR FAHL•ih•kuhl]: A pitlike structure, in the skin, from which hair grows **(110)**

hardness [HARD•nis] A mineral's ability to resist being scratched **(38)**

headland [HED•luhnd] A point of land at the shore where hard rock is left behind and other materials are washed away

health consumer [HELTH kuhn•SOOM•er]: A person who buys and uses health products or services **(126)**

heat [HEET] The transfer of thermal energy between objects with different temperatures

herbivore [HER•buh•vawr] An animal that eats only producers **(278)**

humidity [hyoo•MID•uh•tee] A measurement of the amount of water vapor in the air

igneous rock [IG•nee•uhs RAHK] Rock that forms when melted rock cools and hardens **(44)**

illegal drugs (ih•LEE•guhl DRUHGZ): Drugs that are not medicines and that are against the law to sell, buy, have, or use **(214)**

inclined plane [in•KLYND PLAYN] A ramp or other sloping surface

index fossil [IN•deks FAHS•uhl] A fossil of an organism that lived in many places around the world for a short period of time; it can help scientists find the age of a rock layer

inertia [in•ER•shuh] The property of matter that keeps it at rest or moving in a straight line

ingredients [in•GREE•dee•uhnts]: Substances that are in a product **(128, 162)**

inhalants [in•HAYL•uhnts]: Substances that people abuse by breathing in their fumes **(220)**

inherited trait [in•HAIR•it•ed TRAYT] A characteristic passed from parents to their offspring

inquiry [IN•kwer•ee] An organized way to gather information and answer questions **(16)**

instinct [IN•stinkt] A behavior that an organism inherits

insulator [IN•suh•layt•er] A material that does not conduct electricity well

intoxicated (in•TAHK•sih•kay•tuhd): Strongly affected by a drug **(243)**

invertebrate [in•VER•tuh•brit] An animal without a backbone

investigation [in•ves•tuh•GAY•shuhn] A procedure carried out to gather data about an object or event **(16)**

jetty [JET•ee] A wall-like structure that sticks out into the ocean to prevent sand from being carried away

kinetic energy [kih•NET•ik EN•er•jee] The energy of motion

kingdom [KING•duhm] A major, large group of similar organisms

landform [LAND•fawrm] A natural land shape or feature **(70)**

lava [LAH•vuh] Molten (melted) rock that reaches Earth's surface **(92)**

learned behavior [LERND bee•HAYV•yer] A behavior that an animal acquires through experience

lever [LEV•er] A bar that makes it easier to move things

life cycle [LYF SY•kuhl] The stages that a living thing passes through as it grows and changes

light [LYT] Radiation that we can see

local wind [LOH•kuhl WIND] Movement of air that results from local changes in temperature

luster [LUS•ter] The way a mineral's surface reflects light **(37)**

magma [MAG•muh] Molten (melted) rock beneath Earth's surface **(92)**

magnetic [mag•NET•ik] Having the property of attracting iron objects

magnetic force [mag•NET•ik FAWRS] The force produced by a magnet

mechanical energy [muh•KAN•ih•kuhl EN•er•jee] The combination of all the kinetic and potential energy that something has

metamorphic rock [met•uh•MAWR•fik RAHK] Rock formed when high heat and great pressure change existing rocks into a new form **(48)**

medicine [MED•uh•suhn]: A drug used to treat illness or disease **(204)**

medicine abuse [MED•uh•suhn uh•BYOOS]: The taking of medicine to do something other than treat an illness **(212)**

medicine misuse [MED•uh•suhn mis•YOOS]: The taking of medicine without following directions exactly **(212)**

microscope [MY•kruh•skohp] A tool that makes small objects appear larger **(8)**

microscopic [my•kruh•SKAHP•ik] Too small to be seen without using a microscope

mineral [MIN•er•uhl] A naturally occurring, nonliving solid that has a specific chemical makeup and a repeating structure, Nutrients that help your body grow and work **(36,142)**

mitosis [my•TOH•sis] The process by which most cells divide

mixture [MIKS•cher] A combination of two or more different substances

mold [MOHLD] The hollow space that is left when sediment hardens around the remains of an organism and the remains then dissolve

molecule [MAHL•ih•kyool] Two or more atoms joined together

moon [MOON] Any natural body that revolves around a planet

moon phase [MOON FAYZ] One of the shapes the moon seems to have as it orbits Earth

muscular endurance [MUHS•kyuh•ler in•DUR•uhnts]: The ability to use your muscles for a long time without getting tired **(195)**

muscular strength [MUHS•kyuh•ler STRENGTH]: The ability to use your muscles to lift, push, or pull heavy objects **(194)**

muscular system [MUHS•kyoo•ler SIS•tuhm] The organ system that includes the muscles and allows the body to move

MyPyramid [MEYE PIR•uh•mid]: A diagram that helps people choose a balanced diet **(145)**

nearsighted (NIR•syt•uhd): Able to see nearby objects clearly, while faraway objects look blurry **(119)**

nervous system [NER•vuhs SIS•tuhm] The organ system—including the brain, spinal cord, and nerves—that senses your surroundings and controls other organs

net force [NET FAWRS] The combination of all the forces acting on an object

nicotine [NIK•uh•teen]: A drug, found in tobacco, that makes the heart work harder **(237)**

nonrenewable resource [nahn•rih•NOO•uh•buhl REE•sawrs] A resource that, once used, cannot be replaced in a reasonable amount of time

nucleus [NOO•klee•uhs] The part of a cell that directs all of the cell's activities. A dense area in the center of an atom that contains protons and neutrons

nutrients [NOO•tree•uhnts]: Substances in food that provide the body with energy and building materials **(138)**

nutritionist [noo•TRISH•uhn•ist]: A scientist who studies ways to prepare healthful diets **(145)**

oil gland [OYL GLAND]: A gland that releases oil which coats the hair and spreads over the skin **(110)**

opaque [oh•PAYK] Not allowing light to pass through

orbit [AWR•bit] The path one body takes in space as it revolves around another body

organ [AWR•guhn] A group of tissues that work together to perform a certain function

organism [AWR•guhn•izm] Any living thing that maintains vital life processes

organ system [AWR•guhn SIS•tuhm] A group of organs that work together to do a job for the body

orthodontia [awr•thuh•DAHN•shuh]: The correction of crooked teeth **(117)**

overdose [OH•ver•dohs]: A dangerously large drug dose can cause illness or death **(215)**

over-the-counter medicines (or OTC medicines) [OH•ver•thuh•KOWN•ter MED•uh•suhnz]: Medicines that can be bought without prescriptions **(207)**

paleontology [pay•lee•uhn•TAHL•uh•jee] The study of fossils

parallel circuit [PAR•uh•lel SER•kit] An electric circuit that has more than one path for the current to follow

periodic table [pir•ee•AHD•ik TAY•buhl] A chart that scientists use to organize the elements

phloem [FLOH•em] Vascular tissue that carries food from leaves to all plant cells

photosynthesis [foht•oh•SIHN•thuh•sis] The process in which plants make food by using water from the soil, carbon dioxide from the air, and energy from sunlight **(272)**

physical activity [FIZ•ih•kuhl ak•TIV•uh•tee]: Any movement of muscles that uses energy **(179)**

physical change [FIZ•ih•kuhl CHAYNJ] A change in which the form of a substance changes but the substance still has the same chemical makeup

pitch [PICH] How high or low a sound is

planet [PLAN•it] A body that revolves around a star

plate [PLAYT] A section of Earth's crust and mantle that fits together with other sections like puzzle pieces **(89)**

plaque (PLAK): A sticky substance formed on the teeth by bacteria **(116)**

pollution [puh•LOO•shuhn] A waste product that harms living things and damages an ecosystem **(312)**

population [pahp•yuh•LAY•shuhn] A group of organisms of one kind that live in one location **(296)**

portion control [PAWR•shuhn kuhn•TROHL]: A limit on the amount of food you eat at each meal **(150)**

position [puh•ZISH•uhn] The location of an object in space

potential energy [poh•TEN•shuhl EN•er•jee] The energy an object has because of its condition or position

precipitation [pree•sip•uh•TAY•shuhn] Water that falls from the air to Earth

predator [PRED•uh•ter] An animal that kills and eats other animals **(300)**

prescription medicines [pree•SKRIP•shuhn MED•uh•suhnz]: Medicines that can be bought only with an order from a doctor **(206)**

preservatives [pree•ZERV•uh•tivz]: Chemicals added to foods to keep them from spoiling **(163)**

prevailing wind [pree•VAYL•ing WIND] Global wind that blows constantly from the same direction

prey [PRAY] An animal that is eaten by a predator **(300)**

producer [pruh•DOOS•er] A living thing, such as a plant, that makes its own food **(274)**

proteins [PROH•teenz]: The building blocks of the body **(141)**

protist [PROHT•ist] A single-celled organism with a nucleus and organelles

pulley [PUHL•ee] A wheel with a rope that lets you change the direction in which you move an object

radiation [ray•dee•AY•shuhn] The transfer of energy by means of waves that move through matter and space

reactivity [ree•ak•TIV•uh•tee] The ability of a substance to go through a chemical change

recessive trait [rih•SES•iv TRAYT] A trait that appears only if an organism has two factors for the trait

reclamation [rek•luh•MAY•shuhn] The process of cleaning and restoring a damaged ecosystem **(316)**

reflection [rih•FLEK•shuhn] The bouncing of heat or light off an object

refraction [rih•FRAK•shuhn] The bending of light as it moves from one material to another

refuse [rih•FYOOZ]: To say no to something **(222)**

renewable resource [rih•NOO•uh•buhl REE•sawrs] A resource that can be replaced within a reasonable amount of time

respiratory system [RES•per•uh•tawr•ee SIS•tuhm] The organ system, including the lungs, that exchanges oxygen and carbon dioxide between the body and the environment

resource [REE•sawrs] Any material that can be used to satisfy a need

revolve [rih•VAHLV] To travel in a closed path around another object

rock [RAHK] A natural substance made of one or more minerals **(44)**

rock cycle [RAHK CY•kuhl] The continuous process in which one type of rock changes into another type **(56)**

rotate [ROH•tayt] To spin on an axis

salinity [suh•LIN•uh•tee] The amount of salt in water

sand dune [SAND DOON] A hill of sand, made and shaped by wind **(73)**

scientific method [sy•uhn•TIF•ik METH•uhd] A series of steps that scientists use when performing an experiment **(24)**

sedimentary rock [sed•uh•MEN•tuh•ree RAHK] Rock formed when sediments are cemented together **(46)**

self-medication [self•med•ih•KAY•shuhn]: The process of deciding on your own what medicine to take **(212)**

series circuit [SIR•eez SER•kit] An electric circuit in which the current has only one path to follow

shore [SHAWR] The area where the ocean and the land meet and interact

side effects [SYD ih•FEKTS]: Unwanted reactions to medicines **(208)**

simple machine [SIM•puhl muh•SHEEN] A device that makes a task easier by changing the size or direction of a force or the distance over which the force acts

sinkhole [SINGK•hohl] A large hole formed when the roof of a cave collapses **(82)**

skeletal system [SKEL•uh•tuhl SIS•tuhm] The organ system, including the bones, that protects the body and gives it structure

solar energy [SOH•ler EN•er•jee] Energy that comes from the sun

solar system [SOH•ler SIS•tuhm] A star and all the planets and other objects that revolve around it

solution [suh•LOO•shuhn] A mixture in which all the parts are mixed evenly

species [SPEE•sheez] A unique kind of living organism

speed [SPEED] The distance an object travels in a certain amount of time

SPF (Sun Protection Factor): A sunscreen rating that indicates about how much longer the sunscreen enables you to be in the sun without getting a sunburn, compared with no protection at all **(108)**

spore [SPAWR] A single reproductive cell that can grow into a new plant

star [STAR] A huge ball of very hot gases in space

static electricity [STAT•ik ee•lek•TRIS•ih•tee] The buildup of charges on an object

streak [STREEK] The color of the powder left behind when you rub a mineral against a rough white tile or a streak plate **(37)**

succession [suhk•SESH•uhn] A gradual change in the kinds of organisms living in an ecosystem **(304)**

sun [SUHN] The star at the center of our solar system

symbiosis [sim•by•OH•sis] A relationship between different kinds of organisms **(298)**

system [SIS•tuhm] A group of separate elements that work together to accomplish something

tar [TAR] In tobacco a sticky, dark paste that builds up in the lungs and makes breathing difficult **(237)**

tide [TYD] The rise and fall of the water level of the ocean

tide pool [TYD POOL] A temporary pool of ocean water that gets trapped between rocks when the tide goes out

tissue [TISH•oo] A group of cells that work together to perform a certain function

topography [tuh•PAHG•ruh•fee] All the kinds of landforms in a certain place **(70)**

translucent [trans•LOO•suhnt] Allowing only some light to pass through

transparent [trans•PAR•uhnt] Allowing light to pass through

transpiration [tran•spuh•RAY•shuhn] The loss of water from a leaf through the stomata **(271)**

troposphere [TROH•puh•sfeer] The layer of air closest to Earth's surface

ultraviolet rays [uhl•truh•VY•uh•lit RAYS]: The invisible light waves given off by the sun that cause sunburn and tanning **(107)**

unbalanced forces [uhn•BAL•uhnst FAWRS•iz] Forces that act on an object and don't cancel each other; unbalanced forces cause a change in motion

universe [YOO•nuh•vers] Everything that exists, including such things as stars, planets, gas, dust, and energy

vascular tissue [VAS•kyuh•ler TISH•oo] Tissue that supports plants and carries water and food

velocity [vuh•LAHS•uh•tee] A measure of an object's speed in a particular direction

vertebrate [VER•tuh•brit] An animal with a backbone

vibration [vy•BRAY•shuhn] A back-and-forth movement of matter

vitamins [VYT•uh•minz]: Nutrients that help the body do certain things **(142)**

volcano [vahl•KAY•noh] A mountain made of lava, ash, or other materials from eruptions that occur at an opening in Earth's crust **(92)**

volume [VAHL•yoom] The amount of space an object takes up. The loudness of a sound

water cycle [WAW•ter SY•kuhl] The process in which water continuously moves from Earth's surface into the atmosphere and back again

water pressure [WAWT•er PRESH•er] The downward push of water

wave (WAYV) The up-and-down movement of surface water

weathering [WETH•er•ing] The process of wearing away rocks by natural processes **(54)**

wheel-and-axle [weel•and•AK•suhl] A wheel with a rod, or axle, in the center

withdrawal [with•DRAW•uhl] The painful reaction that occurs when an addicted person suddenly stops using a drug **(215)**

work [WERK] The use of a force to move an object through a distance

xylem [ZY•luhm] Vascular tissue that carries water and nutrients from roots to every part of a plant

Index

VISION Jaguars see better at night than during the day.

They are different

MOVEMENT If possible, jaguars live near water. They are different from most cats—they LIKE to swim!

CAMOUFLAGE Most jaguars have brownish-yellow fur.

YOUNG Jaguar cubs weigh about two pounds, less than most human babies, when they are born. Their eyes are shut to protect them from sunlight.

COLOR Some jaguars have black rosettes and black fur.